AARP
CRASH COURSE IN
ESTATE PLANNING

The Essential Guide to Wills, Trusts, and Your Personal Legacy

MICHAEL T. PALERMO, JD, CFP

DOUBLEDAY LARGE PRINT HOME LIBRARY EDITION

STERLING PUBLISHING CO., INC.

This Large Print Edition, prepared especially for Doubleday Large Print Home Library, contains the complete, unabridged text of the original Publisher's Edition.

AARP Books publishes a wide range of titles on health, personal finance, lifestyle, and other subjects to enrich the lives of 50+ Americans.

AARP, established in 1958, is a nonprofit organization with more than 35 million members age 50 and older. The views expressed herein do not necessarily represent the policies of AARP and should not be construed as endorsements.

The AARP name and logo are registered trademarks of AARP, used under license to Sterling Publishing Co., Inc.

ISBN 0-7394-5073-5

Published by Sterling Publishing Co., Inc.
387 Park Avenue South, New York, NY 10016
© 2005 by Michael T. Palermo
Distributed in Canada by Sterling Publishing
c/o Canadian Manda Group, 165 Dufferin Street
Toronto, Ontario, Canada M6K 3H6
Distributed in Great Britain by Chrysalis Books Group PLC
The Chrysalis Building, Bramley Road, London W10 6SP, England
Distributed in Australia by Capricorn Link (Australia) Pty. Ltd.
P.O. Box 704, Windsor, NSW 2756, Australia

Printed in U.S.A.

This book is an overview of basic legal concepts, not a substitute for a lawyer or an answer to every possible legal question. The laws touched on in this book vary considerably from jurisdiction to jurisdiction, and they can change. Be sure to consult a lawyer knowledgeable about the current laws in your state or jurisdiction if you have a particular legal problem. Names and identifying information have been changed in examples used throughout the book.

Although Sterling Publishing and the author have used best efforts in writing this book, they make no representations or warranties as to its accuracy or completeness. They also do not make any implied warranties of merchantability or fitness for a particular purpose. Any advice given in this book is not guaranteed or warranted, and it may not be suitable for every factual situation. Neither Sterling Publishing nor the author shall be liable for any losses suffered by any reader of this book.

Certified Financial Planner Board of Standards Inc. owns the certification mark CFP®, which it awards to individuals who successfully complete initial and ongoing certification requirements.

To my father

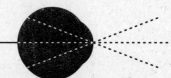

Steptoe & Johnson, and one year as an AARP Legal Counsel for the Elderly Hotline Attorney. Kuhn is an editor and contributing columnist to the *NAELA Quarterly Journal.*

Michael Schuster is an Associate General Counsel for AARP, specializing in intellectual property law, nonprofit law, and elections issues. He is also counsel to the AARP Foundation. In his 26 years at AARP, he has held a variety of legal positions, including those of litigation director, legal trainer, and litigator. Schuster, a graduate of the University of Notre Dame Law School, is an active member of many federal court bars, as well as the bars of the United States Supreme Court, Minnesota, and the District of Columbia.

{Contents

{Foreword

By Ric Edelman, author of *The Truth about Money*

Imagine the flight path of a rocket as it blasts into space. Now imagine taking a ride in a trolley car.

That rocket represents the growing complexity of personal finance, and estate-planning in particular. The trolley reflects the financial knowledge of most Americans.

Houston, we have a problem.

Fortunately, Michael Palermo brings you his many years of experience as an estate-planning attorney in the *AARP Crash Course in Estate Planning*. It's not a "do-it-yourself" guide, for Palermo makes it clear that the reader should work with an attorney. And he's right: consumers need to work with professionals—and not just in matters pertaining to estate planning. After all, no one would perform surgery on a child based solely on reading a book that describes the procedure.

That's why Palermo has written this crash course for you. He knows that the more you know, the less likely you'll be to experience serious problems. It's a lesson all financial professionals have learned: clients get the best results when they have a basic understanding of the topic at hand.

The *AARP Crash Course in Estate Planning* is a handy guide for readers who need to create or update their estate plans. Palermo presents his information in a nontechnical manner (no easy feat for a lawyer!). You can read the book from cover to cover, or skip to whatever chapter addresses your specific concern. Keep pen and paper handy as you read, jotting down questions to ask your attorney later on. If you read the entire crash course, you'll probably fill several pages with important notes.

The two most important themes that emerge from the book are the facts that most estate-planning mistakes are avoidable, and that most family fights are the fault of the deceased. Financial advisors like me and estate attorneys like Michael Palermo see these errors all the time.

As he points out, clients tend to place too much trust in family members, assuming that parents, spouses, siblings, and children will implement decisions that are best for all concerned. Too often, though, the deceased creates problems that the living cannot fix.

Too many times, the deceased fails to anticipate either the problems he or she is creating or the way family members will respond to them. When family members act selfishly—sometimes spurred by their spouses (the dreaded "in-laws")—greed can wreak havoc on the family. Indeed, for most American families, the enemy of estate planning isn't the IRS—it's your own family.

Believe it or not, many parents don't even sign a will. The absence of a document, they mistakenly believe, will guarantee the absence of problems. In reality, that's the surest way to incite family feuds.

The next most common tactic is for Mom and Dad to leave all their assets equally to all their children; that way, they think, no one can accuse them of favoritism. Wrong!

In many families, parents give more money over time to one child than to others—for college, for help in buying a home or starting a business, even for bailing kids out of jail. That leaves the other children to complain that they should get more—not merely an equal amount—from the will.

Parents who want to avoid confrontation sometimes abdicate their role. Can't decide whom to leave the house to? Designate *all* the kids, and let them figure it out! One of my clients did just that: she left a beach condo to her son and daughter equally. The daughter lived nearby, so her family enjoyed using it each summer. But the son lived 1,000 miles away and had money troubles. He wanted to sell the condo. His sister refused. He offered to buy her out. Again she refused. He asked her to buy him out. She refused once more, this time because she didn't have the money. So brother sued sister, and tens of thousands of dollars in legal bills later they no longer speak to each other.

Other parents find themselves in a quandary because they have a "problem child"— an irresponsible person, perhaps involved with drugs or crime, who refuses to grow up. Sometimes the child is a spendthrift, chronically in debt and cadging loans he never repays. Parents typically spend more money supporting and helping problem children than their more mature siblings. Some parents resort to a harsh solution: they cut the problem child out of the will.

Yet that "solution" is anything but. When the problem child discovers—usually not until after the funeral—that he is getting no inheritance, he may turn to his siblings for the financial support once furnished by Mom and Dad. Unprepared for this pitch, the other children feel guilty that the problem child was disinherited—and the problem child takes full advantage of their generosity. Result: the siblings become surrogate parents to the problem child.

Surprisingly, I've also seen parents disinherit their *successful* children. "Mysonthedoctor is doing so well that he doesn't need my money," some parents reason. They leave their money to their other kids—not because they don't love Theirsonthedoctor, but because they figure he doesn't need the money as much as his siblings do. One client's son, a successful surgeon, was crushed to learn he had been disinherited;

he couldn't imagine why. His sister told him he'd been cut out of the will because their parents had spent more money on his education than the others—and besides, he was making more money than them. The way the surgeon saw it, however, his parents had punished him for achieving success. Nor was he able to explain to his own children why their grandparents had left them nothing when their cousins received a great deal.

Another client had twin sisters. While all were still young, their mother died. Their father then married a woman who had two sons; when he died, he left everything to his second wife. She promised to leave to his three daughters everything she got from him, but—you guessed it—at her death, she left everything to her sons. The girls got nothing.

Then there are the missteps caused by well-meaning people who want to help their children inherit assets without having to go through probate or pay taxes. One woman added her son's name to the title of her house. But when the son got in financial trouble, his creditors searched county court records and found he was a co-owner of the house. The creditors sued the son, forcing the sale of the house. The proceeds went to the creditors; the woman lost her home.

Another couple was unmarried, in a relationship of which one family disapproved. A serious auto accident landed one of the partners in the hospital, whereupon the reproachful family barred his partner from visiting—a right they could claim because unmarried partners lack the legal rights of husband and wife. Documents such as a power of attorney or a medical directive could have prevented this tragedy.

As the last two stories demonstrate, estate planning is as much about protecting yourself while you're alive as it is about maintaining happiness for the family after you've passed. Reading these stories, it's easy to see the mistakes these people made. But are you sure you're not making similar errors that could jeopardize your own family relationships?

As you read the *AARP Crash Course in Estate Planning,* consider the tough questions:

- Has every adult in your family—parents, spouse, siblings, children—signed a will?

Does everyone know what it says? Do you know how they feel about it?

- When was your estate plan last reviewed by an estate-planning attorney?
- Does your plan reflect your current wishes?
- Have you asked key people identified in your plan, such as your executor, if they are willing to assume the duties your plan requires of them?
- Do you know what you will receive from your parents? From your spouse?
- Do you know where your parents and spouse store key legal documents?
- Do family members, including your executor, know where to find your legal documents?

Will Rogers once said that even if you're on the right track, you'll get run over by just sitting there. I hope you now realize that it's not enough to jump onto the trolley car, either. You need to climb aboard that rocket—and reading the *AARP Crash Course in Estate Planning* is a great way to start.

{Introduction

A Crash Course Designed to Give You a Soft Landing

This crash course in estate planning began around 1995 as a community college class in Lexington, Kentucky. My goal was to present, in six course hours, the information that my experience as an attorney had shown me most people need to know. This book expands and improves upon my original crash course, addressing those topics that proved to be of greatest interest to my students. It also includes information for anyone expecting to choose—or to be chosen as—an executor or trustee. These are the fundamentals you should understand before committing your plans to paper. Fortunately, none of the facts, terms, or con-

cepts presented here is terribly complicated. In fact, you probably know more than
you think.

● **What is estate planning?** When a person
dies owning property, that property has to
go to somebody, somehow. Any competent
adult can arrange his or her affairs to
choose "who gets what." The process of
making those decisions is a minimal definition of *estate planning*. A good estate plan
provides a legal and practical mechanism to
dispose of your property after death in a
way that acknowledges your wishes and
the needs of your survivors but minimizes
taxes. An estate plan almost always involves a will, but there are other aspects to
it as well, such as the manner in which you
hold title to property, and beneficiary designation forms on which you specify to whom
some kinds of assets will pass (for example,
a life insurance policy payoff).

For many people, an important part of estate planning is putting into a legal document their wishes for their underage children or grandchildren, in case both parents
die prematurely. This includes the choice of
a guardian, guidance as to how the kids

should be cared for, and how funds destined for their benefit should be managed and distributed. Of increasing importance to parents and grandparents in recent years is providing for the special needs of a disabled adult child.

Other people are more concerned with making arrangements to manage their property and affairs in case of their own disability. For still others, the process is also a time to reflect upon nonlegal matters. Many people find great comfort and satisfaction in memorializing for future generations important personal and spiritual values. Of course, too, the process can involve planning for some of the deeply personal medical choices to be made as life nears its end. Whatever your focus, after reading this book you should be ready to begin crafting an estate plan that effectively expresses your intentions and handles your affairs.

● **Why is estate planning important for you?** If you don't decide who's going to be in charge and what's supposed to happen—and then arrange things accordingly—a combination of luck and state law will take over upon your disability or death. There is no way for anyone to enforce your intentions if you have not given them legal effect in one or more of the ways we will look at here— some simple, others complex. Maybe everything will work out fine without a bit of planning. But bear in mind that families can be torn apart in jockeying for legal authority, modest sums of money, or even mundane household items such as a kitchen wall clock or a tissue-box cover.

If you want your wishes to be fulfilled at your death without starting World War III, avoid the following age-old invitations to disaster:

- "Everybody already knows who's supposed to get what."
- "In my desk drawer is a list of my possessions and the persons to whom they should be given."
- "I don't have much. The kids can just come in and divide it among themselves however they decide."
- "I put name tags on the bottom of every knickknack and piece of furniture, so they'll know who gets it."
- "Last year I put all my money in a joint account with my oldest daughter. After I

die, she'll split it three ways with her brothers."
- "All I have is life insurance." (Or, "All I have is an IRA.") "My son is the only beneficiary listed on the form, but I want him to share it with his sister."

In all the often-heard client-to-attorney statements above, the client is asking for trouble. The last one, for example, is all too common. The size of beneficiary designation forms for insurance policies, retirement accounts, and pay-on-death accounts is often unreasonably small. It can be difficult to squeeze in all the kids' names. So parents sometimes assume that if they name one child as the beneficiary, he or she will split everything evenly with his or her siblings. The parents may even issue specific verbal instructions to that effect. Regrettably but not surprisingly, those instructions aren't always carried out.

Many people readily acknowledge the pitfalls of not having an estate plan—in other families. But their kids, so they say, will respect the parents' wishes and never stoop to fighting over the estate. Even if we give these parents and children the benefit of the doubt, what about the kids' spouses? Well-intentioned or not, meddling is an art form with some in-laws. Unless you spell out your wishes in an estate plan, what's to stop your pushy son-in-law, for example, from pressuring your daughter into accepting his way over things that are absolutely none of his business? Never mind that he has no rights under the law; "meddling" is not a legal concept.

Even if you don't "need" one today, a simple will is so easy to prepare there's no reason not to have one. (What if you win the lottery the day before you die?) True, a few people (without small children) use only nonprobate property dispositions (see page 29) in their plan, so their lack of a will does not present a problem. Even then, however, they do have a plan.

● **Do you need a lawyer?** A great deal of self-help is possible in print and online for the person who takes the time to educate himself. But unexpected complications or issues pop up often in legal matters, so you probably *should* see an attorney for your estate-planning, probate, and other legal work—at least for an hour of consultation, if only to answer a list of questions you've prepared in advance. If you know what you don't know, you at least stand a chance of finding the answers. But if you *don't* know what you don't know, then you're asking for trouble by going it alone. Many a client has begun by telling me of his "very simple situation," only to reveal in five minutes' discussion that it was anything but. Better to find out now than later.

Many people have not studied the topic and are at risk of serious family or financial problems after death. Yet they simply refuse to see a lawyer. Sadly, many of these potential estate-planning fiascoes will actually occur. It's going to take lots of luck for things to work out well.

So this book is not intended to be a do-it-yourself guide. Of course, not all do-it-yourselfers are doomed to failure, but they run the substantial risk of overlooking a potential pitfall, opportunity, or some other important factor that would be obvious to an experienced attorney.

As for will- or trust-preparation software, it can produce adequate results in straightforward situations. The catch is that it's difficult to be confident your circumstances are indeed "straightforward" without an attorney's assurance.

Software, however, does not fully cover all the details, contingencies, and specific issues likely to be critical. (I'm aware of no consumer software, for example, that can adequately help somebody deal with the dilemma of leaving a substantial sum to an adult child with an ongoing drug or alcohol problem.) Some clients use software programs just to learn a little and "get something on paper" before consulting an attorney. This is a fine idea.

{ A Closer Look: You might even need *two* lawyers

Many life situations call for everyone involved to seek independent legal advice—a different lawyer for each party. Estate planning is often one of them, especially in the context of marriage. When people with children marry late in life, for example, each spouse is likely to have contemplated the need for a prenuptial (premarital) agreement to ensure that

each spouse's estate will ultimately stay in his or her own family. No matter how loving and respectful the partners are to each other, they recognize unavoidable legal and financial conflicts of interest materialize upon the words "I do."

Once the conflict is acknowledged, fair compromise and agreement are readily possible. This process brings into play a variety of complex laws and issues, so most people understand the need for professional help in preparing a prenup. Although the process is hardly romantic, usually there is no need for hard bargaining or unpleasantness. But you can't compromise and agree with yourself—and neither can your attorney, if only one lawyer is representing both parties. So each partner needs advice from his or her own lawyer—independent representation.

Likewise, there should be independent legal advice for any two people entering a long-term committed relationship, whether it is a formal marriage or not. The law regards married and unmarried people quite differently, but their issues and interests are largely the same—as are the potential conflicts that can be resolved in advance only when each partner has sought out the counsel of his or her own attorney.

Hint: Adult children with parents who have put off estate planning sometimes retain attorneys to consult with their parents to "get things moving." In these and other similar situations, the rule is clear: an attorney owes her loyalty, confidentiality, and best efforts to the client alone, *not to the person paying the fee.*

● When should you review your estate plan? It's wise to review your estate-planning documents—and the estate plan itself—when certain life changes occur:
Changes in whom you want to receive your property: This can occur when someone dies or leaves the family through divorce. On a happier note, someone not included in the original plan can enter the family by birth or marriage. Sometimes a

family member's circumstances change for better or worse, calling for a review of your existing estate plan. For example, if your children are now adults and faring well, the "trust for minor children" written into your will thirty years ago is probably no longer necessary.

Changes in your finances: If your financial circumstances improve, you might want to reconsider the amount and timing of your beneficiaries' inheritance. Tax or business planning might be appropriate. A charitable bequest might make sense.

Changes in your state of residence: If you move to another state, have a lawyer in the new state review your estate-planning documents. In general, a will or trust that is valid where it was prepared will be honored in any state to which one relocates. In most cases, therefore, no changes should be necessary.

In some scenarios, however, it could be difficult for a probate judge in the new state to interpret the law of your former state in attempting to carry out the terms of a will created there. This is especially so when married couples move from community property to common law states, or vice versa. (The difference between community property and common law states is explored more fully in chapter 1.) Sometimes, too, a change in residence makes an estate plan that was simple to begin with a bit more complex. This happens when, for example, a person moves but retains ownership of real estate in the state he just left.

Reviewing your estate plan does not necessarily mean revising it. Many estate plans and the documents that implement them are written to accommodate life's uncertainties. But it is important to be sure, and that's the purpose of the review.

● **How to use this book** Most lawyer-authors (myself included) have an understandable desire to be comprehensive. But trying to cover everything has a downside: the presentation can be difficult to understand, unduly long, and intimidating. I have resisted that tendency in favor of a "broad brush" approach.

Some readers will want to begin with a basic review of estate planning and the most common estate-planning tools, then continue straight through the book. If you don't have time to read cover to cover right now, browse the table of contents to find those topics of greatest interest to you.

You'll have a hard time settling the estate of a loved one or planning your own estate without a grasp of basic property-law concepts. Therefore, I recommend that everyone understand the material in chapter 1, which explains the difference between probate and nonprobate property. If your state follows the law of community property, there is a section on that topic of importance to you.

For those currently going through the probate process following a death in the family, chapter 4 explains the basics of probate and the role of the executor. (You'll find a step-by-step list of executor duties in the appendix.) If you're seeking guidance on more specific issues, later in the book you'll find practical topics, such as asset protection planning (chapter 14) and the selection of those who make estate plans work—executors, trustees, trust advisers, and protectors (chapters 5 and 6).

This book is based on the assumption that it's wise to learn about a subject before you get involved in it, if only to formulate good questions. But when you are finally ready to create your own estate plan, consult a lawyer experienced in this field. An overlooked fact or detail can derail your intentions. That's why you'll see cautionary statements in these pages regarding do-it-yourselfers and occasional reminders of an attorney's value.

Everyone reading this book is motivated by an individual set of life's concerns and questions. The goal of this crash course is to address as many general concepts and issues as quickly and as efficiently as possible. Once you have a general understanding of these topics, you will be able to design—or help your attorney design—a plan that works for you.

{1

Understanding Estate-Planning Basics

Most of us have a fairly good idea of what a *will* is—a simple statement directing how property in your name is to be distributed after your death. What you may not know is that the basic U.S. law regarding wills is more than 460 years old. It originated in England (as did much of American law) with the Statute of Wills in 1540. Before then, primogeniture was the rule—the oldest son inherited his father's land. The Statute of Wills, in contrast, permitted land to be passed upon the landowner's death to whomever he pleased by means of a signed and witnessed document composed of two parts. The portion of the document that *devised* (gave to another) a man's real estate was called the *testament*. But what about a fellow's sword, armor, and other belongings? His personal property (everything besides land) was passed down, or *bequeathed*, in the *will* portion of the newly authorized legal instrument. Although we still call this formal document a "will," you now know why it usually reads "Last Will and Testament" at the top.

Fortunately, you'll be able to get by quite well with no knowledge of that history whatsoever. But there is a reason for mentioning it: in addition to being ancient, the law of property, estates, wills, and trusts is inflexible. Legal documents and details have to be prepared and handled just right. That's why the services of an experienced attorney are crucial to almost everyone in estate-planning and property-law matters.

The concept of a *trust*—as in "trust fund"—is probably vaguely familiar to many of you as well. It, too, is centuries old. A trust is an agreement under which one person formally transfers the title to property to another party (the *trustee*), who then manages it exclusively for the benefit of whomever is named in the trust agreement. In a nutshell, here's how wills and trusts differ: a will passes property directly to someone after the will-maker's death, whereas a trust holds the property for the benefit of another person during the trust-maker's life, after death, or both.

Let's take a look at the types of property you may own, exploring some key facts and concepts about wills, trusts, and other estate-planning tools along the way. We'll also examine the basic steps in probating a will and the duties of the *executor*, the person named in the will to carry out its instructions. Part One concludes with an introduction to tax issues that people with larger estates should consider during the planning process.

1

Different Kinds of Property and the Law

Let's start here: there are two classes of property you need to concern yourself with when planning your estate—*probate property* and *nonprobate property*. Before learning about the basic estate-planning tools at your disposal, it's important to understand what you own, and how the law treats each type of property.

Hint: One who dies with a will is said to have died *testate*, and is called the *testator*. A decedent without a will has died *intestate* (however, there is no such term as "intestator").

Probate

Property All states have a division in their court system responsible for probating wills and administering estates. Most commonly, this judicial entity is designated by a name such as *probate court* or *surrogate's court* (in some states there is no such designation; a regular court of record handles probate). Your probate estate includes any property subject to the authority of this court, whether that property passes according to a will or not. Property that you own in your name alone—and which no one has been chosen to receive upon your death—is probably probate property. This can be real estate, financial accounts of any kind, or just household "stuff."

Attorneys use an important property-law term in wills and trusts in a different sense than regular people use it in everyday conversation. Everyone knows that real estate is real property, or *realty*. In law, however, personal property, or *personalty*, does not refer only to one's toothbrush or watch. Personal property is defined as anything that is not real estate, including tangible items such as a desk or chair as well as intangibles such as financial accounts of all types. In strict legalese, personal property is disposed of by a *bequest*; real estate is disposed of by a *devise*. Often, though, "bequest" or "bequeath" is used in regard to all forms of property.

The best way to explain probate property is as follows: your probate estate is everything you own that is *not* distributed via a *non*probate technique, such as a trust or joint-ownership arrangement. For this reason, it is helpful to begin our study of probate property and procedure with some examples of nonprobate property.

Nonprobate Property

A handful of nonprobate techniques and planning options are available to ensure that your real estate, money, and worldly possessions end up where you want. These nonprobate means of property disposition are extremely useful and common, but not all of them can be used for every type of property.

The critical feature of these property dispositions outside probate is that your will has no control over them. Zero. Absent unusual circumstances, the probate court has no authority over this property either. If you remember nothing else in this book, please remember that. Many people use this fact to great advantage, simplifying their estate plan while saving time and money. Ignorance of this fact, however, could ruin your plan, setting the stage for family warfare once you are gone.

Let's look at the various nonprobate means of property disposition.

● **Gifts** Remember the obvious: if you don't own something when you die, it's not part of your probate estate. By *gift* I mean an outright, complete transfer of realty or personal property (including money) to a person or charity, with no strings attached, *before* you die. In contrast, a property deed stuck in a drawer, for example, with sealed instructions that it be delivered to your child *after* you die, would not be a completed gift. That property would be part of your probate estate.

There are plenty of tax and nontax reasons why a lifetime gift might not be a good idea in your circumstances, however. You should also be aware that if deathbed giveaways leave your estate without funds to pay lawful debts, the probate court could order the gifted property paid back to the estate to satisfy creditors.

● **Property owned by a living trust** If you have created a *living trust* (a trust established during one's lifetime) and formally transferred property to it, that property can be distributed by the trustee to whomever the trust document directs without the probate court's involvement. The retitling of an asset is essential for the trust to have any control over it. Strictly speaking, the transfer is not to the trust itself but to the trustee, who has a legal duty to use and manage trust property for trust purposes only.

● **Property owned jointly with right of survivorship** When each of two or more *joint tenants* (owners) in an asset has a (usually equal) undivided interest in the whole account or asset, the share of the first to die automatically shifts to the surviving joint tenant(s) at the moment of death. The transfer of ownership is complete at that point by "operation of law." *Nothing a will or trust says makes any difference regarding this* *property.* (Of course, there is paperwork to be completed before official records can be switched to the survivor's name alone.) Many married couples own their house, checking accounts, and just about everything else jointly with right of survivorship. There is no requirement, however, that joint tenants with right of survivorship be married.

Alternatively, some states recognize a form of joint ownership known as *tenancy by the entirety,* available only to married couples. In this type of joint ownership, each tenant owns the *entire* property; therefore, neither tenant can transfer his or her interest in the property independently of the other. The advantage here is that creditors of one spouse cannot force the sale of property held as a tenancy by the entirety; the property is not severable.

This stands in contrast to a joint tenancy with right of survivorship, where each of the joint tenants owns a distinct share of the whole property and *can* dispose of his or her interest without the other's consent. In the case of two spouses, a creditor with a judgment against either could collect it by forcing an auction of the couple's home, for example. From the perspective of protecting family assets, tenancy by the entirety is superior to joint tenancy.

● **Tenancy in common** An alternative to joint ownership with right of survivorship is a form of co-ownership *without* the right of survivorship: *tenancy in common*. Here the property does *not* automatically shift to the remaining tenants upon one owner's death. Instead, in this arrangement, each owner (tenant) has a severable interest in the property and is free to sell or bequeath it independently of the others.

Tenancy in common can be the appropriate form of ownership in many situations. For example, when siblings inherit a piece of real estate such as a vacation home from their parents, the best way to hold the property might be a tenancy in common. That way, when one sibling dies, the other(s) could purchase his share from his estate. This would keep the property in the family while allowing the deceased sibling's spouse and children to receive some benefit as well. Recognize, however, that in this type of arrangement, discord between the tenants in common while alive could lead to the sale of one of their shares to an outsider.

● **Beneficiary designation** When you name a person, trust, or charity as the beneficiary of a life insurance policy, retirement account, or anything else, that designation determines who will receive the payment(s) upon your death. This money is not controlled by your will and is thus not part of the probate estate (unless you designate "my estate" or make no choice at all). The proceeds of the policy or account should be transferred at once to whomever is designated, without involving the probate court. Like a will, your choice of beneficiary can be changed.

{ **Warning!** Take care not to let your ex collect

With qualified retirement plans such as 401(k)s, profit sharing, and many pension plans, the account owner's husband or wife has a legal right under federal law to be designated the beneficiary. This spouse must agree in writing to any change in this designation. (This is not so with IRAs.

Note, too, that federal law does not extend this protection to a same-sex spouse, even if his or her marriage was valid under the law of the spouses' state.) Immediately after a divorce, therefore, both ex-partners should review any accounts that designate their former spouse as a beneficiary. Although a will naming a spouse as beneficiary automatically becomes void (as it pertains to the spouse) when he or she becomes an "ex," the same is not true of a beneficiary designation form that directs how funds are to be distributed. So if you are divorced but never bothered to change your designation forms, your ex probably still stands to collect your retirement funds and your life insurance payout if you die right now.

● **Pay-on-death (POD) bank accounts and transfer-on-death (TOD) brokerage accounts** These accounts began as ordinary financial accounts. Because so many people have bank, brokerage, and mutual fund accounts, a convenient way was created to deal with them without probate: a beneficiary designation form is offered at the time the account is started. That's all *pay (or transfer) on death* means—it's the designation of one or more beneficiaries. The beneficiary receives the account funds directly, without going through probate court. This can be an extremely useful and convenient tool—so long as you're aware of how it works.

A Closer Look: A common mistake regarding accounts naming beneficiaries

My father's will named me executor and divided his estate equally among my brother, my sister, and me. So I was surprised to find he had a bank certificate of deposit payable on death (POD) to me alone. None of his other accounts was POD. Someone at the bank probably suggested he use the POD designation as a way of avoiding probate. Dad did not hear well, and he may have just nodded when the bank employee made the suggestion. I knew very well, however, that my father did not intend to give this CD only to me. But by using a POD instrument, that's precisely what he did. Unlike his other property, the CD was not subject to probate.

I would have been within my rights to pocket the money—with or without the knowledge of my brother and sister. They could have then gone to court, arguing that a mistake had been made—that my father lacked the required intent to make a gift of the entire CD to me. That's the truth of the matter, yet it would have been almost impossible to prove.

Instead, I cashed in the CD and gave one-third of the proceeds each to my brother and sister. We're a close family, so the decision was automatic, but I'm sure Dad didn't buy that CD because he was counting on me to be fair and share the money—he just made a mistake. Beware of

this kind of situation; the potential for a family feud is obvious.

• **Contracts** Generally, any kind of written deal you make concerning money or other property will stand after your death (assuming the deal is still possible). Suppose I sign a contract to sell you my tractor for $1,000, with the exchange to take place next week. If I die before then, you could present the signed contract and your money to my executor and insist that he or she carry out the transaction. Never mind that my will gives "all my property of whatever kind" to somebody else; a deal is a deal.

Strictly speaking, it is not a nonprobate disposition when an executor honors a contract. After all, the executor controls only the probate estate. So any money or goods he transfers has to be probate property. In fact, the contract itself is part of the probate estate and, if our example were reversed, the executor could sue the tractor-buyer to complete the sale. The money paid for the tractor would likewise become part of the probate estate. The point to remember is that because my tractor is covered by a contract, it would not pass according to my will. If I bequeathed the tractor to my cousin Bob, poor Bob would be out of luck.

A buy-sell agreement for a business is a common example of a contract that comes into play when one of the owners dies. Under such a contract, the decedent's business partners offer a previously agreed-upon price for the decedent's share of the business, and the executor must accept the payment and sign the papers required to close the transaction. Without this contract, the decedent's share in the business would pass to someone else according to his will or trust, or the executor could sell it to the highest bidder, just like any other property.

A *prenuptial (premarital) agreement* is another type of contract often used to establish a married couple's financial relationship. (This topic is examined in depth in chapter 3.) In most situations, if there is a conflict between the terms of a valid prenuptial agreement and the decedent's will, the prenup takes priority. This is only fair. Otherwise, either party to the prenup, acting alone, could change the bargain simply by writing a will.

Intestacy: Where There's No Will, There's Still a Way

If you have not planned ahead using tools such as a will or the nonprobate means of passing property at death, you are relying on the law that applies in your state when a person dies without having directed to whom his property should go. That is the law of *intestacy* or *descent and distribution*. Remember, however, that this law pertains only to probate property—that which you own alone. As such, it would be disbursed by the probate court according to state law.

State laws of intestacy make pretty good sense. They work as default plans for distributing the property of those who die without a will. But state intestacy laws are also absolutely rigid; they are not customized to achieving a fair result in the eyes of your survivors. The court has virtually no discretion to do the right thing—whatever that might be.

{ A Closer Look:
What happens to your probate property if you die without a will?

Below are general examples of property distribution schemes that show how state laws direct the distribution of a person's probate estate when that person dies without a will. These state statutes vary significantly, however; be forewarned that they contain important details not covered here.

MARRIED WITH CHILDREN Many people wrongly believe that a surviving spouse will inherit all property owned by the deceased spouse, especially if they have young children. That is generally not the case. In this situation, the law of most states awards one-third to one-half of the decedent's property to the surviving spouse and the remainder to the children, regardless of their age.

The court appoints a guardian of the children's property until they reach legal adulthood. Even when the surviving parent continues to have custody of the kids themselves, this property guardian is not always the parent. This arrangement may leave the surviving parent without adequate resources of her own, forcing her to repeatedly justify child-rearing expenses to the court in order to get money for them. If an adult child of the decedent has also died, that child's children—that is, the decedent's grandchildren—would inherit their parent's share to split.

MARRIED WITH NO CHILDREN OR GRAND- CHILDREN In some states, the surviving spouse will inherit the entire estate in this situation—or everything up to a certain value (for example, the first $200,000). In many other states, however, the surviving spouse receives only a specified interest in any real estate owned by the decedent (such as "one-half," or "one-third"). In addition to that value, the surviving spouse usually gets only one-half of the remaining estate. The balance generally goes to the decedent's parent(s), if they are still alive. If both parents are dead, many states split the remainder among the decedent's brothers and sisters.

SINGLE PERSON WITH CHILDREN When a single person with children dies without a will, all state laws provide that the entire estate go to the children, in equal shares. If an adult child of the decedent has also died, that child's children (the decedent's grandchildren) split their parent's share.

SINGLE PERSON WITH NO CHILDREN OR GRANDCHILDREN In this situation, most state laws favor the decedent's parent(s) in the distribution of his property. If both parents are deceased, many states divide the property among the brothers and sisters. In some states, the decedent's brothers and sisters are ahead of the parents in the distribution order.

With or without a will, trust, or any planning at all, the law is designed so the state seldom stands to take your estate, unless you have no children, spouse, or blood relatives. For all sorts of reasons, you probably should have a will. But there's no basis for the common belief that when a person dies without a will the state automatically takes her money—or that a judge picks someone at random to receive her property.

Furthermore, if your spouse has already died, there are no circumstances in which the spouse's side of the family (your brother-in-law, for example) would inherit any portion of your estate. If your spouse is still living when you die, of course, the brother-in-law might eventually inherit "your" property from your spouse as your spouse's brother.

What Is
Your Estate? "What does my estate include?" The simple answer is "everything." As noted earlier in this chapter, easily arranged nonprobate dispositions can keep your property from passing through probate court. That decreases your *probate* estate, but your probate estate is only a portion of your total estate. For almost every purpose, including taxes, your estate is everything you own. Whenever the word "estate" is used by itself (rather than in a term such as

"probate estate") in this book, it means "everything." Your estate includes:

- All property rights and interests owned by you, including half of joint accounts with your spouse. If the other joint owner is not your spouse, your share is defined by law for many purposes as one hundred percent, unless you can show that somebody else contributed to the account or property.
- All property owned by a trust that you control outright, or by a trust over which you have any significant control or strings attached.
- The full value of IRAs and employer retirement plan accounts of all kinds.
- Life insurance proceeds, if the policy is payable to your estate or owned by you and payable to anyone else.

The last item surprises a lot of people, because life insurance payoffs are received free of income tax. Because such payoffs are included in the calculation of estate taxes, however, they can precipitate a nasty tax surprise for the unwary. (Chapter 15 examines ways to avoid this.)

{ **Warning!** Relative wealth: Your estate could attract the gaze of Uncle Sam

Who should be concerned about federal estate tax? For 2004 and 2005, if the value of a single person's estate or a married couple's (combined) estate reaches or approaches $1.5 million, federal estate-tax planning is called for. Tax matters are considered more thoroughly in chapter 8.

Community Property

• **Who needs to know about this? What is it, anyway?** The term *community property* often crops up in discussions about estate planning (and divorce). Derived from Spanish law, it is a form of property ownership between husband and wife that is recognized in Arizona, California, Idaho, Louisiana, Nevada, New Mexico, Texas, Washington, and Wisconsin. The other forty-one states are *common law* states; they follow a marital property ownership system known as American common law, which originated in England.

Three groups of readers should pay particular attention to community property:

1. Spouses who now live in a community property jurisdiction
2. Spouses who now live in a common law state, but who acquired money or property while living in a community property state
3. Spouses who now live in a community property state, but who acquired money or property while living previously in a common law state.

Details of the law differ from state to state, but the defining feature of community property is this: Irrespective of the name(s) on title documents, ownership of almost all the property acquired during the marriage by either spouse is considered to be automatically shared; this means each spouse owns a separate, one-half interest. Likewise, both spouses have an equal share of *all* income (and retirement benefits) from wages and self-employment earned by either spouse during the marriage.

In a nutshell, community property is (almost) anything that is neither *separate property*, nor property owned jointly with right of survivorship. Separate property includes anything acquired by a spouse before the marriage, and brought into it. In addition, in community property states, property acquired by gift or inheritance, or in exchange for separate property or separate money, remains separate.

The income, if any, that separate property produces is treated differently by the various community property states. In California, for example, the income from separate property remains separate property. In Texas, however, income produced by the separate property of one spouse becomes community property. As a practical matter, however, commingling of funds over time can obscure separate-property ownership until finally it becomes impossible to prove that formerly separate money is not community property. This can easily happen with checking and other financial accounts.

Hint: Most community property states allow spouses to change their respective ownership rights in an asset from community property to sep-

arate property, or to joint ownership with right of survivorship, simply by written agreement between
them. Separate property cannot be
changed into community property—
but unless you can clearly prove that
the property is separate, the law will
presume it to be community property.

● **What does community property have
to do with estate planning?** Because the
two equal interests of the spouses in community property are distinct, each spouse is
free to dispose of his or her half of community property in a will. (Note, however, that
neither spouse can sell any portion of the
community property without the other
spouse's consent.) Of course, a deceased
spouse's federal taxable estate contains his
half of the couple's community property.

When a married decedent in a community
property state has no will (dies intestate),
what happens to his half of the community
property varies according to state law and
who the surviving family members are. In
California, for example, the surviving spouse
would inherit half the deceased spouse's

share of the community property, regardless of whether the decedent had any children. The survivor retains the half of community property he or she already owned, as well.

In Texas, if the decedent has no children, or if all his children were also those of the surviving spouse, then the surviving spouse receives all the decedent's community property. But if the Texas decedent had even one child who was not also the child of the surviving spouse, the surviving spouse gets none of the decedent's share of community property. The survivor retains the half of community property he or she already owned, but all of the decedent's half goes to the decedent's children.

A Closer Look: When a spouse acquires assets in a common law state but resides in a community property state

Here's a common scenario: A wife earns and saves money in a separate account in a common law state, then moves with her husband to a community property state. If she dies before her husband while they are both still living in the new state, is the money deemed community property or not?

The answer differs from state to state. California would treat the wife's account as community property, granting the husband a half-interest. Texas, in contrast, would treat the wife's account as it was treated in the common law state where it was earned: because the account was originally in the wife's name alone, Texas would regard it as her separate property and not recognize any interest of the husband in it.

Although community property is basically a simple concept, the devil is in the details. State laws vary, and you can imagine the multitude of circumstances that pose community property planning questions. Tax matters, especially, can become complex. If you are affected by the issue of community property, devote special attention to it. Before attempting to give community property away by gift, in a will, or in a trust, see a lawyer for guidance in understanding the extent of each spouse's property rights.

If you have ever lived in a community property state while married, property acquired there will generally be presumed to still be community property even if you move to a common law state, unless there is clear proof to the contrary (e.g., a written agreement between spouses). So if either or both spouses are or ever were legal residents of a community property state, good records should be maintained. These records should detail the estate of each spouse before marriage, the state of the current marriage, and the identity, value, and source of funds used to buy property during marriage, as well as the legal residence at the time of acquisition. This is essential information in identifying the respective property rights of the spouses; it is important for estate planning and in the unfortunate case of divorce as well.

Life

Estates This is a topic that doesn't fit neatly anywhere, but it comes up in many situations. Because we've been looking at the meaning of "estate," let's discuss the term here. When a person is given a *life estate* in a piece of property (very often, a house and the contents within it), he enjoys almost the same rights in that property as would the "absolute" owner—but only for his lifetime. When the holder of the life estate dies, the property permanently passes to the *remainderman(men)*—one or more people chosen in advance by the original property owner.

A life estate is a grant of property rights, and can be created in a property deed, a will, a trust, a prenuptial agreement, or even an agreement after marriage. The individual situation usually dictates which of these legal documents is used.

The nature of a life estate is illustrated in the common "subsequent marriage" scenario. Assume that a widow who owns a home plans a late-in-life second marriage. She and her new husband decide that he will sell his own house, and that the couple will live in the wife's home. The new bride wants to ensure that her children, not the new husband or his family, ultimately inherit her property. For this reason, she does not put his name on the deed, nor does she leave the house to him in her will. The wife wants to be sure, however, that her husband will have a place to live if she dies before he does. So the newlyweds agree (on paper) that the husband will have a life estate in the house. He can live there until he dies, at which time the property will go to the woman's children (or to whomever she specifies). As a *life tenant*, the husband can do pretty much as he pleases with the house, but of course he cannot sell it. (This kind of understanding can—and should—be put in writing *before* the marriage. Typically, it would be part of a prenuptial agreement, which should always be prepared or reviewed by independent attorneys for each party [see page 17].)

Remember that the rules concerning life estates vary according to state law. For example, property tax is generally the responsibility of the ultimate owner (the remainderman). But the document creating the life estate can specify differently—for example, that the life tenant must pay the taxes. In contrast, the life tenant is generally responsible for maintaining the property in "good condition," a term open to interpretation and argument. To avoid disputes about the responsibilities and costs of property ownership, it is wise to spell out who is expected to do—and pay for—what.

Hint: **With many couples marrying late in life, a number of clients prefer to use a lifetime *right of occupancy* for a spouse, rather than a life estate. If the surviving spouse then enters an assisted-living facility, where she might stay for the next ten years, the children can get at their inherited house as soon as their stepmother ceases to occupy it. With a life estate, they would have to wait until she died.**

If you have a life estate and want to know your rights (or, more importantly, if you want to give somebody a lifetime interest in property you own), please see a lawyer. Much is at stake in seeing that this arrangement works as planned, and it is easy to foul things up trying to do it yourself.

{ **A Closer Look:**
You make the call:
Is this a life estate?

A man is living in his house with his second wife. He dies and his do-it-yourself will reads, "To my wife I give the use of my home and regular household furniture as long as she needs the house for her primary residence."

Who knows what this fellow meant by "needs"? Did he intend for his wife to first seek a bed at the Salvation Army shelter? Probably not. The man's children think he meant, "If you marry a guy three months after my funeral and he owns two nice houses, you won't need to live in my house, so my kids can sell it." This scenario is based on an actual case. The wife *did* quickly remarry such a man.

What did the testator (the will-maker) intend? Unless the parties settle, the court must decide. In disputes such as this, most courts would give the surviving spouse the benefit of the doubt. Judges are human (they're also usually elected officials). No matter what the reality is, no judge wants to appear to be putting a widow out on the sidewalk so that greedy offspring can pocket their inheritance.

No one knows how cases like this might end up—nor does it matter. The lesson is: you don't want your survivors to be in this situation at all. Thousands of dollars in legal fees were wasted in our example; had the testator simply hired an attorney to prepare his will, it might have cost him $500.

CHAPTER 2

Wills and Trusts: Choosing the Right Tools to Make Your Estate Plan Work

At this point you are probably not quite ready to make your choice of planning tools. Although we have mentioned the most fundamental of these tools—wills and trusts—we have not yet examined either one in detail. In addition, we have focused only on background information for you to keep in mind and have not taken individual needs into account. In this chapter we'll explore some life situations that wills and trusts can address, then study the basic features of each planning tool and compare the two.

Hint: If you know that a certain household item has special significance for a particular child, consider giving it to her before you die, or specifically directly doing so in your will. If you don't know how to do this, simply ask the children what they'd like—but be sure to allocate something to everybody. This may minimize the likelihood of arguments among your children.

Determine
Your Needs

There are those, including plenty of attorneys, who act as if anyone lacking a living trust is crazy. On the other side of the fence are those who give the impression that a will is all anyone needs, and that a trust is usually a waste of time and money because so very few people can benefit from one. Even without a law degree, common sense tells you that the truth lies between those two extremes. Rather than worry about what you "should have," focus on your situation: if you died tomorrow, what people and things would need to be taken care of? What are your concerns?

An issue we all share is that our affairs will have to be wrapped up—something that often requires time, effort, and skill. So if you care who your "wrapper upper" is, you'd be wise to identify him or her by naming that person as the executor of your will. (The responsibilities of this position are detailed in chapter 5.)

For now, even if you are of modest means, don't assume that the wrapping-up duties will be trivial. Be realistic. When a person dies, rich or poor, certain matters must be taken care of by somebody—lawyer or not—whether there's a will, a trust, or neither one.

First, there is the funeral. Then bills have to be paid. Personal business and insurance matters must be concluded, such as notifying the Social Security Administration and the employee benefit offices of government, military services, or private-sector companies paying benefits to the decedent.

Final income tax and/or state inheritance tax returns usually must be filed, even if no tax is due. A federal estate tax return might be necessary, too, if the estate is large ($1.5 million in 2004 and 2005). A dwelling may have to be vacated and cleaned up in anticipation of a sale or a lease termination. All kinds of property—from bank accounts to cars to coin collections—must be accounted for, secured, divided appropriately, and formally transferred as required.

These chores cannot be avoided. A certain amount of time, free or paid, is inevitably involved. Obviously, leaving all these details to an attorney or a court-appointed administrator could be expensive, but that won't be necessary if you have named somebody in a will to handle things for you. Failing to name an executor often leads to some kind of problem for the people you most care about—whether right away or many years later.

Wills and Trusts
Can Work Together
Wills and trusts are tools and nothing more. When tackling a household repair, no one starts by choosing a tool and then figuring out some way to make it work. So it is with wills and trusts when the project at hand is constructing your estate plan. Depending on your estate and goals, either a will or a trust—or both

(perhaps with several other estate-planning tools)—may be appropriate.

Wills and trusts are not unrelated or alternative estate-planning options. Many wills, for example, have trusts written into them. These are called testamentary trusts and they come into existence only after death. The testator states that his money or other property is to be placed in trust; the will then spells out how the trustee, or trust manager, is to administer and distribute those assets.

A trust created during the trust creator's lifetime, by contrast, is called a *living trust*. In most cases, a living trust should be accompanied by a basic will. For example, for the overall handling of typical post-death affairs, as a practical matter, the executor of a will is often better situated than the trustee of a living trust. When personnel at the phone company or the motor vehicle department get an inquiry from an executor, they usually have to ask a supervisor what to do—but at least they know that an executor is a deceased person's representative. This is just one reason why a will is strongly recommended even if you create a living trust.

A will is also used to direct how your property should be distributed. You should understand, however, that *a simple will by itself is a fairly limited planning device*; it is useful primarily in uncomplicated situations. This does not mean that a will is suitable only for small estates; to the contrary, a will can be quite adequate for conveying a large estate, even one with numerous beneficiaries and sizable assets. As long as you contemplate only straightforward transfers of property at death, with few if any conditions or strings attached, a will is fine. But a will alone (one that does not call for a trust to be set up) can't do much more than that.

If your goals require a more complex approach, a trust of some sort is probably necessary. What does "more complex" mean? Tax planning, for one thing, or the need to provide for others who cannot appropriately be left a lump sum of money or a piece of property outright. This might include a disabled or financially unsophisticated spouse or other loved one. Frequently, too, a trust is used to manage and distribute money to meet the needs of children or grandchildren. This includes young children who have yet to reach maturity, as well as adult children who refuse to act like grownups or have conniving spouses.

Let's take a look at some "will basics," then do the same for trusts.

{ A Closer Look: A word about domestic partnerships and same-sex marriages

In a great many ways, planning for those in committed, nontraditional relationships involves the same considerations and tools that apply to traditional married couples. Your concerns about loved ones, the disposition of your property, and medical and financial provisions in case of disability can all be addressed with the documents we examine in this book. The "trick"—applicable to *all* estate planners—is to ensure that all documents are written to fit your needs.

That said, there are significant federal income, gift, and estate tax-saving options unavailable to people in these nontraditional relationships. A statute enacted in 1996 denied recognition of same-sex marriages for the purpose of *federal* laws and taxation; unmarried partners have never enjoyed a special status under federal law. A key example is that gifts between same-sex spouses (during life or upon death) do not qualify for the tax-free treatment that traditional married couples enjoy under the federal gift and estate tax law. Another example is the right—provided only to a surviving spouse of the opposite sex—to roll over a deceased spouse's retirement account into her own IRA.

So any special benefits or legal rights granted to unmarried "domestic partners"—whether same or opposite sex—or to same-sex spouses are based on state laws, which vary widely. Any such advantages are limited to matters governed solely by those state laws—state taxation, for example, or the right of one spouse or partner not to be denied an inheritance upon the death of the other. What remains to be seen is the extent to which state courts will honor

laws and rulings from other states, especially if those rulings are quite different from their own.

Will Basics "I just need a simple will" is the first thing many a client says upon meeting with an attorney. Often the client is correct, but frequently a so-called "simple" will, without a trust or other documents, is *not* the best estate-planning option. Unfortunately, much of the public perceives wills as commodity items—and many lawyers are happy to indulge that notion without much professional evaluation.

Before deciding on your needs, therefore, it is crucial to think through some "what if" scenarios about events that could unfold after your death. Ideally, your attorney will facilitate this process. But he or she is not a mind reader, so your active input is essential.

If a simple will covers your situation, fine. But don't assume that thorny matters you've identified disappear if you have not addressed them. What should you put in a simple will? Before trying to answer that question, take a look at the following

clause-by-clause analysis of wh
will can accomplish.

Name your executor This cla
appears at the beginning of the
can be included anywhere in the document.
The executor is given broad authority to pay
your debts and taxes, sell property, settle
your affairs, and distribute your estate as directed later in the document. This person is
your "wrapper upper," so he or she must be
chosen carefully. For married couples, the
executor is typically the surviving spouse,
but almost any trusted person or firm, such
as a bank, can fill the role. (A few states require the executor to be a state resident,
but they make an important exception to allow children or others in the will-maker's
family.) An alternate executor—someone
who will shoulder the task if your first choice
proves unable or unwilling—should be
named as well. (See chapter 5 for additional
important considerations in choosing an executor.)

Make specific bequests to beneficiaries
Such bequests can include either money or
tangible property. For example: "My best
friend, Joe Dokes, gets my fishing rod and

kle box; my daughter Jane gets my an-
que car; my nephew, Jake, gets one thousand dollars; my cousin, Jethro, gets my
Shakespeare collection."

{ A Closer Look: If you sell an item after writing your will

What happens when the will directs that a certain item of property (a coin collection, say) is to be given to a particular beneficiary, but that property is no longer available? The testator may have lost it or sold it, forgetting that it was mentioned in the will. Does the beneficiary get a cash equivalent or a replacement item instead? Not usually. In most states, the would-be beneficiary is out of luck—he gets nothing. The testator's actions have effectively revoked the gift. In this case the gift is said to have been *adeemed*; the process by which this occurred is known as *ademption*.

To avoid any misunderstandings, consider adding the simple words, ". . . if owned by me at my death," after stating to whom the coin collection should be given in a will. This makes it clear that there will be no bequest unless the property is still owned by the testator when he dies.

Dispose of the rest of your property *Residue* is an ancient word used in estate planning, as in "the rest and residue of my property" (or, "my residuary estate"). This consists of anything and everything that remains in your probate estate after the payment of your legal obligations and the distribution of property according to any specific bequests you made earlier in the will. Remember, if there is something you want to leave to someone in particular, spell it out before this clause; doing so will "take it off the table," keeping it from going to someone you did not intend.

Because the value and make-up of your estate at the time of your death can often not be foreseen, it is neither necessary nor desirable to be too specific here. For example, couples married for many years commonly use the language: "If I die first, everything goes to my spouse. If my spouse has already died, everything to my descendants, in equal shares, *per stirpes*." (This is a Latin term that means, in effect, "If a child dies before the parent, that child's children split their parent's share.") Note, however, that a parent is under no obligation to leave anything to a child.

Set up a testamentary trust (if you need one) The above example calls for the distribution of the rest of your property directly to one or more people (a charity could have been included to receive a portion of the estate, as well). Alternatively, the will can state that some or all of your property is to be placed in a trust to be managed for the benefit of your loved ones. (A trust is especially useful if your loved ones include young children or grandchildren, or if your estate is large enough to require tax planning.) The terms of the trust are then set forth, along with the name of the trustee and the powers he is to be given. Very often, all of this runs for twenty or more pages within the will. Remember that a testamentary trust does not really exist until the will is taken to probate court.

Name a guardian(s) for your children When there are children under age eighteen, a will should always be used to name a *guardian(s)* of their *persons* and their *property*. If you feel it is necessary or appropriate, two guardians may be appointed—one over the child himself, and a second (presumably financially experienced) over the child's property. Of course, if a surviving parent is living in the same household, he or she remains the sole guardian of any minor children. When a surviving parent does *not* have custody, however, he or she—unless unfit—still has priority in seeking guardianship and custody of the kids. This is true even if you have named someone else as the children's guardian.

In every situation—but especially if the other parent is likely to be unable or unfit to take custody of the children—at least one alternate guardian should be named, or "nominated." (That is the more precise term, because the court eventually must approve any guardian you propose.) Nominating a guardian can help avoid family arguments; it also provides guidance to the court.

Hint: There is an important distinction between *guardianship* and *custody*. This is illustrated when the caretaking ability of a child's surviving parent is legitimately in question, and the person nominated as guardian (the child's grandparent, for example) comes forward to alert the court. In that situation, the court often appoints a state social-service agency as a temporary guardian. Like any guardian, the state would have full legal authority over the child. The agency might then determine that the grandparent was better suited to have custody, or physical control and day-to-day authority over the child, until the parent proved himself worthy. (Again, it is the strong policy of the law to keep children with their parents.)

Consider carefully the wisdom of naming a young child as the beneficiary of money or other property, even if a qualified guardian is available. Guardianship ends at the age of legal adulthood (usually eighteen, sometimes twenty-one.) From then on, the child exclusively owns and controls any property left to her. Until then, guardianship over a child's property occurs under rigid court oversight. There are obvious good reasons for that, but it is a cumbersome way to manage financial affairs. Periodic reports and accounting to the court might be required, and flexibility is limited by law. Establishing a trust for the child's benefit is far preferable. (Trusts for minor children are discussed in chapter 9.)

{ A Closer Look: Take care how you direct your expenses to be paid

The "pay my debts and taxes" clause is a seemingly innocuous feature in almost every will. It is also a prime example of how easy it can be to foul up your estate plan without realizing it. Here is an example.

Mary, a recently deceased widow, had three children to whom she intended to leave her estate, in equal shares. The estate consists of a $75,000 house and a $25,000 savings account in the name of the decedent alone, plus two $100,000 certificates of deposit. Mary's simple will gives the house and the savings account to Child A. One of the CDs is payable on death (POD) to Child B, and one is POD to Child C. The decedent understood that POD accounts are nonprobate dispositions, so there was no reason to mention them in her will. As far as Mary understood, this simple combination of probate and nonprobate dispositions constituted a good estate plan. It would put into effect her desire to give each of her three children equal monetary value—$100,000. So far, so good.

But the estate will have administrative and other final bills and expenses. Where does the money come from to pay them? Mary's will directs her executor (a son) to "pay my just debts." So that's what he must do—pay all the expenses from the cash available to him, which is limited to the savings account in the probate estate. This means, obviously, that all expenses must come out of Child A's share.

That is not what Mary wanted, yet the executor (no matter who it is) had no choice. Because the CDs left to Child B and Child C were payable on death, they were transferred outside of probate. Those funds were therefore not available to the executor to help pay bills. (The outcome would be even more complicated if the value of the probate estate alone was not large enough to pay a legitimate big claim, such as an unpaid debt of the decedent. In that case, it might be possible under state law for the creditor to recover payment from nonprobate beneficiaries such as Child B or C.)

Had Mary recognized the potential problem and obtained good advice, she could have avoided the unfairness of this situation. Of course, if Children B and C want to be fair to Child A, they are free to contribute to the estate's debts and expenses— but they don't have to do so.

● **Legal formalities and requirements of wills** No special format or "magic words" are required for a valid will, but it must be in writing and signed by the testator (the willmaker.) A videotaped will might sound like a great idea, especially when the testator's mental status might be an issue later. Unfortunately, such a tape would not be recognized as a valid will in any state. (The videotape still might be a good idea, however, just as evidence of the testator's competency at the time the will was signed.)

A typed or printed will must be signed in the presence of two (and in a few states three) witnesses. The witnesses must sign in the presence of the testator and one another, but they need not read the will or know what it says. Such a will is said to be *self-proving* if it contains notarized clauses in which the testator and the witnesses make certain formal recitals. In a nutshell, the parties affirm that all of them are within sight of each other, and that the testator is of sound mind, knows he is signing his will, and has asked the witnesses to so affirm.

{ **Warning!** Can I get a witness? Yes—as long as she doesn't benefit

In most states, if a witness to a will is also a beneficiary, and the will cannot be proved without this witness, the

portion of the will that pertains to that beneficiary/witness can become invalid. (The rest of the will would still be valid, however.) To prevent this, use witnesses who aren't named as beneficiaries.

If a will is self-proving, the witnesses do not have to appear in probate court to verify the document. That's what you want. Otherwise, the witnesses or some other proof would be required to demonstrate the validity of the will. That could be a big inconvenience for your executor, so be sure to make your will self-proving.

A *codicil* is an amendment to an earlier will. Never make written additions, crossouts, or changes on the original document after you have signed it. Instead, a separate page should be prepared, referring specifically to the original will, and executed with the same formalities required of a will in your state. Keep the codicil with the will, and keep it simple. If the desired changes are complicated, subject to interpretation, or potentially in conflict with other provisions of the will, start from scratch and do another will. (Destroy the old one to avoid confusion.)

Some states allow *holographic* wills—written entirely in the handwriting of the testator—with no witnesses required. In these states, however, lengthy, expensive legal battles occasionally arise about whether a letter or some other piece of writing by the decedent constitutes a valid will. Contrary to popular belief, many states do not permit unwitnessed wills, so there is no room for controversy there.

{ **A Closer Look:**
  Read your will carefully
  before signing it

Read your will before you sign it. If you don't understand an item, if something is not right, or if you have any concerns whatsoever, speak up. When my uncle died a few years ago, my father asked me to look over my aunt's old will. At the end of the document, I noticed a slight problem: Aunt Elena had signed her name over a signature line that read,

"GUSTAV BALCH." (I am not making this up.)

Obviously, the attorney had used another client's document as the basis for Aunt Elena's. All lawyers have done this and it is not a problem—*if*, that is, the document has been modified to fit the new client's needs and uses the new client's name throughout. Clients should be fussy about that; it's hardly asking too much. Moral of the story: document-drafting mistakes can and do occur, so carefully read everything before you sign it.

As for Aunt Elena, her will was the first formal paper with a signature line that she had ever seen. She just figured that "GUSTAV BALCH" was legal mumbo-jumbo.

To qualify as a will, a document must appear to the court—looking only at the document itself—that it was intended to be the final expression of the testator's wishes about how his property should be disposed after his death. That is why, even where holographic wills are allowed, a general letter stating one's desires—or a list of property with someone's name beside each item—is probably insufficient.

● **Mental competence to write a valid will**
Most importantly, the will-maker must have *testamentary capacity*. Under the law of most states, this requires that the testator be of "sound mind" when drawing up and signing the document. She must only be aware—generally—of the nature and extent of her property, and of the "natural objects of her bounty." What does that mean? It means that she must understand, for example, that she has three children, who would "naturally" be those to whom a mother would leave her estate. This does not mean she *must* leave her estate to her three children. It means, however, she must realize that her nurses are no kin to her, for example. Additionally, the testator must be aware that by signing the will, she is directing a final disposition of her property.

Most wills attempt to resolve the mental competence issue by having the witnesses sign a blurb at the end of the document stating that the testator is of "sound mind." That standard clause would not settle the matter, however, if somebody complained that the testator was mentally weak and under "undue influence" or duress from another party. But the law bends over backward to reject such claims and uphold wills that appear to be valid on the surface.

It is worth emphasizing that the testator is not required to be mentally sharp, or reasonable. There is certainly no requirement that she be "fair" at all. A perfectly valid and legally defensible will can be made by a testator who is eccentric, weird, or just plain mean. She must only know what she is doing, to the extent described above. If she does, the law will respect whatever disposition she cares to make—subject to lawful claims that must be paid first. Never mind that the testator had been acting "funny" in the months during which the will was written. Never mind that the will unfairly favors one child over the rest. Those facts by themselves would almost never persuade a judge to declare a will invalid. (If a will is voided, the estate is handled according to the state law of intestacy, discussed in chapter 1.)

Hint: Adult children concerned that their parent lacks a will sometimes consult an attorney. The parent's mental condition may be deteriorating rapidly, punctuated by "good days." The law makes it proper for the testator to execute a will during such a "lucid interval"—if, that is, testamentary capacity truly exists at the moment of signing.

● **What if I get married, divorced, or have a child after the will is done?** Marriage generally revokes your will automatically, unless the will expressly states that it is not to be revoked. However, even in a state where your will is not revoked upon marriage, your new spouse can acquire a substantial claim to your estate by renouncing the will and taking a state-determined elective share. (We'll discuss this on page 87.) A divorce and final property settlement bar all claims of the divorced survivor to the estate of an ex-spouse who dies. The estate of the decedent passes by will, trust, or state intestacy law as if the surviving ex-spouse had already died. The same may be true if a spouse abandons the household, even if there has been no formal divorce.

{Warning! Sign off your ex on the dotted line

A divorce generally does not automatically undo beneficiary designations on life insurance policies, retirement accounts, and so on. If you want your ex off the policies and accounts, request and fill out new beneficiary designation forms. Then try extra hard to stay alive until they are placed in the mail.

The birth of a child, unborn when the parent's will was made, is a common occurrence. In many states, such a child receives a share by law equal to what he or she would have received if the parent had died without a will (intestate). However, the law will not require this distribution if the testator-parent left everything to the surviving parent of the omitted child, or if the testator provided for this child outside the will—with life insurance, for example. The share-splitting arithmetic in such situations can get complex—and does not necessarily result in equal treatment of the omitted child. For that reason, revise your will after the birth of a child. Alternatively, when writing your will, include a provision stating that all future off-spring should be counted in for a full share, just as if they had been named originally. A grandparent whose will names her grand-children as beneficiaries should consider a similar provision referring to any future grandchildren. That way, living and unborn grandchildren receive equal treatment un-der her will—if that is what the grandparent wants.

{ A Closer Look: What to do if your will comes under attack

Will contests, in which the validity of the will is attacked, are typically mounted by people who were omit-ted or feel slighted by their share. In some states, a *no-contest clause* can be inserted in a will to automati-cally exclude anyone who challenges the will in court. This can be an espe-cially useful tool if the would-be challenger can be anticipated. In that case, it might be worthwhile to leave this person a "little something."

Once he learned in probate court—if not before—that he had something to lose by challenging the will, the dispute would become far less appealing.

It is unlikely, however, that any state would enforce a no-contest clause against someone who comes forward with a legitimate attack against a will. For example, "Mom didn't know what she was doing. My brother-in-law put the paper in front of her and told her to sign it." Or, "My sister is Dad's executor. She just had a garage sale at his house and kept the money for herself."

● **A spouse's right to renounce a will** Your will (or trust) might not be the last word in determining what your spouse receives. If a surviving spouse is not satisfied with a deceased mate's will, he or she can renounce it. Rather than accept whatever inheritance the will specifies (if any), the survivor can elect to take a share of the estate (sometimes called an *elective share* or a *forced share*) that is spelled out by state law. In many states, this share is approximately equal to a spouse's intestate share of the estate—what the survivor would have gotten had there been no will at all. (One-third to one-half of the decedent's estate is a good ballpark estimate.) In some states, a surviving spouse's elective share starts low and increases with each year of marriage to a maximum of fifty percent.

Hint: A surviving spouse must exercise his or her *right of election*—renouncing a will in favor of the spousal elective share—by filing paperwork with the court, usually during the probate process, within a time period set by state law. This time limit is generally months, not years, so if this might affect you, don't sit on your hands—see a lawyer.

The right of election—that is, the option of renouncing a will—is a legal device originally intended to protect a wife. Historically, all of a family's property might be titled solely in the husband's name. The elective share protects a woman (or a man) from being deliberately or accidentally written out of a spouse's will. A husband with all the couple's property in his name alone, for example, might write a will leaving all of it to his children by a previous marriage. Under state law, the wife could file a petition in probate court to take her elective share of the estate. Likewise, in a state that recognizes same-sex marriage, the right to an elective share would be available to both spouses.

Hint: **Merely being separated generally does not terminate a spouse's right to elect against the will. Living apart under circumstances that indicate an intent to divorce or permanently abandon the marriage, however, may terminate that right.**

Not only does the size of the elective share vary among states, but so does the definition of "estate" that is used in the calculation. Does "estate" mean "probate estate," or does it refer to everything the deceased spouse owned? Property can be kept out of the probate estate in any number of ways. If a dying spouse uses these nonprobate dispositions to minimize or eliminate the probate estate, does that mean the survivor gets an elective share of little or nothing? If so, it would be possible to effectively cut out the survivor's right of election simply by using nonprobate dispositions for all of one's property.

Such a result, whether intended or not, would thwart the purpose and policy of the law in establishing the spousal elective-share, which is designed to respect the marital union by protecting surviving spouses. For unrelated but perfectly good reasons that we explore throughout this book (such as planning for disability), living trusts and other probate-avoiding techniques have become commonplace. People marrying later in life might have estates of quite different size. The better-off spouse might fully intend to provide for his or her new partner by updating account names and beneficiary designations—but never get around to it. That's why the issue of defining a surviving spouse's right of election has taken on even more importance.

Many states now base a surviving spouse's elective share on a concept called the *augmented estate*. For practical purposes, the augmented estate is everything a person owns, not just his or her probate estate. is the trend in the law. But the law move slowly, so many places still restrict the right of election to the probate estate only.

Even in probate-estate-only states, how-ever, it would not be surprising to see a judge rewrite the spousal election law. This might happen if, for example, a particular case presents heartbreaking circumstances. Additionally, courts everywhere have age-old remedies to undo property transfers of all kinds when such transfers have clearly been made to shirk one's legal obligations. (This is among the most important powers of the American judiciary. The concept of achieving justice by canceling gifts, sales, or other arrangements, under limited circum-stances, applies to every field of law, not just estate planning.) The bottom line is that it is probably not possible to totally disinherit a spouse—unless the two of you have reached an agreement to that effect.

● **Retirement plan benefits must be pay-able to a spouse** Under federal law, a mar-ried person's account in a qualified retire-ment plan sponsored by an employer—that is, a 401[k] plan, a profit sharing plan, or a

—must be payable to his or her n the employee's death, unless has signed a waiver of that right. >es not apply to IRAs. Moreover, since the rule is a matter of federal law, which does not recognize same-sex marriage, it is not applicable to a same-sex spouse.) Remember, too, that in the community property states (Arizona, California, Idaho, Louisiana, Nevada, New Mexico, Texas, Washington, and Wisconsin), the increase during marriage in virtually any retirement savings plan or account balance (including IRAs) is considered to be community property. This means a surviving spouse is automatically entitled to half the total account value under state law.

● **Children have no legal right to anything under a will** You are under no obligation to treat all your children alike in your will, or even to treat them fairly; a child has no legal right to your estate if you direct otherwise. Unlike spouses, children can be disinherited. All that's required is a valid will stating the parent-testator's desire to do so. (It is not possible, however, for a parent to avoid the duty to support his minor children until they reach legal adulthood.) The reason for the common practice of leaving one dollar to a child who is to be cut out of a will is to demonstrate that the child was not merely forgotten—which is important. If you intend to take such a drastic step, include in your will language to the effect that "I have intentionally made no provision in this Last Will and Testament for my son/daughter, _____."

Although no explanation for disinheriting a child is legally necessary, it might be wise to offer one anyway. The law assumes that a person does not intentionally disinherit his children. Therefore, if a disinherited child challenges the will in court, a judge might wonder, for example, whether the other children exerted undue pressure on the testator's decision. If a child is not mentioned at all in a deceased parent's will, he or she could also argue that the omission was only due to forgetfulness or dementia, indicating the parent/testator's lack of mental capacity. If the unmentioned child was alive when the will was written, the law in most states asks: "Was the omission intentional?" If so, the kid is out; the reason is irrelevant. For example, it's common for one parent to bequeath everything to the other—thus leaving nothing directly to the children—on the assumption that the surviving parent will provide for the family. Alternatively, if a child is not mentioned in a parent's will but was given something outside the will (such as life insurance proceeds), that is generally interpreted as evidence that the parent omitted the child from the will on purpose.

If a testator wants to avoid leaving property to a child born after an earlier will was written, it is critical to revise the will. Without a new will issuing instructions to the contrary, the law assumes that the parent/testator simply neglected to update his will, *not* that he wished to disinherit the child. Generally, the child is then entitled to the intestate share—that is, whatever he or she would have received had the parent died without a will.

Trust Basics: Sometimes a Triangle Is a Good Thing

● **What is a trust and what are the roles that make it work?** We work with and understand a trust by understanding the roles of the people associated with it and the things it owns. A trust is based on a legal relationship—a contract among three parties: the *grantor* (also called the settlor or trustor) establishes the trust, while the *trustee* administers it, according to the terms of the trust document, for the benefit of one or more *beneficiaries*.

Hint: A trust can be difficult to understand. For a mental image, think of a trust as a big vat into which the grantor "pours" his assets. The trustee takes care of the vat and controls the spigot to dispense funds, all for the exclusive benefit of the beneficiaries.

This section explains and explores these three roles and their interplay. In most family trusts, the grantor himself is one of the trust beneficiaries until he dies; he may also serve as his own trustee, at least initially. These multiple hats can obscure the fact that the three roles—grantor, trustee, and beneficiary—are quite distinct.

Understanding the "moving parts" of trusts is essential to appreciating the flexibility and utility of trusts in planning for a wide variety of family situations. We'll look at some of them later on, as well as trusts designed to meet specialized family needs. But first let's clarify the basic concepts and jargon.

The Grantor The grantor is the person who prepares the trust document—usually nothing more than a written contract agreement—with the help of an attorney. The grantor decides the goals of the trust and sets forth what the trustee should do. (There can be more than one grantor, as often happens with married couples.) For example, if the plan is to send Junior (a trust beneficiary) to college, the trust document would instruct the trustee to pay for it. Alternatively, the trustee might be given discretionary authority to do so, depending on the situation when the boy turned eighteen.

The grantor holds up his end of the contract by contributing property, such as money or real estate, to the trust (technically, to the trustee, on behalf of the trust). That is the trust *principal* or *corpus*. Alternatively, the grantor can make only a promise to contribute property in the future—as, for example, when an empty trust is set up to receive and manage the proceeds of an insurance policy to be purchased on the grantor's life.

Although plenty of empty trusts exist, it's always a good idea to make some nominal funding (such as one hundred dollars in a bank account) at the time the trust is created. Some states do not allow empty trusts. Even if "dry" trusts are permitted, funding a trust shows that it is more than a mere piece of paper.

The Trustee The trustee has the highest of legal responsibilities to do two things: 1) manage the trust property and keep it safe, and 2) see that the trust property is used only for the purposes defined by the grantor in the trust document. The trustee must have money or property available in order to do anything. At some point, assets must be formally transferred to the trustee; the trustee's name should be used in the documents of ownership. Even when somebody is serving as his own trustee, real estate deeds and financial accounts must be retitled in order to be owned and controlled by the trust. To place your mutual fund account in a living trust, for example, you would have to change the legal name of the account owner to something like "Jane Doe, trustee of the Jane Doe Living Trust, under declaration of trust dated _____."

What if you are in poor health and you ask your brother, for example, to serve as trustee? Should you worry that by titling your property in his name, you'll be giving it away? No. The trustee has only *legal ownership* of trust property. The law prohibits a trustee from using the property for anything but the welfare of the beneficiaries and other business of the trust. The name of each account reflects that your brother owns it only as trustee. In addition, financial institutions should require authorization—in the form of the trust document itself—before they will accept instructions from a trustee.

The Beneficiaries The beneficiaries' role can be pretty easy. At a minimum, all they need do is accept whatever the trust provides them. In many instances, however, strings are attached: the beneficiary must do something to qualify for his benefit. That's the motivation behind many trusts. For example, a trust could stipulate that $25,000 be paid to a beneficiary only if he quits smoking for a year or graduates from college.

Some attorneys have become quite creative at drafting trusts that give the beneficiaries themselves broad say-so as to how the trust assets will be managed and distributed. Usually, if the grantor wanted the beneficiaries to have such power, it would be easier to skip the trust and just give them the property outright. But for very large estates, an absolute gift might not be advisable for tax and asset protection reasons.

• Types of Trusts

Living and Testamentary Trusts Trusts can be *living* (established during the grantor's lifetime) or testamentary (established by the grantor in his will). A living trust usually entails an immediate, formal transfer of property into the trust. In contrast, because a testamentary trust is established in a will, the transfer of assets into the trustee's name does not occur until *after* death and probate.

Some people opt for a testamentary trust because they are not yet ready to make any kind of property transfer. They may not fully understand the concept of a trust—living or testamentary—following their first exposure to the subject. The thought of transferring property to a newly created living trust may be confusing or intimidating. A testamentary trust, on the other hand, allows them to avoid this step.

The catch, however, is that a testamentary trust only delays the property transfers until after your death, when someone else has to deal with them. At that time, two transfers of each asset might be necessary: 1) a transfer from your name into the testamentary trust, and 2) a transfer from the testamentary trust to the ultimate beneficiary.

A testamentary trust can have other drawbacks: for one thing, unlike a living trust it requires that the will be probated and does not come into existence until then. For another, state law may dictate that a testamentary trust file a financial accounting with the probate court each year (living trusts have no such requirement). Such filings become public records, meaning a loss of privacy as well as an administrative burden.

On the other hand, accountability to the court might be a very good thing in some situations. If the testator has made a poor choice of her executor or trustee, the mere existence of a judicial watchdog might pre-

vent misconduct. This can be
vantage to creating a testar

As with virtually all
choices, there are pros and co.
of a testamentary, as opposed to
trust—if you need a trust at all. Lea.
about and discussing them is one reason
why it's a good idea to see an attorney.

Revocable and Irrevocable Trusts A living trust can also be *revocable*, meaning the
grantor can revoke (terminate) or modify it
at any time for any reason. This *revocable
living trust* is what people usually have in
mind when they first ask about trusts. Alternatively, a grantor can establish an *irrevocable trust*. This type of trust can almost never
be revoked or modified by the grantor in any
significant way.

Grantors sometimes fail to grasp the full
impact of that last sentence: it bars the
grantor from terminating an irrevocable
trust, blocking her from changing it or withdrawing assets—even in an emergency. An
irrevocable trust is usually an independent
entity under the law, with its own tax ID.

Hint: A typical family living trust
should be accompanied by a *pour-*

will. **This document allows any
assets not formally transferred to the
trust during the decedent's life (such
as property acquired after the trust
was created) to be "poured over" into
the trust—becoming part of the trust
principal—at the decedent's death. A
pour-over will should be included in
the cost of drafting any living trust.**

**As for testamentary trusts, a
grantor is of course unable to change
the terms of a trust created under his
will after he dies, so these trusts are
always irrevocable. (Before death,
however, the grantor is free to change
his will, including any testamentary
trust it directs to be created.)**

A Closer Look: What happens when you transfer community property to a trust?

If you live in a community property
state and use such property to fund a
living trust, the trust becomes the
owner of the property. At that point

the property is "community" no longer. This fact presents an important and potentially complicated issue to discuss with your attorney. In most cases, the property should be clearly identified as having been community, and the trust should specify that the property will revert to its community character if the trust is revoked. Otherwise, the character of the property might become unclear. (The character of the property can be important in case of divorce; it may also have tax implications.)

● **What you need is a trusty trustee** When a client consults a lawyer about how a trust functions, the question often comes up, "Can I do this or that?" The answer is almost always, "Yes, but. . . ." Knowing that you might not be around yourself, you want someone (a trustee and/or adviser) who can faithfully use discretion to fulfill your intentions, given a future set of facts that can't possibly be predicted today.

When a grantor does not trust anyone enough to grant them discretionary authority, it is tempting to spell out every trust provision so "clearly" that the trust terms become too rigid. There are innumerable ways that too much "ruling from the grave" could unexpectedly thwart your intentions. Take the simple example of a trust that authorizes "payment of tuition and expenses at a four-year college or university" for the grantor's children. What if a serious, enterprising kid is not interested in a four-year stint, but wants to take a six-month night school course to become a computer-networking technician? The trustee would probably feel compelled to refuse to pay the tuition. After all, the trust says "four-year college," not "school" or "higher education." Maybe the grantor originally dreamed of sending his child to Harvard; but were he alive today, one has to assume, he would happily help his son with any serious educational pursuit. If so, he could have used words giving the trustee more flexibility. But he didn't, so the trustee's hands are tied.

Even better, the trust might have provided guidance, but allowed the trustee discretion to make the kind of decisions the grantor probably would have made if he were still around. That's what choosing a trustee is all about: deciding who, when the grantor is gone, can be trusted to know—and to do—what the grantor would have wanted. (That's why they're called *trust*ees.)

Generally speaking, any grantor would want his trust funds and property wisely managed and used only for the goals and purposes he set out in the trust document. This may demand a variety of skills and expertise, requiring different people to tend to the job. The management function and the human component of the trustee's job are explored separately in chapter 5.

Comparing Wills and Living Trusts

• **Resolving your post-death affairs** A selling point for living trusts is that they are not probated. However—and especially if you have been exposed to a living trust sales pitch or seminar—be realistic about what a living trust can do for your survivors. The following caveat is worth repeating: when a person dies, certain legal, personal, and financial matters must be taken care of by somebody, whether there's a will, a trust, both, or neither one. Avoiding probate does not mean that all these chores can be avoided as well. For most people in most states, the benefits of the simple living trust have been greatly exaggerated, along with the problems (if any) experienced in probate.

On the other hand, when a decedent's property and investments are already held by his trust at the time of death, the alternate or *successor* trustee (assuming the decedent had been his own trustee until death) might have an easier time than he or she would without a trust. The new trustee can step right in and write checks from the trust to pay bills. If the trust does not call for money to be paid out immediately, the new trustee need not trouble himself with the other accounts and property. After all, the trust (officially, the trustee) owned the accounts the day before the decedent/grantor's death and the day after as well. The only change is that someone else (besides the grantor himself) now wears the trustee's hat.

{ A Closer Look:
Avoiding probate when
the executor is far away

My old friend Steve called recently for some advice after his mother died in New York. Her estate included a modest house and little else. She had a will. Whereas a living trust is not usually recommended in such a simple situation, this proved to be an exception: a trust would have been a good idea.

Even though probate in New York is not a problem in itself, the executor has to be physically present, at least briefly, to oversee it. That becomes difficult when the decedent's two sons—her only survivors—now live in California. Had a living trust been created to own the house, however, Steve, as the backup trustee, would have been able to list the property with a realtor and negotiate its sale by phone and fax. A single brief trip to New York to attend the sale closing would then have sufficed. As things stand now, though, neither Steve nor

his brother has authority to deal with their mother's house until one of them appears in probate court 3,000 miles away to be appointed executor.

Of course, this is so only because the grantor took the time to transfer assets from his name to the living trust. Had the grantor not made these transfers during his lifetime, they would have to occur after his death, thus eliminating an important advantage of using a living trust.

Indeed, by using just a will—or by creating a trust but then failing to transfer accounts and other property into it—you force your executor to deal with each account separately. For example, your executor could change the name on each item from "decedent" to "Estate of decedent; Joe Dokes, Executor."

In a likelier scenario, the executor would close all the accounts and have their cash value sent to him by check. He would also open a checking account on behalf of the estate to pool these account proceeds as they came in (for later distribution to the beneficiaries). Multiple account transfers and closings can be time consuming. Not surprisingly, half the battle is finding the right person to talk to and getting their correct address. When calling a huge mutual fund company, for example, an executor should not be surprised if at first it seems that the death of a customer was a totally unexpected event.

Hint: Leaving this kind of dirty work to a lawyer can be expensive. Your executor, trustee, administrator, or other survivors should therefore consult an attorney on an hourly basis only to answer post-death questions and to handle tasks such as preparing real estate deeds and making court appearances (if your executor feels uncomfortable going alone). Your executor or other survivors should be willing to handle clerical and administrative chores such as account closings and insurance claims. No legal training is required for these duties.

{ A Closer Look:
Don't expect your debts
to disappear with a trust

Strictly speaking, some living-trust hype is true: if you have a trust, the trustee can write checks doling out estate assets the day after you die— if that's what your trust document calls for.

But don't get the idea that's all there is to it—as if the trustee, unlike the executor of a will, doesn't have to worry about your financial responsibilities. If the executor of your will lacks the funds to pay legitimate claims and debts, your creditors don't have to abandon what they're owed and withdraw from the financial field of battle. Instead, these resourceful types can legally discover information about your trust and look there for payment, assuming the claim is large enough to justify the legal fees to pursue it. So if all trust funds and property have been distributed immediately but it later turns out that your executor cannot

pay estate obligations from the probate assets available to him, the hasty beneficiaries or trustee (or both) could be held personally liable.

Ultimately, a living trust is not a cure-all. Its usefulness in your situation will depend a lot on what you own and the way you want it distributed (or retained for investment) at death. If you hold a multitude of financial accounts or real estate properties, centralizing them all in a living trust can be a tremendous convenience to those you leave behind. If you do not, a living trust may be less attractive.

● **Comparing costs** The up-front cost of preparing a living trust is greater than that of preparing a will. However, people thinking about using a living trust to avoid probate tend to focus on probate costs—specifically, attorneys' fees. (Court costs and filing fees for probating a will are relatively low in most states.) In many places, probate attorneys charge clients a percentage of the probate estate's value. This can result in unreasonably large fees for handling a simple estate—for example, one in which a decedent owns just two bank CDs that happen to total six figures. Such fees may be permitted by law and even specified in an official schedule of attorney's fees, but they are not required by law.

If saving a probate attorney's percent-based fee is the only reason you want a living trust, you—or, more likely, your executor—can find somebody willing to handle probate on an hourly-fee basis. Shop around; wills, trusts, and estate work constitute a complex area of law, so attorneys in this field are expensive. Even with a high hourly rate, however, the total fee is often far below a fixed percentage—*if*, that is, the estate truly is a simple one to settle.

Keep in mind, too, that using a living trust to avoid probate does not guarantee that you can likewise elude professional service fees. A trustee is likely to need professional help for many of the same reasons an executor does: appraising and selling property, drafting deeds, answering questions, interpreting her duties under the document. This point is seldom raised; instead, a living trust is customarily portrayed as if it would save one's survivors all the expenses incurred in the probate alternative.

Chapter 8 explores tax matters in depth. For now, note that a typical, simple living trust, by itself, will not save estate taxes—fees, maybe, but not taxes. (For estate tax savings, married people can use a technique in which the living trust of the first spouse to die splits into two separate trusts; see chapter 11.)

● **Disposition and ongoing management of property** Unlike a trust, with a will the executor's management ends soon after completion of his legal duties, perhaps with a final report to the court. The administration of a decedent's estate in probate occurs under court authority. The level of supervision varies among states, but the court always has jurisdiction to hear objections from beneficiaries regarding the handling or distribution of the probate estate. This can be a powerful tool to help prevent misconduct and ensure that the testator's wishes are carried out. With a living trust, however, there is no court involvement upon the grantor's death unless a lawsuit is filed. This is a much slower and less practical remedy for a beneficiary with a legitimate grievance than she would have in probate court.

On the other hand, trusts allow for much greater flexibility than do wills. Many simple wills provide that once both parents are gone, everything they owned is distributed equally among the children, regardless of their differing needs. With a will, the typical way to be fair is simply to be equal. Unfortunately, no one can tell what the future might bring. Since they are ongoing, trusts can allow for greater discretion in responding to future events and circumstances.

● **Providing for young children and grandchildren** The chance of leaving assets to minor children may be the greatest disadvantage of using a will without a trust. Many simple wills call for everything to go to the surviving spouse, which might be fine—if there is a survivor. The potential problem is that most such documents name the children as secondary beneficiaries upon the death of the second parent or in the event of the simultaneous death of both parents.

If the parents die while the children are minors, a court must appoint a guardian over the children's inherited assets. Guardianship is a cumbersome form of property management; it requires regular reports to the court. If the inherited amounts are substantial, and if whomever you've chosen as the children's personal guardian lacks investment management skills, the court might not appoint the personal guardian to be the children's property guardian as well. If another, more qualified family member does not volunteer for the role, the judge may turn to a local professional, who'd be paid a reasonable fee from estate funds. Most important, guardianship usually ends at age eighteen. At that point assets must be distributed outright, giving a young adult exclusive ownership and control of any property left to her. The beneficiary is still a child in many respects, yet legally the guardian must turn over her money (or other property) with no supervision. A similar scenario pertains when a grandparent leaves a large sum directly to a grandchild: the grandchild's property guardian (her parents, unless the court finds it necessary to appoint someone else) will likewise be obliged to give up all control of the money when the child turns eighteen.

If you plan to leave significant assets to your young children or grandchildren but do not want your estate to eventually fall into the hands of teenagers, a trust is the way to go. This purpose can be served by a testamentary trust as well as by a living trust. A trust can dictate that would-be teenage inheritors receive distributions only at a later age, when they have (presumably) developed more maturity and financial responsibility. Until then, a trust can allow almost unlimited flexibility in the management of estate assets. Rather than being constrained to spend equally on each child, the trustee can respond appropriately to the unique abilities and opportunities (or disabilities or illnesses) of each child. This is the approach most parents take while alive.

● **Planning for your disability or incapacity** When it's appropriate to plan for your disability or incapacity, a living trust can be a useful tool. (A will is of no help in this regard because it has no effect until death.) Because the assets in a living trust are already controlled by a trustee who can make financial decisions, the estate owner's resources can be managed and used for his benefit in the event he suddenly becomes incapacitated. That is why it's crucial that an alternate or successor trustee be named, especially in the common arrangement where the grantor initially serves as his own trustee.

If two spouses (or other committed partners) serve as co-trustees, their trust documents should be worded to allow either to act independently. That way, one of them can assume control if he or she senses that the other is becoming unable to do so.

Hint: There is a difference between a *co*-trustee and a *successor* trustee. If a trust has two co-trustees, each has power over the trust's assets from the moment the trust is created. The trust-creator can limit that power by requiring the other co-trustee's agreement in all decisions involving the assets; alternatively, the trust agreement can allow either co-trustee to act independently. A successor trustee has no control at all over the trust's assets until the original trustee or co-trustees die or become incapacitated and can no longer handle the position.

When the original trustee (or all co-trustees) becomes disabled, the successor trustee takes over. It is therefore imperative that the trust document define "disability" or "incapacity," specifying the events upon which the successor trustee should step in. If the disability is temporary, the original trustee(s) can resume the position if desired.

Having a living trust can thus allow one to avoid a lengthy legal-disability hearing in which the court appoints a guardian over one's person and property (guardianship is discussed in greater detail in chapter 3). A living trust also avoids ongoing court supervision of financial decisions. (Because a testamentary trust by definition does not exist during a grantor's lifetime, it cannot offer this benefit.)

Hint: A simple, effective, and inexpensive way to provide for the management of your affairs in the event of incapacity is a *durable power of attorney*—so called because it remains in effect even if you become disabled. All powers of attorney become void at death, however, meaning the person who holds the power of attorney can no longer act on your

behalf once you die. Durable powers of attorney are presented more thoroughly in chapter 3.

● **Ownership of real estate in multiple states** If you own out-of-state vacation, farm, or rental real estate, consider a living trust for that reason alone. If the property has already been transferred by a deed to the trust, it can be sold or distributed upon your death more easily than if it is titled in your individual name. In the latter case, the property must go through probate court in the state where it is located. This process, called *ancillary* probate, must be undertaken in addition to the probate in your home state. Even though that's not a big deal in most places, it becomes problematic if nobody is living in the ancillary probate state to handle it. For transfers of real estate in certain states, such as Florida, it's also wise to have witnesses to your signature on the trust and follow the formalities required there for wills. This may be necessary to ensure that the property deed can be properly recorded.

● **Time and publicity** Probating a will takes time—at least six months. The trustee of a trust, however, can begin distributing property according to the grantor's wishes immediately after death. Probate records are open, but a trust document is private. Oftentimes, neither of these factors is of practical concern to the survivors. But when they are, they can cut both ways.

The delay and publicity that probate causes actually offer a significant potential advantage: they put the world on legal notice that now is the time to come forward with claims against the decedent. If creditors do not present their claims against the estate to the executor within a limited period (six months is common), they may be barred from doing so forever.

That rigid period may not apply to claims against your trust. It almost certainly would not apply if no legal notice was published in the newspaper (the probate of a will usually includes this public notice; the management of a trust does not). This lack of notice could be especially important if you are involved in a profession or business that might leave potential claims against you "out there" when you die.

If an estate has enough assets to satisfy all its obligations, there is generally no reason the executor or trustee cannot properly make partial distributions to eager beneficiaries well before closing the estate. If, however, there is doubt about the estate's ability to meet the decedent's obligations, beneficiaries should be told to sit tight. This is the case both for a will and for a trust.

{ **A Closer Look:**
Privacy and the probate process: you can't hide from prying eyes

Most privacy concerns about the probate process are overblown. True, anything filed with the probate court becomes a matter of public record. This might force a family business, for example, to reveal its financial woes to any competitor or customer who cared to look. Privacy might also be an issue for the rich and famous. But in the typical case, who cares? How many of us have ever gone to the local probate court clerk's office to look up somebody's will or estate inventory out of pure nosiness? In my experience, privacy alone is seldom much of a motivating factor in the decision to use a living trust.

Trust

Scams The Internet has encouraged the proliferation of dishonest (or simply stupid) promoters of trust schemes promising impossible tax benefits. If you see a Web site or get an email promising tax breaks that seem just too good to be true, remember what life has taught you and don't be a sucker. If you are already involved in something like this, you have probably made a big mistake and should consult an attorney at once.

The IRS has identified two broad types of "abusive trust schemes" or "abusive tax shelter arrangements," one foreign and one domestic. The hallmark of these scams? They both promise enormous tax benefits with no real change in the taxpayer's control over—or benefit from—his income or assets.

● **Foreign trusts** One type of bogus arrangement involves setting up one or more trusts in a foreign country that allows financial secrecy and imposes a minimal tax burden. Trust promoters selling these schemes contrive various shell-game transactions and improper expense deductions that make it difficult to track income from the trust. These funds are ultimately distributed or made available to the original owner, sometimes through the issuance of a credit card. The promoters claim these distributions are tax-free.

That's nonsense, of course.

Unless specifically exempted or excluded by law, the income from these arrangements is fully taxable—as is all income to U.S. citizens from any source in the world. If a U.S. citizen transfers property to a foreign trust he created that has even one American beneficiary, the income earned by that trust is fully reportable by the taxpayer under his own Social Security number.

This is not to say that all foreign-based trusts are abusive or promoted by hucksters. They might make sense as part of an asset-protection plan for a very small percentage of people with substantial wealth— those who face an above-average risk of *future* legal claims too large to cover with insurance. A reputable attorney who drafts these trusts will be quick to advise his clients, however, that no income tax benefit accrues from them.

● **Domestic trust scams** The second type of abusive trust on the IRS target list is domestic. These arrangements are marketed on the Internet under a variety of brand names; examples of their come-ons follow. They are usually referred to as *pure trust organizations* (or as pure trusts, sovereign trusts, constitutional trusts, liberty trusts, or common law trusts). Their common feature is an array of completely false promises, including the claim that creditors cannot seize pure-trust property, and that the trust can be used to make ordinary living expenses tax-deductible, while its income is tax-free.

Here's a Web site deal for you:

The first LIBERTY PURE TRUST you order (for you to manage) is usually $995.00. If you decide you'll need more, all additional Trusts to the same customer are just $595.00 each!

Another Web scam promoter beckons:

Lawfully Stop Paying Taxes! $1650 for 3 "Iron Clad" Pure Trust Organizations

These pitches would be funny if people didn't take them seriously: every year, hundreds of unsuspecting investors fall for similar pitches wasting their money and risking serious legal trouble. Fanning their gullibility is the extensive legal and constitutional "analysis" that most pure trust Web sites offer to support the supposed legitimacy of pure trust tax "advantages." Some of these arguments are so well articulated they make for entertaining reading, but all of them are utter baloney.

If you've never heard of the pure trust, claims one promotional Web site, we attorneys are to blame:

If you search the web for information about "Pure Trusts," you'll find some sites which claim that there is no such thing as a "Pure Trust!" If you investigate, you'll discover that, almost without exception, these sites are hosted by lawyers who are not able to make money with "Pure Trusts." In other words, if you use a "Pure Trust," you are not filling the lawyer's pocket with your money. They do NOT want you to learn that an alter-

native to their expensive *"Trust Agreements"* has existed for over 236 years!

If these trusts can do everything the scammers claim, why haven't estate lawyers rushed to embrace them? That's something the promoters—who apparently have no compunctions about lining their *own* pockets with money—never quite make clear. (One reliable indicator of a trust scam: I have never seen one of these sites that mentions the promoter or the resident legal "expert" by name.)

To be clear, the promised tax "breaks" and protection from creditors are bogus, not necessarily the pure trust itself. Indeed, the IRS simply ignores these arrangements, obligating the taxpayer himself to pay whatever tax is due on his trust income. In short, pure trusts get the same treatment from the IRS and the courts as that given any typical living trust. As far as Uncle Sam and other creditors are concerned, the grantor and his trust are one and the same. Therefore, run for the door if anybody claims:

Establishing a trust will reduce or eliminate income or self-employment taxes.

Not true. Here's the law: like any other income, all trust income is fully taxable unless specifically exempted or excluded by law. It's pretty simple—and only fair; if you control the trust and its income, you are responsible for paying the tax owed on that income. Finally, some additional myths on the Web:

Your living expenses may be paid by the trust and deducted on your personal income tax return.

You can transfer your residence into the trust and begin taking depreciation deductions on your personal income tax return.

These statements, too, are totally false. Your living expenses are not deductible, and no depreciation deduction is allowed for a house used solely as your residence. These are classic instances of the "too good to be true" rule. To immunize yourself from their lure, remember that the IRS deems fraudulent any trust established to hide the true ownership of assets and income or to disguise the substance of financial transactions.

Taxpayers are legally responsible for their own actions. You cannot hide behind the counsel of a so-called "adviser" who turns out to be a crook. Even if you're allergic to lawyers, see an attorney about any tax-motivated financial or business arrangement you are contemplating. Your attorney is accountable to the state bar association for what he or she does. Internet "advisers," "experts," and trust promoters are accountable to no one—they don't even give you their names.

{ **A Closer Look:** AARP casts a gimlet eye on living trusts; when and why it pays to keep your distance

Based on sound advice and document preparation by their personal attorneys, many people use living trusts today. Like any tool, however, a living trust is not suitable for every person or every situation. That's one reason why *AARP does not sell or endorse any living trust documents or services, nor does it work with any*

*company that promotes or sells them.** Therefore, *you should never see AARP's name associated with any living trust document, advertisement, or other promotional effort.* If you do, it is intentionally misleading.

Public misunderstanding of tax laws has combined with largely unjustified fears about the probate system to create an opportunity for living-trust scammers. Older persons are bombarded with newspaper ads, direct mail, slick promotional materials, and even high-pressure seminars overstating the advantages of a living trust. Unethical salesmen then try to obtain a consumer's financial information and persuade her to "act quickly" in order to buy insurance, annuities, or other investment products that might be totally unsuitable. People living on limited incomes should be particularly cautious. An AARP survey in 2000 found that since 1991, the greatest increase in living trusts was among survey par-

*AARP sponsors the AARP Legal Services Network, whose participating attorneys will draft trust agreements for their clients.

ticipants with annual income less than $25,000. Yet this is the group least likely to benefit from a living trust.

Unscrupulous living trust promotions often try to create the impression that AARP sells or is somehow affiliated with living trust products or services, or that AARP endorses the use of living trusts in general. Not so! AARP never has, nor will it do so. Estate planning should be a personalized process. The goal is to produce documents that have been truly individualized to fit the circumstances—not "Your Name Here" commodities.

3

Beyond Wills and Trusts: The Rest of the Estate Planner's Toolkit

Though wills and trusts are the best-known estate-planning tools, several others are worth considering too. Planning for physical or mental incapacity—as well as critical or end-of-life medical decisions—should be concerns for all of us. For many, second (or subsequent) spouses present myriad estate-

Hint: It's important to let your family know about your health-care wishes, and where your advance medical directive documents are stored.

and financial-planning issues, as well as conflicting family priorities that must be addressed. Special documents and powers will likely be necessary to develop the best estate plan for you.

Each document described in this chapter is relatively simple—in theory, at least. They all address different present and anticipated life situations. We consider them in one chapter, however, because each of them can expand the scope and utility of your will or living trust to fit your specific needs.

Durable Power
of Attorney
This simple, inexpensive document provides great bang for the buck. Coupled with a will and an advance medical directive (see page 143), the *durable power of attorney* (DPOA) is for many people a superior alternative to the simple living trust in planning for disability or incapacity. (A DPOA, however, does not address the other reasons to have a trust.) Not only is the DPOA more familiar to people than the concept of a "trust," but its cost is far less than that of preparing a trust.

A durable power of attorney is a document in which one person, the principal, authorizes his *attorney-in-fact* to act on his behalf. The law regards the attorney-in-fact as the principal's agent, so we will use the term "agent" here. Most people should have a DPOA if and only if there is someone trustworthy beyond the shadow of a doubt to handle the responsibility it entails. The scope of the power granted in a DPOA may be narrow—it may apply only to the agent's sale of the principal's house, for example— or it may be nearly boundless. (One of the few authorizations a principal cannot grant to someone else with a DPOA is the power to make his will.)

Whatever he does, the agent has a *fiduciary duty*—a duty to the principal to act only in the principal's best interests. This important concept is examined in more detail in chapter 5. Even though the attorney-in-fact does not have to be a lawyer (and usually is not), some DPOA documents refer to the attorney-in-fact as "my attorney" for short. This can be confusing—another reason we refer to the position as the principal's agent.

Hint: At a minimum, the DPOA should be executed with sufficient formality to allow it to be recorded with the official real estate records where your property is located. Some parties also require that your signature on the durable power of attorney be guaranteed by your bank—not just signed by a notary public. This is especially so with regard to real estate transactions. If your agent might need to buy or sell real estate on your behalf, make sure he is acting under a DPOA that the other parties have approved in advance.

{ **Warning!** Some durable tools are designed to dematerialize

A durable power of attorney is an enormously useful tool. Many people don't realize, however, that it ends as soon as the person who granted the DPOA dies. After that, the agent named in the DPOA has no authority at all (unless he or she is also the executor of the decedent's will), and the DPOA document itself becomes void.

● **When is a durable power of attorney useful?** Here are two reasons to use a DPOA:

1. By allowing a busy or absentee party to authorize somebody to act in her place, a DPOA can make business or financial transactions much easier to complete.
2. In the event that a person becomes disabled or incapacitated, a DPOA can delegate broad authority over his affairs, minimizing the disruption of his financial life.

To be useful in a wide variety of currently unknown possible scenarios, a durable power of attorney must be extensive, reciting a laundry list of specific business or financial powers pertaining to any situation (hopefully) the agent might face on behalf of the principal. On the other hand, many do-it-yourself power of attorney forms contain only broad language that is short on specifics. When presented with such a DPOA, a retirement plan administrator, for example, might balk at honoring it if the document did not explicitly authorize the actions contemplated by the agent—say, a withdrawal.

Experience shows that if particular tasks

of the agent can be foreseen, it may be wise to sign several durable powers of attorney, each with a single focus. For example, you could have one DPOA allowing the agent to handle only your accounts at the Big Bank, and another that only authorizes him to deal with the Little Bank on your behalf. There are several advantages to this approach, though it involves more legwork initially than executing just one document at your lawyer's office. All banks, insurance, and financial service companies have their own DPOA forms available at no charge. Once filled out, they keep the forms conveniently on file, and if your agent needs to act under the power of attorney, anyone at the institution will accept it—no need to call their legal department, which is often necessary when someone presents an attorney-drafted document.

● **Durable POAs in the event of disability or incapacity** The durable power of attorney is useful in estate planning because it remains valid in the event you later become disabled or incompetent. (Even if *you* take a licking, your DPOA keeps on ticking.) To achieve this purpose, the law requires it to include a statement such as: "This power of attorney shall not be affected by my subsequent disability or incapacity, or by the passage of time." That sentence (or similar wording) is what makes the power of attorney "durable." Without such a stipulation, state law would render the POA inoperative immediately upon the disability of the principal—precisely when it is most needed. (Bear in mind that we are not dealing with health care POAs here. Those are known as advance medical directives; see page 143.)

Assuming one has a trusted agent, the durable power of attorney can easily and inexpensively provide the peace of mind sought by many people planning for possible disability. Note, however, that although the DPOA can help avoid the need for court-appointed guardianship, if a guardian is in fact appointed, he is usually authorized by state law to terminate the DPOA. In a few states, the law automatically terminates an existing DPOA at the moment a guardian is appointed for the principal. In other states, the agent continues to act unless the guardianship court finds that the agent is abusing the powers granted by the power of attorney. In these states, the court starts from the presumption that you want the person you selected to make decisions for you; it excludes from the guardian's authority those powers you gave your agent.

{ **Warning!** A power of attorney can be an invitation to abuse of power

Most durable powers of attorney take effect immediately. That makes it possible for the agent to act independently, behind the principal's back, even if the principal is healthy. To put it bluntly, you could get robbed—a deplorable but regular occurrence among the elderly. This unsettling prospect should give you serious pause before granting your agent the wide-ranging powers inherent in a power of attorney. If you have any doubt about the trustworthiness of your agent, a typical DPOA, which confers far-reaching authority, is probably not right for you. As an alternative to having no DPOA at all, consider a DPOA in which you define as narrowly as possible the powers given to your agent.

● **The springing power of attorney** A less common variant of the durable power of attorney is the *springing* power of attorney, which "springs" into action only upon the principal's disability (rather than taking effect immediately upon signing). Most attorneys advise against using a springing POA because it can pose a big problem: there must be some kind of determination of the principal's disability before the springing POA becomes operative and therefore acceptable to whomever it is presented by the agent. A springing POA might stipulate, for example, that two doctors examine the principal and attest to her disability, or simply that her regular physician do so. This involves delay and expense, at best. At worst, the principal, her doctors, or her family may squabble over the degree of the principal's disability. Until that is resolved, banks or other financial institutions would refuse to recognize the agent's authority to do anything. In that event, the matter could wind up in court—the very thing you wanted to avoid.

The springing POA exists primarily because some people feel uncomfortable delegating power today, while they are still healthy. Although that sentiment is under-standable, you should also consider the se-rious potential drawbacks of a springing POA before you sign one. If you can't trust the agent not to act prematurely or improp-erly, pick another agent. Estate-planning decisions like this should always be in-formed, but seldom are they right or wrong.

● **Granting a DPOA: legal and practical considerations** In order for a durable power of attorney to be valid, the principal must be of sound mind when he signs it, even if the document is intended to be valid during subsequent disability. (The princi-pal's signature on the DPOA must also be notarized.) The rules for determining sound-ness of mind for a DPOA are probably not as clear-cut as those for establishing testa-mentary capacity to make a will: although some state laws may require greater mental capacity to prepare a valid DPOA than a will, a DPOA should be valid even if it was signed during a lucid interval within a pro-longed period of incapacity.

● **Useful DPOA provisions to discuss with your attorney** In addition to a wide variety of "standard" financial- and business-transaction powers a typical DPOA confers, there are a number of other useful but often overlooked provisions that you'd be wise to discuss with your lawyer. Five of the most common ones appear below:

The power to create, amend and transfer your assets to trusts for your benefit. This is extremely important. It allows flexibility in implementing an estate plan in the event of the estate owner's incapacity. This provision can be especially useful because a POA cannot authorize the agent to write someone else's will.

The power to handle tax matters and deal with the IRS. In the past, the IRS has insisted that its own POA form be used. Now, a specific provision in the taxpayer's own document, conferring appropriate authority, will be honored. Many POA forms lack this clause.

The power to handle retirement accounts and investments. These assets are likely to be substantial. Retirement plan custodians and administrators are appropriately cautious about letting anybody else play with your money. These people, too, will probably require specific authorization in the power of attorney before allowing your agent to act on your behalf. Alternatively, the plan administrator may provide a pre-approved durable POA form.

A compensation clause. If your agent is a family member rather than an unrelated professional, should he be paid? If the agent is likely to spend considerable time managing your affairs under authority of the DPOA, a reasonable hourly fee is fair.

The power to make gifts. Owners of large estates often use annual tax-free gifts of up to $11,000 per recipient to gradually pare down their taxable estates. Others may be free of such estate tax worries but simply enjoy giving money to their children and grandchildren. If an agent is to administer the principal's affairs under a POA, the principal might want him to start or continue making gifts. If so, the power to make gifts must be specifically authorized and precisely spelled out, especially if the principal wants to allow the agent (a daughter, for example) to make gifts to herself. Giving an agent the unrestricted power to make gifts can be disastrous if the agent twists your faith into an opportunity to enrich himself.

A specifically worded gift-giving power is

useful for clients who may need to have their assets retitled (in the name of a spouse, for example) in order to qualify for Medicaid nursing home benefits. Medicaid issues are extremely complex and beyond the scope of this book, but some people should consider them further with an attorney.

Guardianship and Conservatorship

An unfortunate fact of life for the elderly is the possibility of mental and/or physical incapacity. Terminology varies among the states, but *guardianship* generally refers to the overall care and custody not only of a person who needs protection, but of his property as well. *Conservatorship* generally refers to the custody and control of the protected person's money and property only. Guardianship and/or conservatorship involve a court proceeding. They are the least desirable alternatives to using a durable POA or living trust to plan in advance for disability.

The relationship of the guardian or conservator to the person in her care (the *ward*) is much like that of parent to child. The law, quite rightly, considers it a very big deal to strip an adult of his independence and impose that relationship upon him. For this reason, the process of obtaining court appointment as a guardian or conservator involves considerable time and money.

Details vary by state, but usually an office in the local county courthouse handles guardianship. Often, this is a probate court function. The first step is a petition to the court by someone asking to be appointed guardian. In some areas the court clerk's office has blank forms and instructions so that people need not hire an attorney, but usually you will need one.

What happens next accounts for the unavoidable delay, and perhaps expense, of this process. Although most people act from honorable motives, the court must decide whether a full guardianship is necessary, or whether guardianship can be limited to the ward's person alone or to his property alone (the latter case being a conservatorship). Sometimes, for example, matters would be more convenient for an adult child serving as caregiver if she were also her parent's legal guardian. The court would probably not grant such guardianship, however, if the parent objected to it.

The court generally requires a hearing, at which an evaluation of the disabled person by medical or mental-health professionals must be presented. The petitioner seeking guardianship is often the one who must arrange and pay for these examinations and reports. Additionally, in most places the court appoints a lawyer to represent disabled persons and requires periodic reports from the guardian if one is appointed. This is a further safeguard that no competent person will be railroaded into a guardianship because he is too weak or too intimidated to speak out. The court must also determine who is the most capable and appropriate person to serve as guardian or conservator, and what sort of authority he or she should be granted. Once the guardian/conservator has been appointed, he or she must make periodic reports to the court about how the guardian/conservator is caring for the ward and managing the ward's money.

Living Wills and Other Advance Medical Directives

Advance medical directives (AMDs) are documents that address a variety of complicated medical, legal, and ethical situations that we may confront during serious illness, incapacity (including coma), or near the very end of life. Every state recognizes the patient's right to make fundamental choices as to the care and treatment she will or will not receive at such times. These choices are addressed in documents that go by various names, such as *living will* and *health-care power of attorney*. All have the same general purpose, so they are known collectively as AMDs.

Whether you have signed an AMD or not, your consent must be obtained for your medical treatment as long as you retain the capacity to make and express decisions for yourself. This leaves you solely and totally in control. If you have an AMD, you can revoke or modify it at any time, provided you are still capable of doing so. Once your treating physician concludes that you are incapable of making decisions or giving your consent, however, the AMD goes into effect.

Many people have heard of a living will, but few realize it is often a narrow form of AMD. In most states, the living will speaks only about life-prolonging measures (such as cardiopulmonary resuscitation) and applies only when death is imminent without such measures, or when the patient is in a "persistent vegetative state." A living will would therefore be of no use to a patient who needs a decision about chemotherapy, exploratory surgery, or dialysis (none of which is classified as life-prolonging) but is unable to give that consent. For this reason, you should consider an AMD that is comprehensive in the medical situations it deals with.

• **Designating a health-care agent** Most of us planning along these lines hope to "cover all the bases." To do this, appoint someone to speak for you on these matters when you cannot, and prepare a comprehensive medical directive of your wishes. In all states, the patient can select a *health-care agent,* a *health-care surrogate*, or a *health-care proxy* (all three terms are equivalent). The health-care agent can be authorized to make any health-care decision the patient could have made if he had decision-making capacity, as long as it conforms to accepted medical practice and the patient's wishes.

The agent need not be chosen only in anticipation of death. He can be empowered to deal with temporary incapacity, too. Because a disabling medical crisis can occur suddenly, it's best to draw up one of these documents long before you reach the status of patient. That way you'll have time for a detailed discussion with your proposed agent, at which time you can communicate your values and what you would want to have done (or not done) under various "what if" scenarios. Be sure he or she understands and accepts the emotional burden the health-care agent's role carries.

● **Preparing and executing an AMD** Generally, no specific format is required of an AMD, although some states have more rigid requirements than others as to the wording of the document. Most states have laws that include a sample form for appointing a health-care proxy or for creating a comprehensive advance directive. In many states, the use of these forms is optional, or they need be followed only "substantially." Given the document's simplicity, it should not cost much to have a lawyer draft one for you, especially if it is done at the same time as your will or trust.

An AMD can also be prepared without an attorney. The best place to start is an official form (if available) from the statute books of your state. A great deal of information and state-specific sample forms are also available on the Internet. An excellent source is Partnership for Caring, a national nonprofit organization that advocates on behalf of dying people and their loved ones (www.partnershipforcaring.org). If you are in a hospital, nursing home, or other facility, consult the patient's advocate about making an AMD.

If a lawyer does not draft your AMD, make sure you don't just copy an "official" form and sign it unchanged—unless, of course, it reflects what you truly want. The form can and should be personalized to some extent to reflect your unique values and instructions. If changing an official form creates any doubt about its validity, talk to a lawyer.

When it comes to signing and witnessing an AMD, the required procedures vary. Notarized signatures from you and two witnesses are advisable. This might exceed what's necessary in your state, but it should help ensure that your AMD will be recognized in other states, too. There should be a clause in which the witnesses attest that they know you personally, and that you appear to be of sound mind and under no duress or undue influence. Further, you and the witnesses should acknowledge that the document being signed is, in fact, your advance medical directive.

It is crucial to follow—or surpass—the signing and witnessing requirements imposed on AMDs by the law in your state. If the document is not executed perfectly, it could be invalid, keeping medical personnel from following its directions.

● **A good witness is hard to find** Under the law of many states, the following people, who might be at your side during a severe illness, are not valid witnesses (basically, anyone who could potentially gain by your demise is disallowed):

■ Your treating physician
■ A health-care provider or her employees
■ A health-facility operator or its employees
■ Anyone related to you by blood, marriage, or adoption
■ Anyone entitled to any part of your estate under an existing will or by operation of law

• **Your agent's authority** The scope of your agent's power is intentionally broadly worded, giving him the authority to make any decision that you personally could make to obtain or terminate any type of health care. (Even vested with this authority, your agent and doctor still must follow your directions, if you are capable of communicating them in any manner, now or later.)

Most AMDs are worded to become effective upon your incapacity to make health-care decisions. That point is determined by your doctor. You may specify other effective dates or other criteria for incapacity—stipulating, for example, that any determination of your incapacity requires the judgment of two physicians. Don't make it too complicated, lest your agent have trouble establishing his authority with your health-care providers. You can also direct that the power granted in an AMD will end at a specified later date, or upon a particular event, such as your release from the hospital after surgery.

The health-care agent's role is a tough one, so give your proxy a great deal of guidance in making what may well be extraordinarily difficult and painful decisions. Talk to your agent about any limitations you wish to have placed on your treatment, such as the refusal of blood transfusions, psychosurgery, amputation, or abortion. Be sure your agent knows that you want her to act in that capacity. Clearly communicate to her your wishes and values. If your agent doesn't know what you might prefer given a variety of medical possibilities, instruct her to make a choice for you based on what she believes to be in your best interests.

Most state laws make it illegal to compel a health-care provider to follow the directions of your agent, especially when doing so would violate the provider's conscience. (In most states, the provider is required to transfer you to another who is willing to comply.) To ease health-care providers' concerns about complying with your wishes, some AMDs state that medical personnel and others who follow the agent's duly authorized instructions should be absolved of legal liability for the consequences of doing so. Otherwise there could arise a situation in which a provider feared withdrawing treatment, even at the agent's command, because of the specter of a lawsuit by the patient's family months later.

● **Powers to be included in the AMD** Readily available AMD forms vary widely in their wording and appearance. To give your agent meaningful health-care decision-making authority, your own AMD document should grant the agent the following basic powers:

■ To consent, refuse, or withdraw consent to any and all types of medical care, treatment, surgical and/or diagnostic procedures, medication, and the use of mechanical or other means to affect any bodily function, including (but not limited to) artificial respiration and cardiopulmonary resuscitation

■ To authorize your admission to or discharge from (even against medical advice) any hospital, nursing home, or other facility

■ To authorize any medication or procedure intended to relieve pain, even though such treatment might lead to bodily damage, drug addiction, or hasten the moment of (but not intentionally cause) your death

■ To refuse or discontinue life-sustaining treatment

Perhaps the most critical provision in an AMD is the expression of the patient's

wishes about "life-sustaining" or "life-prolonging treatment." (These terms are equivalent; different state statutes may use one
or both of them interchangeably.) If you
want your doctors to employ maximum life-
sustaining or life-prolonging efforts, an AMD
should be used to alert everyone to that
fact. If that is not what you want, make certain your agent knows what your wishes
are—and be sure you document those
wishes in your AMD. Here is how some
AMDs express the point (yours might word
it differently):

*I do not want my life to be prolonged and I
do not want life-sustaining treatment to be
provided or continued if my agent believes
the burdens of the treatment outweigh the
expected benefits. In making this determination, my agent is to consider the relief of
my suffering, the expense involved, and the
quality of my continued existence, as well as
the length of time by which the proposed
treatment is likely to extend my life.*

People differ widely on whether artificial
"nutrition and hydration" are considered
"life-sustaining treatment." This is just one

more reason why it's important to make your preferences known, especially if you live in a state where withholding food or water is legally prohibited unless the patient has authorized it beforehand in writing.

"Nutrition and hydration" refers to the introduction of food and water into the body through a feeding tube or intravenous fluid lines. Under all circumstances, appropriate noninvasive care—spoon feeding, for example, or moistening the mouth—should be expected to continue.

There are several other easily overlooked matters of practical importance to be considered. You should also decide if you want your agent to be authorized to:

- Make contracts on your behalf for any health-care-related service or facility, including placement in a nursing home
- Hire and fire medical or other support personnel for your care, without the agent's becoming financially responsible herself for such arrangements
- Enjoy the same access to medical records and information to which you are entitled

The federal Health Insurance Portability and Accountability Act of 1996 (HIPAA) requires health-care providers to limit the release of medical information. HIPAA also imposes severe penalties for violations. Your AMD should therefore include a clause along these lines:

I intend for my agent to be treated as I would be with respect to my rights regarding the use and disclosure of my individually identifiable health information or other medical records. This release authority applies to any and all information governed by the Health Insurance Portability and Accountability Act of 1996. The authority given my agent has no expiration date and shall expire only in the event that I revoke the authority in writing and deliver it to my health-care provider.

■ Make post-death decisions on organ donation, autopsy, and disposition of your remains. These three matters must be confronted immediately following your death. If it is important to you to make anatomical gifts of your organs, include specific authority in the AMD for your agent to do so. Without it, she will probably be unable to approve such a step.

{ A Closer Look:
A word about autopsy,
burial, and cremation

People differ greatly in their attitudes towards an autopsy—if one is suggested or seems to be called for—as well as in their preferences as to burial or cremation. Our loved ones likewise have different, but deeply held beliefs. Some people seek closure and resist an autopsy under any circumstances; others will be anguished without "all the answers" they hope an autopsy will provide. There are those who would have a traditional religious service and burial even for one who did not embrace religion. Others in the family may feel it is more appropriate to the life just ended to cremate the remains and spread the ashes someplace special.

It would be a shame to diligently plan your affairs to avoid ill-will among your survivors, only to leave a couple of emotionally charged matters unaddressed, possibly setting the stage for bitter disagreement. So provide as much guidance as possible to your agent. Indicate clearly your wishes as to your remains. Discuss the circumstances under which you believe an autopsy would or would not be appropriate. Despite their personal preferences, those you leave behind will almost surely agree and be content with any decisions they know reflect what *you* wanted.

● **Problems to anticipate** If you have made the decision to refuse treatment, medical providers must, by law, honor it. Before imposing this duty, however, the law requires that they be informed of your instructions. That is where problems can arise. As a practical matter, it is up to you to ensure that everyone expected to follow your instructions has received a copy of your AMD. True, under federal law, hospitals and nursing homes are required to ask about your AMD, but there is no guarantee the actual document will find its way into the right hands when needed. So without some extra effort on your behalf, the doctor or hospital might not know about the AMD. Have several original documents prepared for signing initially, so they can be freely distributed to those close to you (but save some to take along on trips).

Even at home there are practical issues to consider in the event of a serious medical crisis. First, of course, the AMD must be handy to be of any use. The Emergency responders are not going to wait to do CPR, for example, while the family rummages through desk drawers. Second, these personnel are generally required by law or their own policy to administer life support and transport patients safely to a hospital. If this is so, there is little one can do until the patient arrives there. Some states have developed procedures that allow emergency medical personnel to refrain from life-support efforts under certain circumstances. If this is important to you, find out how you can get an "out-of-hospital do-not-attempt-resuscitation order." As a practical matter, though, it is unrealistic in most cases to expect emergency personnel to instantly determine the likelihood and extent of recovery; their job is to stabilize the patient, and every second counts.

Finally, for those lacking an AMD, most

states have laws that authorize family members, in a specific order of kinship, to make some or all health-care decisions. Even without such statutes, doctors and hospitals routinely rely on close family members to make decisions if, that is, they are available and in agreement. Knotty problems are likely to crop up, however, when the family does not know (or cannot agree upon) what the patient would want in a given situation. This uncertainty can spark family disharmony and extra unpleasantness at an already stressful time.

The Ethical Will

Seemingly a new idea, the *ethical will* has in fact been around for thousands of years. It is a way to express and pass on to others your love, values, beliefs, lessons learned in life, and hopes for the future. An ethical will is not a legal document, but it can constitute your spiritual or personal legacy.

● **The origin and purposes of an ethical will** The idea of the ethical will can be traced back to the Old Testament:

And Jacob called unto his sons, and said, Gather yourselves together, that I may tell you that which shall befall you in the last days. [Genesis, 49:1]

In the Bible, Jacob renders his ethical will in the form of a blessing spoken to his sons from his deathbed. Although Jacob had harsh words of rebuke for several of his twelve sons, all were blessed to some degree and would enter the land of Canaan.

Today, while there is no prescribed format for the ethical will, most people write theirs as a letter to loved ones, expressing what they would like their survivors to know—not to have—after they are gone. (Others write ethical wills at significant points in their lives, then share them while they are still alive.) Some people prefer to capture their ethical will as a videotaped presentation; in fact, creative services have popped up that offer just this service.

The ethical will can also serve to explain estate-planning decisions—those set forth in your formal, legally binding will or trust documents—that your survivors might misinterpret or misunderstand. It might clarify, for example, why the children's inheritance is being held in trust until they reach age thirty-five; why certain lifetime gifts were made to one child but not to another; or why somebody is getting more than the others. Formal estate-planning instruments typically lack any such explanation. These documents tend to be long and confusing enough as it is, without much room for extra verbiage.

Hint: **Don't be confused by the word "will" in the phrase "ethical will."** *The ethical will is not a legally binding document.* **It has nothing to do with worldly property.**

Great comfort and peace of mind often cascade from an ethical will. For one writer, an ethical will might be an affirmation of shared family values. For another, perhaps it is the first step in reconciling with an estranged family member—a written balm that begins to heal emotional wounds.

Although an ethical will is designed to contain a lot of personal history, it is not meant to be a lengthy autobiography. Rather, it's a way to get to the "bottom line"—to impart to loved ones some of the wisdom acquired from your life experiences. For example, you could use it to share inspirational stories that might otherwise disappear from the family memory.

For now, neither lawyers nor the public are widely familiar with the ethical will. Because the expressions of the ethical will are not legal in nature, they have not traditionally been included in the formal estate-planning process. But what better time to consider this simple tool for leaving a personal legacy? Attorneys are beginning to awaken to this fact.

● **Creating your ethical will** One of the people doing the awakening is a physician and former hospice medical director named Barry Baines. Caring for a dying patient several years ago, Baines suggested that the man write an ethical will as a way of alleviating his anxiety over the significance of his life. The patient, rich in experience, felt immediate relief and peace upon completing the document; his writing, the man realized, had indeed left something of value to the world.

Profoundly moved, the compassionate Dr. Baines began to advocate the ethical will from that moment on. His Web site, www.ethicalwill.com, offers suggestions on drafting an ethical will. (Another good resource is Jack Riemer's inspirational book, *So That Your Values Live On: Ethical Wills and How to Prepare Them.*)

Often, the hardest part is just getting started. That's why the ethical will writing software available on the Web site is so useful. It can start you off with a line or two about several things you'd like to share. One category of thoughts, for example, concerns the importance of family: "As I've grown older, I continue to value the family more and more." From there, you can add your own thoughts or move to another topic, such as "the importance of honesty" or "learning from mistakes." Even if you don't consider yourself good with words, this exercise can produce an enduring document that your survivors will always cherish.

Prenuptial
Agreements
People normally don't associate prenuptial agreements with estate planning. But estate-planning issues are in-

variably involved when a married couple has such an agreement. It's important to be aware of the law when creating both your prenup and your estate plan.

A typical *prenuptial agreement* (also called an *antenuptial agreement* or a *premarital agreement*) establishes the responsibilities of husband and wife for joint living expenses and other agreed-upon outlays in the course of a marriage. The document might call for a 50-50 split of expenses, for example, or it might stipulate that each spouse deposit a certain amount of money per month in a joint checking account to pay bills. For people of ordinary means, a prenuptial agreement usually states, in essence, that "What's mine is mine, and what's yours is yours."

In signing the prenup, each partner agrees that the other's estate plan will be allowed to stand. Generally, the plan of each spouse upon death is to distribute his or her own estate to his or her own children or others, not to the surviving spouse. In a prenuptial agreement, therefore, each partner in the marriage gives up certain rights she or he would otherwise have under the law. These include the right to reject the will of the deceased partner in order to take the spousal elective share instead (or the intestate share, if the first spouse to die does not have a will).

- **A special kind of contract** A prenup is simply a contract. If it's done right, the court will honor it. Because the subject matter involves marriage and family, however, the law scrutinizes premarital agreements far more closely than it does ordinary business contracts. The courts are universally interested in ensuring that these agreements are fair to both parties.

Experts agree that two factors are key to preparing a valid prenuptial agreement: each party must fully disclose all financial information, and each party must have the advice of a separate attorney in establishing the terms the parties will live by. If these principles are violated, the agreement is likely to be thrown out of court in the event of a dispute. (By the way, don't forget the obvious: unless there is a legal dispute, the court won't get involved at all.)

- **Living arrangements for the survivor** An important part of the prenuptial agreement is a written understanding about living arrangements for the survivor after the couple marries and one of them dies. Will the surviving spouse be able to afford to maintain (approximately) the lifestyle—or even the dwelling—the couple had shared? If the answer is "no," consideration should be given to providing the survivor with the means to do so. If, for example, you have a prenuptial agreement in place, but it's easy to see that the death of one spouse will create serious financial hardship for the survivor, your prenup is probably no good. The survivor would have to suffer in silence, which is probably not your intention, or challenge the agreement in court, which is definitely not what your children want. The survivor's argument would be simple: despite appearances when the agreement was signed, it simply was not fair, or the survivor would not, in fact, now be left in such dire circumstances. The court might be persuaded that enforcing the agreement would be "unconscionable."

The survivor could ask the judge to set aside the prenup and give him or her at least a portion of what the law would allow without a prior agreement. Unlike a case involving an ordinary business contract, the court might very well be sympathetic to such a request. But never mind the court; sound personal financial planning makes it essential to do some budgetary forecasting so that both parties can predict where they will stand if events leave them on their own again.

{ A Closer Look: Work through the "what ifs" when preparing a prenup

A couple of years after my mother died, Dad married a good woman I'll call Laura, and they entered a pre-nuptial agreement. Their attorneys did a good job overall, but failed to address one matter.

Laura and Dad's scenario is common: one spouse-to-be sells a house and moves into the other's home. That was Laura. The prenup allows Laura to live in Dad's house for as long as she wants to after his death. When she dies or moves elsewhere, however, the property goes to my sister, my brother, and me.

So far, so good.

The agreement makes Laura responsible for real-estate taxes on the house. But the prenup also states that she must pay the cost of "minor repairs (under fifty dollars)." About *major* repairs, however, the document is silent. That seems to imply Laura is not responsible for those—but then who is? Dad's three children? We never signed anything, so how can we be bound? We can't be, and besides, what if we lacked the funds when the repairs were needed?

"Fortunately," the furnace had to be replaced soon after Dad's funeral (good thing he never saw the bill!). This gave me a chance to show my understanding that Dad would have wanted me to take care of the problem, so I paid the bill from the estate checking account. That was one big future problem taken care of right away. Then, as executor, I decided to set aside funds in short-term CDs earmarked for additional repair work.

But what might have happened

otherwise? What if something big had gone wrong after I wrote checks to my brother, sister, and myself to distribute the liquid portion of the estate? One possibility would be for Laura to pay the repair costs out of her own pocket, then place a lien for that amount on the house. That way, she or her children would recover her expenses when the house was eventually sold.

Meanwhile, it's clear from the prenup that no one had foreseen this issue. So if you are drafting such an agreement yourself, remember that a lack of foresight and planning today will invite conflict later.

4

The Ins and Outs of the Probate Process

As chapter 1 made clear, the probate estate is simply any property subject to the authority of the probate court. (The many assets and accounts *not* subject to probate constitute the nonprobate estate.) Probate is often portrayed as an expensive nightmare—something to be avoided at all possible costs. In

Hint: The executor's responsibilities can be significant. Before naming someone the executor of your will, make sure you have asked her if she is willing to serve in that capacity.

most situations in almost every state, however, probate does not deserve this reputation. Probate is generally not a bad experience—unless a family squabble breaks out, in which case all bets are off. (The probate process itself seldom causes such disagreements.)

This chapter's explanation of the probate process is addressed primarily to executors. If you are preparing an estate plan, however, keep reading; not only will you discover what's involved in probate, you may pick up ideas along the way for making your executor's job easier.

The Big

Picture The following pages describe the probate process in a way designed to help you understand the big picture.

Probate is initiated in the county of the decedent's legal residence at death. As mentioned earlier, the probate court is usually a lower level court in the state system, but it may be referred to by another name—often, the surrogate's court. A clerk at your county courthouse can help you find the right office.

A will cannot be drafted in such a way as to avoid the probate process. If there are probate assets—with or without a will—probate is necessary. But streamlined procedures do exist to handle the settlement of small estates (those worth, say, $100,000 or less) or uncomplicated larger ones. In a few states, the procedure for small estates is so expedited that a trip to probate court might not even be required but that is because of the estate's small size, not because of the way the will was written. Most wills in most states, therefore, are subject to probate. If the situation is not complicated, however, the process is nowhere near as bad as many people fear.

{ **A Closer Look:**
Two states where probate
might give you sticker shock

If you live in California or Florida, consider an estate plan that avoids probate. Florida probate rules dictate that every personal representative of the deceased (such as the executor or administrator) "shall be represented by an attorney admitted

to practice in Florida," unless that personal representative is the sole beneficiary of the will. So much for your executor doing it herself or trying to avoid costs! Moreover, both states' laws authorize—and attorneys often adhere to—a fee schedule based on a percentage of the estate. This results in high fees in many cases where not much legal work is necessary. As for California, court fees were increased in 2003.

Significant details of the probate process vary greatly by state, but three basic steps remain constant everywhere:

1. Take inventory and manage the decedent's estate
2. Pay the decedent's lawful debts and taxes
3. Distribute whatever is left of the *probate* estate according to the terms of the decedent's will, or, if there is no will, according to state law.

It's all fairly straightforward. If you were the executor, you'd probably do this with the estate anyway, whether you were required to or not. Likewise, as the decedent you would want someone to do this for you, whether they were required to or not.

When someone dies without a will, the probate court appoints an administrator to handle these matters. Typically the surviving spouse or an adult child of the decedent is appointed. But if there is family disagreement, the judge can turn to a public administrator or to a knowledgeable local attorney, either of whom must be paid with estate funds. Because assets disposed of outside the probate process are part of the nonprobate estate, they are not the executor's or administrator's legal responsibility. As a courtesy, however, the executor/administrator frequently serves as an intermediary between the beneficiaries of the will and an insurance company, for example, to facilitate the payment of policy proceeds (a nonprobate asset).

Hint: *Seek cyber counsel.* **Most or all state bar association Web sites have specific information for your state on topics covered only generally here. County courts, including the probate or surrogate's court, are**

increasingly going online. Yours is likely to offer an outline of procedures, a Frequently Asked Questions page, and maybe sample forms to download as well as a phone number. If your county is not online yet, some other county in the state probably is; it should have substantially similar information and instructions.

• **Filing for probate** The probate process begins with the filing of a Petition for Probate of Will and Appointment of Executor, or something similar, with the court. This relatively short document asks for basic information such as the decedent's Social Security number, date of death, next of kin, and so on. This can be done with or without the help of a lawyer; some states give out preprinted forms so people can do at least that much themselves. Just don't forget to bring money for filing and other administrative fees, such as a newspaper legal notice announcing the probate to potential creditors.

This first step is usually taken by the person named as executor, or any other interested person who possesses the original will. If there is no will, somebody must come forward and ask the court to be appointed as administrator, instead of executor. (The same or a similar form is used in this situation.)

The person filing for probate should order multiple certified copies of the death certificate, with raised seal. (No one will honor an ordinary photocopy.) Death certificates are issued by a government agency such as the local health department, but the funeral home often procures some for customers as a courtesy. You will need the death certificate in many situations related to settling the estate, such as dealing with financial accounts and the Social Security Administration.

{Warning! Documents can harbor unpleasant discoveries

Check the death certificate carefully right away. When my stepmother went to the Social Security office after my father's death to inquire about benefits, she was surprised to discover that his death certificate listed him as a widower! (I hadn't noticed

the mistake either.) Because the erroneous information had already been entered into official records, a long delay ensued in getting the document corrected.

In many states, a brief trip to court is required soon after the initial Petition for Probate is submitted. At that time, a judge or clerk inspects the will to see if it appears genuine and valid on its face: Is it signed? Witnessed? Does it look like it was intended as a will? (If the document says "Last Will & Testament" at the top, that's a good indication, but it's not necessary.) At this point, the judge or clerk also should ask to see the death certificate, to make sure that reports of the decedent's death have not been greatly exaggerated.

Hint: The executor-to-be is limited in what she can and should do until the will is probated by the court; until then, she has no official authority over the estate. Common sense dictates, however, that she perform a few simple tasks (maintain real estate and notify Social Security, for example) before her appointment as executor. Above all, the executor-to-be should see to it that car, home-owner's, and other insurance premiums are paid on time (assuming she can access estate funds to do so). These coverages should be kept up until the covered property is no longer owned by the decedent's estate. If the decedent's car will be used by someone not named as an insured driver on that car's policy, notify the insurance company at once—even before the burial or cremation.

● **Postmortem popularity** Any heavy lifting in probate is obviously not going to be done by the will-maker. To give your executor a break he'll thank you for, get organized: gather all relevant information and put it in one central location, then be sure your executor knows where it is. If you can't find something, now is the time to get replacement copies (or, at least, to alert the executor-to-be about what's missing and how it might be located or replaced). Your executor will need the following items:

- Your Social Security number
- Prepaid funeral and/or cemetery plot deed/information
- Auto and property hazard and liability insurance policies
- Life insurance policies (check to see if the beneficiary designations are as you want them, especially if you have been divorced)
- Other insurance policies—health or long-term care insurance, for example that might cover expenses of your final illness
- Safe deposit box location, number, keys, and password if required
- Checkbook(s) and other important information for all bank and financial accounts, including mutual funds and brokerage accounts
- Pension, profit-sharing, IRA, and other retirement plan information (again, double-check the beneficiary designations, especially if you have been divorced)
- Real estate deeds and corresponding mortgage loan statements
- Recent tax returns
- Prenuptial agreement or postnuptial agreement
- Divorce or separation agreements

- Business buy/sell agreements and suc-
cession-planning documents
- Will and living trust documents, including
any statements for financial accounts or
deeds for real estate you have transferred
into the trust
- Military discharge papers, divorce decree,
or adoption papers.

● **Admitting the will to probate** If everything appears to be in order, the court issues an order "admitting the will to probate," or some similar proclamation that the
will is "official." The will is then recorded by
the court clerk. Usually, this is a routine
matter. State law might require public notice
of the probate proceeding to potential creditors by the publication of newspaper ads. If
creditors do not respond within a certain
time (often, six months), their claims cannot
be enforced later on.

Even if not required, notice by publication
is a good practice. If there are claims out
there—valid or not—it's best to force them
out of the woodwork immediately. Without
legal notice to the public, it would be unfair
to impose a claims-filing deadline, and the
law does not do so.

The court order also formally appoints the executor. This appointment confers full authority on the executor to handle the decedent's accounts. The executor is given a certified court document, often called the *Letters Testamentary*, that will be honored by financial institutions and others. If the terms of the will create a new trust, the court in some states also issues *Letters of Trusteeship*, a document empowering the trustee in like fashion.

● **Notice to named and unnamed heirs** Occasionally, somebody claims the document being offered for probate has been *revoked* by a later will and is therefore not valid. Very rarely, somebody objects to the Petition for Probate on the grounds that the document being offered to the court—the will—is in fact a forgery. Whatever the objection or claim, it must be brought to the judge's attention before she can do anything about it. Whoever has a gripe must go to court at once. That is why state laws require that notice of probate be sent to the beneficiaries named in the will, as well as to those people (usually the spouse and/or children) who would inherit the estate if the will proved to be invalid, whether they are also named in the will or not.

Laws differ as to whether this notice must be sent before or right after the will is presented to the probate court. In New Jersey, for example, I could send letters formally notifying my stepmother, brother, and sister only after my successful trip to the surrogate's court. Elsewhere, the notice might be sent out before the will is probated to any and all interested parties to come to court and *show cause*.

Hint: What is a *show cause order*? A court often issues a show cause order when a party in any type of case has asked the judge to do something. To be fair, the law requires that everyone who might have a stake in the outcome of the case be given notice of the request—and a chance to present their position on the matter—before the judge makes a decision.

In the context of probate court, a show cause order usually means, "Somebody has brought a document to court they claim is John Doe's will.

The court is going to examine it. If you do not want that document admitted to probate for some reason, this is your chance to come forward and *show cause* why not." Notice and an opportunity to be heard— that's "due process of law."

Now the beneficiaries are put on notice to pay attention as the executor performs his duties-and to take action if they feel he is not. (Executor misconduct is examined further in chapter 7.) Also, at this point, a spouse who feels she was improperly left out of the will should immediately make her election against the will and claim her statutory share of the deceased spouse's estate. Moreover, if the will calls for something unexpected ("I leave everything to the Flying Saucer Society"), the family can now look into the possibility of mental incompetence, duress on the decedent, or outright fraud.

People who receive a notice of probate don't always recognize that it might call for them to object to or raise a claim against the estate. The notice itself does not tell the recipient precisely what, if any, legal issues he should consider or actions to take. But the law assumes that a notice of probate would alert a responsible person with an interest in the estate to seek legal counsel if necessary to find out where he stands.

Hint: **If you have an interest in a decedent's estate, you can keep important transactions from happening behind your back by filing a written *demand for prior notice* with both the court and the executor. Such a filing, authorized in most states, compels the executor to alert you in advance to any action regarding the estate, such as a property sale. This gives you time to take action before it is a "done deal."**

Once probated, a will is a public record, as are all motions and court orders that are filed. These papers may be viewed by anyone, along with the final settlement and inventory of estate property. So even without individual notice from the estate, any member of the public can see the will and find out what is going on simply by visiting the probate court office.

Duties of
the Executor

Being the executor of a will can be a time-consuming position. This section traces the executor's duties and financial responsibilities. Will-makers can use it to get an idea of what the executor must go through, while anyone who has been named an executor can use it to scout the territory ahead. The appendix provides a detailed checklist of tasks.

● **Immediate tasks** In the weeks after his appointment, the executor:

■ determines whether a streamlined probate procedure is available (this usually applies only to estates limited in size and/or number of beneficiaries; does the entire estate go to the spouse, for example?)

■ presents his Letters Testamentary to financial institutions (and any other party with whom estate business must be conducted) to enable him to take inventory and control of the decedent's assets.

■ opens an estate checking account to use for paying bills and as a collection pot for various accounts or sale proceeds. The estate's Employer Identification Number from the IRS will be needed to open this account.

- uses estate funds to keep hazard and liability insurance in full force and to otherwise manage and secure estate property.
- requests formal appraisals of all real estate to establish its value as of the date of death.
- reviews final bills and other claims against the estate as they come in, paying those deemed valid and rejecting the rest.

● **Distributing estate property and managing claims against it** The executor may sell real estate and personal property, but she should not begin the final distribution of any property or sale proceeds until the end of the waiting period specified by state law. (Six months is typical.) A waiting period before distribution of property, even if one is not required by law, is a practical idea: it allows time for final bills and all creditor claims against the decedent to surface. (It may be possible in your state, however, to make early partial distributions if the remaining estate assets are sure to be sufficient to meet any valid claims.)

Whether there is a will or not, most states

provide an allowance to be set aside for the surviving spouse and children. This is usually a fairly modest amount. These survivors take a specified dollar value off the top of the estate before any creditors, heirs, or beneficiaries receive their bill payments or their shares of what remains under the will (if there is one) or under the state law of intestate distribution (if there is no will). These allowances vary greatly among states, but some reach five figures.

{ A Closer Look: The family dynamics of estate planning

My Aunt Jane called recently to discuss a situation that she recognizes as a problem in the making. She has two adult children, Patrick and Ann. Patrick was going through some rough times when he moved back into the family home following the death of his father (Jane's husband) ten years ago. Since then, his two grown sons came to live there as well.

Patrick and his sons are in the

construction and home remodeling business. They've done well at times, but they can't seem to put together twelve good months in a row. Meanwhile, they've kept the house in good repair and made some additions, but they have paid rent only sporadically. The house represents Aunt Jane's entire estate, which her will directs is to be divided equally between Patrick and Ann. The house will clearly have to be sold, and everyone knows that Patrick can't afford to buy out his sister.

Aunt Jane's health has begun to fail over the past few months, but Patrick seems unaware that he might ever have to find another place to live. Ann's husband recently died of cancer, however, leaving her a forty-five-year-old widow with three kids. Ann is surviving somehow, but when her mother dies, she will desperately need her half of the estate.

Foreseeing conflict, Aunt Jane called to ask if there was something she could "put in writing" to resolve this problem.

"Yes," I told her. "It's called a will, and the one we did last year is crystal clear. You don't need to do any more writing; you need to sit down with Ann and Patrick and do some talking." Whether brother and sister talk about this before or after their mother's death, Patrick will surely point to the value his improvements have added to the property, while Ann might focus on her brother's years of rent-free residence there.

At my strong suggestion, Aunt Jane chose Ann as the sole executor, abandoning her earlier idea to name the two children as co-executors. When her mother dies, Ann will therefore have the legal authority to decide how to value (if at all) Patrick's claim that he should be compensated for increasing the value of the house. She will have the power to determine a selling price for the house—and to start charging Patrick a fair rent until it's sold. As landlord, executor Ann will also have the right to evict her tenant/brother if he fails to pay.

That's about all "something in writing" can do in this situation, but that's not what Aunt Jane wants. She wants her children to remain close to each other. What's needed here is family communication, not more legal documents.

Claims against the decedent might include a request by the decedent's associate for repayment of a loan he made to the decedent. In other cases, someone might demand payment for injuries received in a car accident caused by the decedent a few months before his death. The executor reviews these claims and the supporting proof, pays those he deems valid, and rejects the rest.

If claims are not made in writing to the executor within a time frame provided by law, they may be barred forever. For such a bar to be effective, however, the law requires that the world must have been notified of the death. This is why the executor should publish a legal notice in the newspaper that the estate is in probate.

{**Warning!** An executor can't lose sight of his obligations

Some states allow the executor to make partial distributions of property to beneficiaries before the claims-filing deadline passes—but he'd better keep ample funds in reserve to meet such claims. If a valid claim is presented on time but the executor has already doled out everything, he has violated his duty—and he could be liable to the creditor out of his own pocket. The creditor also might seek recompense from the beneficiaries themselves. After all, legitimate claims should be paid before the beneficiaries see their first dime.

If a claim is presented on time but denied by the executor, the rejected claimant then faces another deadline: he must file an objection with the court or a lawsuit against the estate within a certain time limit. If that happens, the executor may use estate funds to pay a lawyer to defend or settle the suit. If the time limit expires with no further action by the creditor, however, the claim is dead.

{Warning! Pay special attention to secured loans

A mortgage loan secured by real estate is in a separate category from other, unsecured debts of an estate. The bank that holds your mortgage, for example, would not have to line up with other creditors to recover the balance owed on its loan. If it appears that mortgage payments are likely to go on without interruption, the bank may very well agree to continue the loan in some form. But if the bank feels it necessary, it can usually demand to be paid in full, or go to court to have the house sold. That's not how banks make money, however, so be sure to keep up any mortgage payments during the administration of the estate. This deprives the lender of a reason to force payment of the loan in full.

Once the required waiting period has passed, and all legitimate claims, debts, and expenses have been paid, the executor can distribute the remainder of the property as the will directs. (If there is no will, at this point the administrator distributes the estate's property according to the state law of intestacy, discussed on pages 40–43.) Unless the will specifies otherwise, the executor generally has the discretion to distribute the beneficiaries' shares in cash or in kind. For example, he should honor the will's instructions about property specifically left to somebody unless selling that property is necessary to pay estate debts.

Hint: It's smart practice for the executor to get a receipt from each beneficiary acknowledging that he has received all to which he is entitled.

{ **A Closer Look:**
What to do when a will-
maker outlives a beneficiary

What happens if a will beneficiary dies before the testator does? If the will addresses this possibility, the executor merely follows its instructions. If the will does not do so, it depends on state law and the identity of the deceased would-be beneficiary.

Generally, if the deceased beneficiary is a blood relative of the testator, that beneficiary's children divide his share equally. If the deceased beneficiary is unrelated, however, his children would get nothing. The gift would lapse, becoming part of the "rest and residue" of the testator's estate (also called his *residuary estate*).

Regardless of what the law says, the deceased-beneficiary situation can lead to disputes—unless, that is, the testator has anticipated it. The best solution is for the testator to name a contingent beneficiary—someone who will receive the gift in question in the event the will-maker outlives the originally intended beneficiary. Alternatively, the testator can specify that if a beneficiary fails to survive, his bequest is to be included and distributed with the "residue" of the estate.

● **Final accounting** Finally, the executor or administrator usually must submit a report or final accounting for approval by the court. The degree of detail and formality required depends largely on how much is demanded by other interested parties, such as creditors or suspicious beneficiaries. If there is no tension and all are in agreement, this step can probably be taken care of in abbreviated fashion, or waived altogether. Even if no formal final accounting is required, the executor should prepare an informal settlement statement. This will serve as a lasting record that the job was properly done—or bring to light any irregularities while they can more readily be corrected.

At this time, beneficiaries or other interested parties (such as creditors) can file objections to the final report, or to other actions by the executor (if they have not done so already). They can ask that the judge intervene in some way, forcing a hearing to settle the case. This might happen if, for example, a beneficiary felt he had not receive all to which he was entitled under the will, or a creditor objected that the executor had ignored his claim.

The point to remember is that if you have a complaint of any kind against the estate or the executor, don't wait to bring it up. Don't stew about it for three years before calling a lawyer to see what your options are. At that point, they would probably be zilch. The law places great importance on finality. This is true in all kinds of cases in courts everywhere. People are responsible for keeping up with what is happening in legal matters that might affect them—and for getting advice about where they stand and what they should do.

If you ever discover that "something's up," legally speaking, but you don't understand what it is or why, don't be silly and do nothing. See a lawyer and find out right away. Otherwise, pray you don't need to go to court a few years from now to complain about it. You won't get much sympathy when explaining to the judge that you did get "some legal paper a while back," but recycled it with the junk mail.

● **Executor compensation and other fees**
The executor is entitled to reasonable compensation, often limited to a certain percentage (five percent, for example) of the property in the probate estate. Some states observe a sliding scale of fees pegged to the size of the probate estate. Either way,

the fee allowed by law is typically based on the estate's value, not the complexity or difficulty of administering it.

The court may allow extra executor compensation stemming from her handling of some special matter. Professional fees (those for lawyers, accountants, and appraisers) are also permitted. These fees must be reasonable. (Some states have official guidelines for "reasonable" attorney's fees.)

{ A Closer Look: Your executor's fee— take it or leave it?

A client asked me, "I've recently been appointed as executor of Aunt Sadie's will, which also names me a beneficiary. Am I better off, tax-wise, taking my fee or not?"

From the beneficiary's standpoint, inheritance money is free from federal income tax. The executor's fee, however, is taxable income. Thus if the beneficiary/executor opts *not* to take his fee, the result may be a slightly larger, income-tax-free inheritance. If the sole beneficiaries are you and your spouse, for example, it makes sense to skip the fee.

On the other hand, if there are other beneficiaries, not taking your executor's fee leaves that money in the estate to be shared with the others. Depending on the number of other beneficiaries, you might end up with more money by taking an executor's fee and paying income tax on it.

Those who argue that probate must be avoided often cite unduly large probate attorney's fees. That point of view, in my eyes, overlooks two key facts.

First, no matter how much estate planning has been done, someone must tend to the administrative and "housekeeping" tasks that loom after a person dies. Legal fees can be saved if the executor or family members are available and able to do some of these tasks themselves for free, or at least for less than a lawyer's hourly rate. Second, the executor can curb fees by finding professional help willing to work at negotiated rates, rather than the maximum allowed by law.

Although the executor's job entails effort and serious responsibilities, the pitfalls are often overblown. Absent his own negligence or wrongdoing, the executor is never personally liable on claims or lawsuits against the decedent or the estate itself. Nor is he liable for a poor return on estate investments, as long as those, if any, chosen by the executor are appropriate.

5

Who's in Charge Here? Choosing Your Executor and Trustee

Now that we've examined the tasks facing an executor or trustee, let's consider the positions themselves. In many respects, the same legal rules bind the executor of a will (or the administrator of an intestate estate) and the trustee

Hint: Be sure to discuss the role and its duties with your executor-to-be. It's also a good idea to discuss your choice (and your reasoning) with those family members who weren't chosen.

of a trust. Each of them has a *fiduciary relationship* to the beneficiaries of the wills and trusts they serve. (This is why executors, administrators, and trustees are sometimes referred to collectively as fiduciaries.)

The law pertaining to wills and trusts derives from ancient England, but it is based on timeless common sense: your executor or trustee has the highest legal duty to "do right" on behalf of you and your beneficiaries. The fiduciary relationship dictates that your beneficiaries' interests are paramount. The executor or trustee must be scrupulously fair—and is forbidden to take advantage of his position.

Your executor or trustee is responsible for managing your assets, conducting your affairs, and fulfilling your legal and financial obligations when you cannot—or don't want to—do so yourself. For any number of reasons, not all of us have other people in our lives who can realistically be considered for these responsibilities. Therefore, an important first decision in selecting an executor or trustee (or successor trustee to serve after your death) is whether to use an individual or an institution, such as a bank. This chapter explores both options. Whatever the ultimate choice, discuss your decision with everyone affected by the disposition of your estate.

Let's begin by focusing on the kind of person who would make a good choice. This will most likely be someone in your family.

Naming a Family Member as Your Executor or Trustee

People often choose a loved one "automatically." In many cases, their choice is undoubtedly the person best suited for the role. The choice of any individual as your executor or trustee always carries the possibility of squabbling among your survivors, if there are more than one. Ideally, to keep the peace, the person selected should be acknowledged by the other beneficiaries as being fair. At a minimum, *you* must feel confident that your choice will be fair-minded, whether he gets credit for that quality or not. Your designee should have common sense, including the wisdom to seek and heed sound professional advice when it is called for. Finally, your executor or trustee should be the type of person who gets things done—neither a procrastinator nor likely to be flustered and stymied if problems arise.

When one of several adult children is selected to serve as the executor or trustee for one or both parents—a typical family scenario—a number of issues can arise. It is therefore wise to communicate your decision to all concerned. Hopefully, any sibling resentment or potential problems will surface while you are still around to respond. Consider also whether it's appropriate to address the question of the fee to be taken by the child as executor or trustee. That can be a big point of contention that may be avoided if the matter is discussed and an understanding reached.

● **Naming a child as executor** Naming a child as your executor probably presents fewer pitfalls than naming a child as your trustee. With the former, the duties are more limited in duration, there is less need for "judgment calls," and no investing for the long term is generally required. No matter how simple a child-executor's job should be, suspicion or rivalries in the family pose the potential for bickering. Even if your executor-to-be is currently close to her siblings, it's wise to think ahead and avoid putting her in a difficult situation in the future. There are innumerable ways conflicts may arise, depending on what the executor must do to fulfill her responsibilities and the relationships between family members. My Aunt Jane's case (recounted on pages 187–89) is a good example.

Recall that my Aunt Jane has a son living in her house, which must be sold upon her death so that her estate can be equally divided between both her children. Her son is going to have to leave; she has chosen her daughter, Ann, as executor. I have advised my aunt to discuss the situation candidly with her son in the near future. If he recognizes (and hopefully accepts) the inevitable, he can plan accordingly and minimize friction with his sister. If my cousin Patrick seems unlikely to cooperate, however, a confrontation is unavoidable. Ultimately, he might have to be evicted.

In choosing Ann as her executor, Jane should be confident that Ann will have the assertiveness to claim her rightful share. Otherwise, Jane could avoid putting an unmanageable burden on Ann by choosing an impartial, diplomatic third party capable of taking strong action if necessary—me, for example.

{Warning! Keep sentiment out of your choice of executor

Naming multiple children as co-executors or co-trustees is usually (but not always) a bad idea, in my opinion. This is primarily because it requires two or more people to agree to—and sign off on—everything. When one child is not well suited to the task but you don't want him to feel left out, it's invariably a mistake to assign it to him anyway. Including that child as a co-executor or co-trustee will very likely complicate matters at best; at worst, it will invite costly disagreements or bitter personal disputes. If this is a potential problem, consider using as your executor or trustee an institution or a trusted family friend or attorney. Better yet, choose the qualified child you want to serve, then sit down with everyone and discuss why you made that decision.

● **Naming a child as successor trustee**
When the parents have a trust (assume it is a living, not testamentary, trust), the issues differ from those involved in administering an estate in probate. In a typical living trust, the parent-grantor initially chooses to be his own trustee. His trust assets are usually not too complicated, so ongoing professional advice may be unnecessary.

In many situations, however, the grantor is uninterested or unable to continue managing his assets after transferring them to the trust. Unless the grantor lives forever, a backup trustee will eventually be needed; the trust document should identify this successor trustee. The grantor obviously wants his successor trustee to share a similar investment philosophy; the successor trustee must also possess the experience necessary to handle the amount and kind of assets placed in trust. (We are limiting our focus at this point to money management, not "human" qualifications.)

With married couples, spouses often serve as the first successor trustee for each other's trust. (In community property states, where a single, joint family trust is used more often, the spouses typically start as co-trustees, but either of them can act alone if necessary.)

In some families, an adult child who is well qualified to eventually serve as trustee may be named a successor trustee. Often, however, that choice is made without considering a few key practical matters. Depending on how the future unfolds, the child may serve as trustee for many years of his parents' lives. This could happen because one or both parents suffer an early disability, or because they simply get tired and turn the trustee's job over to him. Some parents assume that a child who has done well for himself financially automatically knows how to invest money for others. This is understandable but not necessarily logical; making money is one thing, but managing it—especially for others—is another matter entirely.

The investment time horizon and risk tolerance of most parents, for example, is probably quite different from that of a successful forty-year-old daughter in mid-career—as it should be. The daughter need not be a professional money manager to understand that difference and invest wisely. But it would be a mistake to assume that she is prepared to take on the investment responsibility for her parents' money, even when her good intentions are beyond question. It's therefore a good idea to frankly discuss with your child whether she and you feel comfortable with her making financial decisions on your behalf.

A much different money-related concern stems from the fact that the child-trustee is almost surely a trust beneficiary. Therefore, he immediately confronts at least the opportunity to give himself preferential treatment. If there are other beneficiaries, especially siblings, they might view the child-trustee with jealousy or suspicion—with or without justification.

This can turn into an enduring source of family strife. Once bad feelings develop among siblings (and their spouses)—especially over money—reconciliation becomes difficult. This doesn't necessarily mean you should not name a child as your successor trustee; it simply means you should give the matter thorough and serious consideration before taking such a step.

If you decide not to name a child as successor trustee, you will probably need to select an institutional trustee, which we examine next.

{ A Closer Look: How to divide household goods without creating a house divided

An almost universal duty for the executor (or trustee or court-appointed administrator) is to divvy up household property among several children. For this chore alone, you want somebody with the skills and patience of a referee. This may seem like a trivial issue; my experience tells me it is anything but. While this portion of an estate is likely to be relatively insignificant in financial terms, it has riven families, triggering heartache and resentment.

The potential divisiveness of candlesticks, china, and family photos can be easy to overlook. After all, your will probably directs that all your possessions are to be divided equally. So where's the problem?

Let's start with the word "equal." Does it mean each beneficiary gets a batch of household goods of equal monetary value? Or that each gets the same number of things? Does a brace of candlesticks constitute one item or two? Is Mom's jewelry to be distributed as a collection, or is each piece in it a separate item? Alternatively, should everything simply be auctioned off and the proceeds equally divided?

As a practical matter, it's best to give the executor some discretion in these choices. But it is also wise to remind the child you've chosen as executor to apply her diplomatic skills to the job. Even when no sibling rivalry is apparent, convene a family powwow at the time you put your estate plan together. Get everybody on the same page to determine if any lurking issues need to be addressed while you are still around to do so.

Banks and Other Institutional Trustees An institutional

trustee—generally a bank or trust company—should be named if a child has been ruled out and there are no other appropriate trusted friends or family members.

● **Fee schedules** The fees these institutions charge are a percentage (usually about one percent or less) of the amount under management. But all of them levy a minimum annual fee, which may depend on the mix of trust assets and whether some or all of your money is invested in "house" brands. This minimum yearly fee will typically be at least $1,000 to $2,000, and probably more like $3,000 to $4,000. As a practical matter, this dictates a minimum account balance in order for the fee to be reasonable on a percentage basis (i.e., about two percent at most, hopefully less).

If active, day-to-day management is required of the trustee, this would entail a fee at the higher end of the schedule. In this case, an account of $250,000 to $500,000 probably would be required to make sense. On the other hand, if the grantor has only a lump sum of cash to be placed by the trustee in a common investment fund, less work—and therefore a lower fee—will be involved. In that case, an account as small as $100,000 might be feasible at some banks or trust companies. These ballpark estimates are just for money management and related administrative tasks. When the trustee's duties require actual decision-making about expenditures or distributions to beneficiaries, there will be additional fees for the time spent doing that.

Hint: To make investments and monitor their performance, institutional trustees generally use committees; these include a customer's trust officer and others. In trusts where it is called for, there is also a trust committee to determine the needs of the beneficiaries and the most appropriate use of trust funds, as set forth in the trust document. A committee is no substitute, of course, for someone who knows the beneficiaries well. If an individual close to the family has been named as a *trust adviser* or *trust protector* (a role discussed in chapter 6), he can give the institutional trustee his input and advice, enabling the trustee to make decisions that are more informed and personal in focus.

The fee question is just one reason why it is a mistake to name an institution without discussing that selection in advance with a trust officer. At a minimum, you should feel personally and philosophically compatible with that person. There should also be a frank discussion about whether the institution really wants your business. The schedule of fees and services offers the first clue as to whether the institution caters to trusts the size of yours.

• **Levels of management** Find out if the institution is willing to undertake the type of trusteeship you want. At one end of the spectrum, you may want the institution to assume total investment control. ("Don't bother me. Just send an account statement every three months.") This arrangement is always acceptable to the institution, which probably offers several common funds oriented toward different objectives. It may have bonds available to provide maximum current income, or "growth" stocks to maximize long-term gain.

Many grantors, however, are reluctant to give the trustee complete discretion; they want to retain some degree of involvement with their investments. Having enjoyed considerable success handling their own investment portfolios, grantors often simply want a trustee to stay the course, and "not fix what ain't broke." Most institutional trustees today will accommodate you on this.

Other grantors are willing to allow the institutional trustee wide discretion as to individual selections—but only within a well-defined class of investments. Still others demand nothing more than to be consulted, or to give the final "yes" or "no" to any proposed investment decision. All of these options (and many variations on them) are available, but you have to ask.

Trust institutions are cautious by nature—and that's a good thing. They are particular about the powers and authority that a prospective customer's trust document grants the trustee. They all insist on reviewing the document before accepting trusteeship. Some will not modify their standard arrangements to suit an individual customer. If your estate is big enough, many trust institutions will bend their rules or fees to land the account. For these reasons, be sure to devote considerable thought and investigation to selecting an institutional trustee.

● **Pluses and minuses of institutional trustees** One obvious disadvantage of using an institutional trustee is the fees it charges. Another is the lack of personal insight such a trustee has into the dynamics of your family, although that's not a relevant factor in every case. Sometimes, however, the institutional trustee's distance from the people involved is a blessing. An institutional trustee will have no problem playing "bad guy" in situations that might make a family trustee uncomfortable. This can come in handy when trust beneficiaries—typically the grantor's adult children—make requests for funds that would be unwise to grant but difficult for their mother, for example, to refuse if she were the trustee of her deceased husband's trust.

A clear advantage of the institutional trustee is professional money management and related services, such as tax accounting and preparation. A less obvious edge: The institution has the financial resources and insurance necessary to make good if trustee negligence ever causes a loss. Rarely does an individual trustee have the liability insurance required to cover his actions as trustee. Keep in mind too that the individual is almost surely a member of the family or someone close; if anything gets seriously bungled it would be difficult and unpleasant to complain about his perform-ance, much less sue him for negligence.

{ **A Closer Look:**
  Some notes on investment
  management

In the past, some institutions in-sisted on quickly selling new trust customers' existing assets and rein-vesting the funds in portfolios *they* felt comfortable managing. For some people, this was a foolish move from the tax and investment point of view. Under ancient principles of trustee-ship, however, the trustee who con-ducted the sale could claim it was simply preserving capital by limiting it to ultra-safe bonds and maybe a few stocks.

Modern investment theory, how-ever, explicitly directs a fiduciary money manager to look at the big picture—not every investment in every trust must be ultra-safe. After all, even if we assume a moderate future inflation rate, if the growth of trust principal does not keep up, there could be a stunning loss in trust value in ten or twenty years.

Therefore, successful long-term investing almost invariably involves some degree of risk. Talk frankly to the people at the bank or trust company to ensure that you and they see eye-to-eye on investment policy.

The Business Side of the Executor's and Trustee's Job

What would you expect the law to require of someone who has accepted this important position? In a nutshell, the law says that he (or it) should do only what is in the interests of the people for whose benefit the money or property is being held. According to the law, executors and trustees have a fiduciary relationship to the beneficiaries of the wills and trusts they serve.

In many family situations, there is no need to think about the executor's or trustee's role. This is often so when, for example, a husband leaves everything to his wife of many years, who is also named as the executor of his will and the trustee of his trust. Their children stand eventually to inherit whatever is left under their mother's will or trust (and maybe their father's as well).

Meanwhile, the mother manages things for her own benefit only. Depending on how the documents are worded, she may have a theoretical duty to her children not to waste the estate. But she is unlikely to do this anyway. As a practical matter, the children are unlikely to question her handling of money, and there is probably no one else with an interest sufficient to permit him to ask for an accounting.

When the mother dies and her children settle her affairs and distribute the family property among themselves, one of them often serves as executor and/or trustee— and is then held accountable by the others. Although most wills—and the law—give the executor wide discretion in handling property and the affairs of the estate, the law does not permit an executor or trustee to give himself preferential treatment—ever. The world would be a better place if everybody kept that in mind. Sadly, they do not;

fiduciary misconduct is a regular occurrence.

● **Understanding the fiduciary relationship** A fiduciary relationship exists when two parties assume—through a will, a trust, a power of attorney, or some other agreement—certain roles regarding money or property: one person (the maker of the will or trust, for example) places a special trust and confidence in another person (the fiduciary). This individual (or institution) has a duty to make her very best effort and use all her skill, care, and good judgment to act in all the beneficiaries' interests in investing, distributing, and otherwise handling the property entrusted to the fiduciary. The law requires an executor or trustee to look out for you, even—*especially*—if you are not looking out for yourself.

Accordingly, the law forbids an executor or trustee from acting in any way contrary to the interests of the beneficiaries. When the fiduciary is also a beneficiary herself, she need not put her interests below the others. But she should not seek an extra or special benefit for herself in relation to the property under her management. A person acting in a fiduciary capacity is required to make full financial or other appropriate disclosures to those placing trust in her. None of this is expecting too much. After all, an executor or trustee has agreed to assume a special position of confidence and legal duty, and is likely being paid reasonably for services rendered.

If an executor or trustee violates his fiduciary duty and a loss of assets results, he might be ordered to pay compensation personally (or as an institution) to the beneficiaries. This does not necessarily mean that the executor or trustee is liable if a portfolio of blue-chip stocks happens to decline in value during a general market slump. On the other hand, if the executor or trustee neglected to use available funds to pay a fire insurance bill and a piece of estate property burned down, he could be held liable to the beneficiaries for the loss.

Hint: The fiduciary relationship is radically different from ordinary business relationships. For example, I have an honest plumber who understands that taking care of customers is always good for business. But

even if I have confidence in him, he has no high legal duty to me. Everyday business transactions are often governed by "Look out for number one" and "Let the buyer beware." Not so with an executor or trustee.

● **The Prudent Investor Rule** Most states spell out the obligations and standards to be met by an executor or trustee in managing the estate's investments in a law called the *Prudent Investor Rule*. There are a few slightly different versions of the rule, but all are based on financial common sense. The basic rule can be paraphrased as follows:

A fiduciary shall invest and manage assets held in a fiduciary capacity as a prudent investor would, taking into account the purposes, terms, and distribution requirements expressed in the will or trust and the other circumstances of the estate. To satisfy this standard, the fiduciary must exercise reasonable care, skill, and caution.

The word "reasonable" appears frequently throughout all areas of the law. Ultimately, when there is a dispute, the court must decide whether that standard has been met. It is only fair, however, that compliance with the Prudent Investor Rule be determined in light of the circumstances prevailing at the time of the executor's or trustee's decision or action, not in 20/20 hindsight. The rule requires a good standard of conduct—not necessarily a good outcome.

● **Review and management of assets** Within a reasonable time after accepting the job, the executor or trustee should review the assets of the estate or trust and make an independent determination about which, if any, should be sold. One might assume that the decedent would already own exactly the kind of assets appropriate for carrying out his wishes. This is not always true, however. The executor or trustee must therefore quickly make sure the property in the estate or trust investment portfolio jibes with what the decedent has decided is to be done. If a widow is supposed to get monthly income according to her husband's trust, for example, a piece of undeveloped land won't do the trustee any good—even if it's worth a million dollars. He might have to sell the land and invest the proceeds to make cash available to pay the widow on a regular basis.

Although the Prudent Investor Rule applies to the executor of a will, it is generally of more day-to-day importance to a trustee. This is simply because the trustee might be called on to manage and invest trust assets for many years. The tenure of an executor, on the other hand, is often limited to a year or less and may involve nothing more than cashing in a few CDs, paying some bills, filing some paperwork, and cutting checks.

If the decedent owned stocks, bonds, real estate, or other assets, decisions would have to be made about how best to distribute them in accordance with the will (for example, transfer the deed to a farm, or sell it and issue a check). The executor is often well advised to get input from the beneficiaries before doing so. But there usually is not much "investment" called for, as long as everything is safe for the short term.

Fortunately, some corollaries to the basic Prudent Investor Rule provide guidance as to what an executor or trustee (or any fiduciary) can and should do. The most significant of these are summarized below. When a fiduciary violates his duty and acts improperly, resulting in a loss of money, those who suffered the loss—typically the beneficiaries—can sue. (If the fiduciary is a sibling rather than an institution, however, actually collecting any court-awarded money could be a different matter entirely.)

- **Important corollaries to the Prudent Investor Rule**

1. An executor or trustee must make a reasonable effort to verify information about the investment and management of estate or trust assets.
2. An executor or trustee is allowed to hire and rely on a professional financial adviser, provided that he chooses the adviser with care and periodically reviews the adviser's decisions.
3. The executor or trustee must diversify investments unless there are special circumstances.
4. An executor or trustee must consider many factors in investing and managing property. Some are fairly predictable:
- General economic conditions

- The possible effect of inflation or deflation
- The expected tax consequences of an investment decision
- The anticipated total return (income plus price appreciation) of each asset

5. An executor or trustee is supposed to consider other factors as well (and this is where the job can get interesting):
- Other financial resources of the beneficiaries
- A particular asset's special relationship or special value, if any, to the purposes of the trust or estate, or to one or more of the beneficiaries
- The need, if any, for regular income, as well as the potential for investment growth, if that is important

The problem with that last factor is that regular investment income and long-term investment growth are most commonly associated with quite different types of investments. A widow in need of current income might want her late husband's trust to own only safe, reliable U.S. Treasury notes. She is not interested in investing for the long term. Her children, by contrast, often stand to receive a share of their father's wealth only much later. They might therefore favor investments that pay little or nothing currently but show the greatest chance of increasing in value over many years.

● **Considering multiple beneficiaries** When an executor or trustee has more than one beneficiary to think about, he is obliged to do a balancing act. He must act impartially in investing and managing the assets, taking into account the beneficiaries' differing interests. This is a tall order. But there is a solution: when writing your will or trust, specify your priorities to provide the executor or trustee with guidance in determining the appropriate investments.

For example, a lot of people might want to say, "The primary purpose of this trust is to take care of my spouse [or other loved one] until he or she dies; the trustee is authorized to spend whatever the trustee feels is necessary to do this, even if that leaves nothing for my children." A grantor or testator with children in college and an independently wealthy spouse, in contrast, might give the trustee entirely different guidance.

The Human and Practical Side of the Trustee's Responsibilities
This reality is worth repeating: when you are gone, your trustee will be counted on to know—and to do—what you would have wanted. That should be the trustee's guiding light—and yours as well when selecting the trustee. The focus is on trustees here because their jobs, more than those of executors, involve the "human touch." The executor's financial and administrative duties in probate do not usually demand as much close and ongoing interaction with the beneficiaries. Probate is all business (one hopes), and then the case is closed. This is often not the case with trustees.

The business aspect of the trustee's job—the *minimum* level of responsibility that will be required of all trustees, executors, and administrators—is much easier to define and comment upon than the practical, human side. How much of the human touch is needed or expected from the trustee hinges on the circumstances of those who are left behind. Let's consider a couple of hypothetical situations to illustrate the ends of the spectrum.

In plenty of cases, little is required of the executor or trustee. When a widow dies and leaves three grown daughters, for example, one of them is likely to have been named the successor trustee of the family trust, once both parents are gone. Assuming the three sisters are all responsible adults, it is also likely that the trust directs the trustee simply to divide everything equally and terminate the trust. In that case, the trustee would probably not have to deal with any personal issues.

When parents with small children both die prematurely, on the other hand, the scenario is quite different. Even if the parents had the foresight to set up a trust to hold the life insurance proceeds and any other funds available to raise their children, the question remains: "When the parent-grantors are gone, who can be trusted to know what they would have wanted—and then carry that out?" Here, obviously, is where maximum personal insight and attention—the human touch—is most desirable.

Let's extend this hypothetical scenario to make another point. Spouses often create a joint trust or separate trusts that are basically alike. Each spouse typically serves as the successor (backup) trustee or co-trustee for the other. In these cases, parents might name a bank as the second successor trustee, without much thought, just in case they die together in an accident.

Regrettably, sometimes that is just what happens. The successor trustee might then be a committee at a bank—somewhere—trying to make important evaluations or judgments of a kind no one ever contemplated leaving to a stranger. The professionals at the bank, though well intentioned, would surely recognize their lack of personal insight.

How to prepare for this situation? Just as a family member serving as trustee can turn to financial pros to fulfill his fiduciary responsibilities, an institutional trustee can look to the family for help with its "human" responsibilities. You can name a trust adviser or advisers in the document. Most institutional trustees welcome that kind of help, but they do not want to be held liable for improperly acting upon the adviser's input—or, conversely, for failing to heed it. The trust therefore must clearly articulate the adviser's degree of authority.

The *trust protector* offers estate planners another means of supplying a trust with that personal touch. This role is examined in the next chapter.

{ A Closer Look: Some decisions should be kept in the family

As a fifteen-year-old sophomore, Sally was clearly the best member of the high school dance team. Tragically, both her proud parents were killed in an auto accident the summer before her junior year. Sally grieved with her younger brother, Billy, and the two went to live with their guardian, Aunt Marge.

Sally eventually found comfort in dancing, and began planning to make it her career. A teacher at school thought she had a good chance of being accepted at the prestigious Juilliard School in New York. Being in a position to offer a strong recom-

mendation, the teacher called Aunt
Marge to discuss the possibility. He
told Marge to use $40,000 per year
(including airfare, spending money,
and so on) as a bottom-line cost figure in making her decision. It would
take Sally four years to earn a Bach-
elor of Fine Arts degree.

Even though she was the children's guardian, Marge explained,
she had direct access to only a relatively small sum that had been left in
the parents' names. Sally's father
had been covered by a $250,000 life
insurance policy at the time of his
death, but it was payable to an irrevocable trust he had created. The
trustee at this point was a bank that
had changed names since the trust
was written. Marge spent that after-
noon on the phone, finding the appropriate trust officer.

She'd never seen the trust document, Marge explained to the young
trust officer, but she had always as-
sumed its funds were earmarked primarily for Sally's and Billy's college
educations. Would the trust consider

an arts school such as Juilliard a college, Marge asked the trust officer— and, if so, would the trust pay for Sally to attend it?

The officer told Marge that a three-person committee, acting as trustee, would make the decision after reviewing the terms of the trust. Though the officer was neither equipped nor eager to make decisions about a teenage girl's future in dance, he and two other employees of an out-of-town bank would now have to do just that. Just as the child's parents would have done, this institutional trustee had to determine whether Sally had the talent and long-term commitment to justify the cost. Would it become the break of a lifetime or an expensive diversion?

The trust committee knew the trust was being administered for two children, not just one. Whereas the document did not require equal spending for each child, and it seemed likely that the $250,000 trust principal, plus earnings, could easily cover the expense of four years at Juilliard, other questions had to be considered. There would not be enough to send Billy to an equally expensive college, should he apply there, or to graduate or professional school afterward if that became his goal. Was that fair? Meanwhile, if Sally proved ill-suited to a performing arts career, limited funds would remain to start her on a more traditional path.

Fortunately, the decision did not have to be made in the blind. The attorney who drafted the trust, having contemplated just this kind of dilemma, had *specifically authorized* the institutional trustee to rely on Marge's input as an adviser on family decisions such as the one at hand. The trustee could therefore follow her suggestion without worrying about breaching its fiduciary duty. Marge felt certain that Sally's parents would have encouraged their daughter to apply to Juilliard, so that's what Sally did—and she was accepted. Everyone is satisfied that the decision was made by the family, as it should have been.

6

Using a Trust Protector: Someone to Trust besides Your Trustee

A *trust protector* can be thought of, in part, as a trust adviser, a position that has been written into trusts for years, although it is still not the rule. But a protector has real authority, so the role is not strictly advisory. Think of the protector as a "super" adviser, with a big

Hint: A trust protector can resolve family dilemmas that arise after you are gone—ideally, with an understanding of what you would have done in a given situation.

"P" on his chest. Day to day, the trustee alone manages assets and disburses funds uneventfully. But when a beneficiary's personal issue or situation must be confronted, or if the trustee himself falls asleep at the helm, the protector swoops in to save the day. (This is about as exciting as estate planning gets.)

Until recently, this role has been routinely, and almost exclusively, built into foreign asset protection trusts. But there is nothing exotic about using a trust protector. It is such a good idea, in fact, that lawyers are using it more and more in all kinds of trusts for all kinds of clients. There are certainly some complications and issues to resolve in using a trust protector and it is not practical for everyone. But it is a way to build flexibility into an estate plan and provide oversight of the trustee.

Viewed in that light, much of our discussion here will still be relevant to people who do not incorporate a protector in their trusts. After all, the situations and issues addressed by a protector exist even when a trust does not have one. The following can help you recognize some of the scenarios that might arise and have to be dealt with during the life of the trust.

Introduction to the Role and Its Duties

A trust protector is empowered to make "judgment calls," based (hopefully) on the protector's personal relationship with the beneficiaries. Consider this example of the trust protector's role: When parents are alive, they will take into account their children's readiness, maturity, and needs before giving out money to them. If the parents have passed away, however, in plenty of cases the successor trustee is a bank, ill-suited to making these kinds of judgments. It might be a good idea to have a family member—an aunt or uncle, for example—empowered to make decisions on distributions to the children based on their stage in life and long-term goals.

The role of trust protector gives a grantor peace of mind when setting up the trust, especially when young ones are involved. While planning the best for their toddler, for example, parents/grantors would be foolish not to recognize the uncertainty in life. Who knows what kind of person this child might marry, or what kind of mistakes he might make in his youth? A mandatory trust pay-out could easily be the worst thing possible at some distant date. On a more positive note, what if life presents a promising op-portunity to a deserving child, young or adult, who needs a few bucks to make something happen? If the parents are not around, these are the kinds of purse string decisions a protector can make. The leeway given to the protector can be narrow, wide, or in-between—as long as it's spelled out in the trust.

● **Why use a protector AND a trustee?** Certainly, the important trust protector pow-ers can effectively be given to a "regular" trustee, and in many cases that's a good idea. But designating different parties to serve as trustee and protector is often dic-tated by the people and circumstances in-volved. A grantor might have a brother who is perfect for making family decisions, but who doesn't want or couldn't handle the fi-nancial and accounting aspects of trustee-ship. The role of trust protector is ideally suited to making use of a family insider's wisdom without giving him responsibilities that require a different set of skills easily delegated to a professional trustee.

Using a single person (or institution) to wear both hats will also defeat a significant purpose of having a protector to begin with—the watchdog function. Even if your choice of trustee is ideal, it can't hurt to have somebody to monitor things as time goes by. What if your sister is doing a great job as trustee, but becomes terribly distracted by a health or other crisis in her own family? What if the bank merges and the trust department moves to Timbuktu and your trust officer is never heard from again? Actually, "protector" really is the best name for this job: he can replace your trustee if events call for it, protecting your assets and plan from mismanagement, neglect, or even disaster.

Powers to Give
the Protector Trust protectors by the
nature of their role are given power to make significant changes to the trust. But there are a number of potential pitfalls, so it is probably wise to limit that power to a scope

commensurate with the anticipated need. Rather than start with a long list of things the protector can do, begin with a blank page. Your attorney can be of real help here.

The more important powers are as follows:

- The power to replace the trustee (and/or any other investment advisers) is perhaps most useful when the trustee is an institutional trustee. There are a wide variety of settings in which this can become important. So put this at the top of the list.

- Powers of an administrative nature, such as amending the trust as needed to deal with future tax or legal changes, unforeseen circumstances, or minor errors in the trust document.

- The power to determine the amount and timing of trust disbursements. If the issue of future payments to trust beneficiaries such as the amount and/or timing of disbursements is of concern to the grantor, the protector can be given broad authority over this matter. For example, sometimes it's best for a protector familiar with the family to determine disbursements at the time they are contemplated. On the other hand, if there are only two adult children as beneficiaries and they are both level-headed and responsible, why complicate life by allowing the protector to be involved with the distribution of money to them?

{ **Warning!** Don't give your trust protetctor too much power

Some trusts give the protector authority to make any amendments to the trust document that are necessary, in her opinion, to fulfill the grantor's intentions—or simply to be "of benefit" to the beneficiaries. Does this mean the protector is free to rewrite the trust? If so, what are the trustee's duties? There are so many questions and potential problems related to this kind of far-reaching power that granting it may be asking for trouble. Give this considerable thought. Discuss with your attorney whether this degree of power is necessary or desirable in your situation.

{**Warning!** Take care in allowing a beneficiary to name a new trustee

For years, plenty of trusts have been written giving the beneficiaries themselves the power to change the trustee. This kind of provision in a trust must be used and drafted cautiously; if not, it opens the door to all sorts of problems. Carelessly tossed into the trust document, a beneficiary's power to replace the trustee might result in the trust's assets being exposed to the beneficiary's creditors, or included in his own taxable estate. To be safe, the trust should almost never allow a beneficiary to name a new trustee who is related or subordinate to the beneficiary. As a practical matter, this will usually rule out a lot of names. With this in mind, many attorneys limit beneficiaries' ability to change the trusteeship only to an institution.

Who Should Be Your Trust Protector?

This question is tricky, especially when you consider who should *not* be the protector. For various legal reasons, the list of who usually should *not* be the protector includes:

1. The grantor's spouse or children
2. Any other beneficiary of the trust, especially if the protector would have even the *potential* power to benefit himself or his dependents.

As with a beneficiary who also serves as trustee, having a beneficiary serve as trust protector could expose the trust's assets to that beneficiary's creditors or increase his taxable estate. There are also practical reasons why a grantor would be asking for trouble by giving a child some of the common powers given to trust protectors. Consider the power mentioned previously, to make decisions on distributions to the grantor's children (which includes the protector/child himself) based on their individual circumstances and needs. Obviously, this kind of discretion could be used by the protector/child to favor himself. The protector's brothers and sisters may regard even totally proper management with suspicion. The grantor is better off leaving any discretionary judgment calls to a knowledgeable third-party protector with no interest in the trust.

But who is the best candidate for the role? As the brief discussion and examples above suggest, ideally you want a family insider with good judgment and no direct or indirect interest in the trust. You also want someone you feel comfortable asking and *who is willing to serve*. (Remember to ask first; that's a minor detail not to forget.) This is a simple but demanding list of requirements. Indeed, not having the right person is the biggest problem with the protector concept.

Your siblings are a good place to look for candidates. Your children's aunts and uncles might be close to the kids and, even if not, they've at least been around long enough to know what's going on. Not surprisingly, when brothers or sisters are not available, most grantors will choose a close friend or another relative who isn't a beneficiary of the trust. (With the latter choice, the issue is often age—you'd like somebody about your age or younger, certainly not much older.) When all else fails, sometimes a long-time family financial adviser or attorney will do. Such professionals would have to be paid a fee, however, for time actually spent on trust matters. Otherwise, protectors typically serve without pay.

Some trusts create a two- or three-person committee of protectors. That's fine, but think about it carefully first. Life has taught us all that doing things by committee sometimes creates more work than it saves. If you have one good candidate in mind, you're lucky. Go with him alone unless there's a reason to use a committee. Any other good people can be used as alternates. But if it comes down to a tough decision, a single wise protector can ask the family for all the advice he needs. In many situations, requiring two or more people to formally agree on anything can be problematic.

Defining and Limiting the Trust Protector's Powers A good trust protector in the right situation can work won-

ders for a particular estate plan. There are some significant caveats and issues worth examining, however. In addition to *defining* the powers your trust protector has, it's also important in many cases to include a clause in the document to *limit* her responsibilities and potential liability. This might address some valid trepidations of your would-be protector and make it easier to find someone to take the job.

For example, we have said that a protector needs good judgment and sensitivity when called upon to offer guidance on family matters. Sounds simple enough. But does that mean the protector assumes a duty to make regular family checkups? Is the protector supposed to keep tabs on your adult children at all times? If she authorizes a trust distribution for what is, supposedly, a worthy cause, is the protector liable for not knowing that the money is really going to pay off a gambling debt? Thinking it through, no one in her right mind would ever be a protector, if she felt that was the level of responsibility called for in the trust document. Thus, it is important when providing for a trust protector to minimize potential future issues and uncertainties regarding her duties and expected standard of care.

Respected attorneys have widely different views on the degrees of legal responsibility (much or little?) the protector should be given—and be prepared to assume. Perhaps there is a middle ground, where the protector has a duty of "ordinary care." That's simply the attention or skill that a reasonable person would use under similar circumstances. This is what the law expects of us in most day-to-day life situations anyway. (Of course, what "reasonable" means is usually open to debate; that's why we have lawyers, judges, and juries.)

The nature of the trust protector's duties is a matter to be carefully discussed with your attorney—as well as the candidates you are considering. Just keep in mind that it does little good to write a "job description" so demanding that no one wants the position. That might be better, however, than empowering a protector in a trust document that leaves a lot of unanswered questions.

{ A Closer Look:
Protector powers in trusts
for the disabled

In some family situations involving disabled children, a trust protector might be given the power to make changes or direct the trustee to take actions necessary for compliance with new laws or frequently changing rules. Attorneys who work with these families find this flexibility extremely useful and important. There are onerous restrictions on the benefits a disabled person can receive from a trust and still qualify for state assistance with housing, medical care, and so on.

In a carefully designed *special-needs trust* for a disabled beneficiary, a protector can be authorized to make changes in the trust in response to changes in the eligibility rules for government benefits. This can be critical, because unfortunately, prohibitive care costs and the unavailability of insurance for them usually make reliance on public assistance a financial necessity. The laws and regulations in this area are changing constantly, and no one can predict far in advance all the rule changes that might necessitate changes in the trust document.

Don't Forget the Trustee

The trustee needs to know where he stands, too, in terms of his level of responsibility for implementing the protector's decisions. When a protector exercises the power to do something—for example, amend the trust provisions or give out money—is the trustee obliged to make an independent determination about whether it's a good idea? We have considered the protector's role as watchdog of the trustee. Does it work the other way around, as well? It's probably not supposed to.

Remember that the protector exists in large part to make judgments and decisions the trustee is not qualified to handle. Therefore, it makes little sense to place upon the trustee the burden of evaluating the desirability of the protector's actions. But a trustee at all times retains his fiduciary role under state law. That's a high degree of responsibility and creates a potential liability to the trust if anything goes wrong. So most trustees are unlikely to sit back and let the protector do as he pleases.

Trustee liability regarding the protector's actions (or nonactions) is likely to be a particular source of concern for an institutional trustee. For one thing, a bank, unlike Uncle Fred, will be aware of this issue in the first place. More to the point, the bank knows it's a much more inviting target for lawsuits than most Uncle Freds. Trustee liability vis-à-vis the trust protector is another matter to be discussed with your attorney, as well as with the would-be trustee and protector.

Helping Your Trustee and Trust Protector

Do Their Jobs There are at least two categories of crucial information to include in your trust that could be of immense value to your trustee, protector, and beneficiaries. Remember, if it's not written down anywhere, nobody is going to know what you decided during that thoughtful discussion in your lawyer's office except your lawyer, of course, and she probably won't or can't discuss it for ethical reasons.

● **Spell out the ground rules** One class of input the trust should provide is administrative or functional—establish the ground rules. What will be the rights and obligations of the trustee, the protector, and the trust beneficiaries in dealing with each other? Who is supposed to do what? If the protector is required to approve or disapprove some action by the trustee, how does he do it? Just do nothing? Send a letter? What if the protector doesn't know about the proposed action by the trustee? Is the trustee required to give the protector notice?

It's not important to answer these questions here. There are many other "what ifs" we could include, as well. The preliminary decisions, for discussion purposes, can be safely left to your attorney. Just be sure that they are answered in the trust document, everything is explained in an understandable way, and you feel completely comfortable. This added batch of considerations is unavoidable if two parties (trustee and protector) are to be given concurrent authority over a trust and its assets.

Hint: If you fail to define everyone's turf and your expectations in a trust arrangement, there will be unresolved issues when you are no longer around to clear them up. Whether these blossom into full-blown problems will then depend largely upon circumstances or luck. This is asking for trouble. All this might make you wonder whether incorporating a protector into your trust is worth the effort—and it might not be. Perhaps an informal family adviser to the trustee would do just as nicely.

• **Make your priorities clear** The other information that might help everyone deal with your trust is more philosophical in nature. How about a statement of the guiding principles and values that should be used in administering your trust? Not many documents actually have a section like this. Obviously, an institutional trustee is likely to need this more than a close relative who already knows you well. But the need for such guidance is likely to be better addressed as the use of trust protectors catches on.

An awareness of your priorities could be especially helpful to trustees and/or protectors in the many life situations that require a balancing of competing interests. For example, if a wife knows that her second husband is well off, her trust might be primarily intended for the ultimate benefit of her children, who are not her children by her present husband. As a safety net for the husband, a secondary purpose of the trust—as far as the wife/mother is concerned—might be to provide for his "health, maintenance, and support."

But "support" is certainly open to different interpretations. If only a "safety net" is contemplated, then maybe she should say so. That would provide practical guidance to the trustee, while not tying his hands. On the other hand, spouses frequently intend that the entire family estate should be at the disposal of their spousal survivor. The amount, if any, that their children receive is of secondary, or maybe no, importance. Clarifying priorities such as these in writing would avoid problems and makes sense, especially since it's so easy to do.

Some grantors feel comfortable giving the trustee or protector only a broad statement of principles to guide their exercise of discretion. For example, the trust might direct the protector simply to act in accordance with what the protector believes the grantor would have wanted, considering the facts and circumstances at hand. That kind of statement would leave little room for reasonable argument over the authority of a trustee or protector to take almost any action—in good faith, of course.

Sometimes, it's hard enough to get people to do what they're supposed to, no matter what your precautions. But eliminate as much ambiguity in your wishes and outlook as possible. This will allow your trustee and protector to better serve your interests with less effort and uncertainty. A guiding statement of values also helps weaken the position of anyone such as a troublemaking beneficiary who might not be in tune with your plan.

7

When Things Go Wrong

A carefully thought-out plan and properly drafted documents should provide smooth sailing for most executors, trustees, and estates. But anytime multiple people are involved, the potential for conflict exists, so let's look at problems that sometimes arise.

Hint: Be careful when choosing your executor. An executor (or an attorney-in-fact or a trustee, for that matter) is in a position to misuse funds and take advantage of his power. Put the wrong person there, and you virtually guarantee the failure of your estate plan.

Executor Misconduct

I get more email from my Web site on the topic of executor misconduct than any other, by far, but there is not much to be said. Misconduct happens. What can be done? The truth is that it's very difficult to get a court to remove an executor. Never mind if the executor has "attitude problems," doesn't tell you anything, is insensitive, slow to act, or generally a jerk. This is the person the decedent chose. You're probably stuck with the choice, so try to be nice.

Actual misconduct is about the only legal basis for executor removal and it can be hard to prove in court. But as a practical matter, even if you have clear evidence the executor has mishandled estate property, or given himself preferential treatment (assuming he's also a beneficiary, such as an adult child), it's unlikely the judge will be able to make you completely happy at the end of the day. The fact is that an executor (or attorney-in-fact or trustee, for that matter) is in a position to misuse funds and take advantage of his power. Put the wrong person there, and you have virtually guaranteed the failure of your estate plan. There is simply no good legal remedy.

{ A Closer Look: When legal action cannot solve the problem

I had an executor disqualified in probate court on behalf of a client (his brother) years ago. It was a classic case of winning the battle, but losing the war.

There had been, overall, fairly blatant misconduct that was easy to prove to the judge. She could see exactly what was happening, even though the executor-brother had an "answer" for everything. So we won, and the evil executor-brother even had to pay my client's (the good brother's) attorney's fee for the hearing. But when the dust settled, the evil brother still failed to account for (in other words, managed to steal) a watch of great sentimental value and some other items. The judge had done everything we asked, but my client was angry and still holds a

grudge against me. Even though we won, the judge was not about to send the SWAT team out to secure the premises and prevent my client's watch from being removed. So it "mysteriously" disappeared.

That's because even if you achieve victory in court and have the executor disqualified, the victory is likely to be bittersweet. Tangible property long "known" by all in the family to be in the parents' home might become "lost." Money in the bank can be improperly spent by an unworthy executor—somebody who wouldn't have a dime to pay back even if he were successfully sued over it. To have any chance of success, however, sit down with an attorney as soon as possible to see where you stand. If the errant executor knows somebody is on his case, he might straighten up—at least a little. Especially when items of the decedent's household property are being improperly removed, time is your enemy. There's no paper trail and it's almost impossible to prove anything.

It makes sense that it is difficult to remove the decedent's choice of executor. Unfortunately, however, the consequences of that fact are not always appreciated by people writing their wills. This is one of those problems that has no real solution. You simply must do your best to avoid it.

Challenging

a Will Contrary to popular belief, it is *very* difficult to successfully challenge a will. The two most common legal grounds for attack are often interrelated:

1. The testator lacked *testamentary capacity* (mental competence) to make a valid will, and/or
2. The testator fell victim to the *undue influence* of another, so that what was written does not reflect the testator's true, freely made choices.

There is a strong presumption in the law against both arguments.

{ A Closer Look: The curious case of the will-maker who couldn't spell her own name

Although will contests that go to a jury trial are rare, I happened to take

part in just such a case as this book was nearing completion. The trial went fine, as lawyers like to say, until we got to the verdict. But despite the disappointment (or perhaps because of it), I'm compelled to share a valuable lesson: do things properly. Even if your state allows you to write your own will, as mine does, don't do it! Do, however, notify everyone who should know of your plans.

For years there had been a daughter-mother relationship between my client (I'll call her Louise) and an elderly woman (the decedent) with no children of her own. Louise had successfully gone to probate court with a piece of notebook paper making a testamentary disposition (a will) that she claimed (and I still believe) the decedent had written in her presence. The handwritten document, filled with crossed-out words, stated (verbatim):

_____, [the decedent], want Louise [last name] to have my house and everything in it at my dat death.

my will is at the bank at they [indeci-
pherable]
She is so good to me
I don't owe anything but to Louise
[Decedent's signature] Age 100 Aug
27.
[Note: This was her correct birthday.]

My client had hesitated for months
to come forward with this document.
Meanwhile, when the decedent's attorney went to her safe deposit box
to retrieve the will he'd prepared
years before, he claimed it was not
there. A short time later, however,
the bank staff found it—torn neatly in
half—revoked. (The torn document
called for most of the decedent's estate to go to her church.) The bank's
logbook of access to the box showed
Louise had never been there, but the
implication was made that somehow
she was responsible for destroying
the decedent's prior will.

When it appeared there was no will
to direct otherwise, the decedent's
entire estate was to be divided

among her nieces and nephews by a court-appointed administrator, according to state law. But after the probate court ruled that Louise's document qualified as a will (pertaining only to the house and its contents), the administrator filed an appeal and asked for a jury trial. The verdict was that the document accepted by the probate court was not a will because it was not, as my client claimed it was, in the decedent's handwriting. I don't believe Louise was a forger, but apparently the jury did.

It didn't help our case that the decedent appeared to have spelled her name two different ways, both of them wrong. Other facts, too, created doubt in jurors' minds about my client's truthfulness. It was unfortunate, but a trial lawyer has to play the cards he is dealt. Win or lose, however, the bottom line would have been the same: this kind of scenario should never be allowed to happen in the first place.

● **Testamentary capacity** With respect to testamentary capacity, we learned earlier that the law doesn't require much in the way of mental sharpness. The testator doesn't even have to be able to name the president, for example, or know the date. Capacity to make a will requires that:

1. The testator understood the nature and extent of his assets. (Did he know, very generally, what he owned?)
2. He understood who his family members were and that he was (or was not) naming them in his will.
3. He realized that in signing the will he was directing where his assets were to be distributed upon his death.

If these questions are all answered "yes," testamentary capacity exists. You can see, therefore, that a lack of mental capacity at the time the will was signed is extremely hard to prove. This is especially so given that the law requires the judge to lean toward a finding that there *was* adequate testamentary capacity.

■ Who could even file such a challenge? It could not be just a family insider or friend. It has to be somebody with a potential iron in the fire—a disinherited child is the most frequent example. He would stand to gain if the will were declared invalid because he would then take a share of the estate under the state law of intestacy (or else an earlier will, if any, might be admitted to probate instead).

■ The child's argument would be, "Look, Dad entirely forgot about me. He *must* have been crazy or incompetent." That's why it is wise for a testator to specifically state in a will if he intends to leave a child nothing. It is not necessary, however, to leave one dollar or provide a reason. The disinherited child would have little chance of success in attacking a will that specifically mentioned him—at least not on the basis of a lack of testamentary capacity.

● **Undue influence** *Undue influence* is another legal argument that could void a will. This is just a little easier to prove, especially when there is evidence the testator was mentally weak, even if not to a degree that testamentary capacity was gone. Let's look at the two components of undue influence in reverse order. "Influence" exists when someone in a close relationship with the testator "persuades" him to leave his property in a manner he would not have done without the "persuasion." The influence rises to the level of "undue" only when it becomes a form of mental coercion—taking advantage of the circumstances.

Every case has to be judged on its own merits, but we can say what does *not* generally constitute undue influence. For example, it would not, by itself, be considered *undue* influence if a man's new wife or girlfriend nagged or sweet-talked him into favoring her over his children in making his will, even if the result was quite unfair under the circumstances. The question asked by the court is: "Was the testator's final decision freely and independently made—was it his own?" The law presumes that it was and proving otherwise is hard.

Unless somebody puts a gun to the testator's head, there is probably no single event or action that can be identified as being unduly influential. However, imagine a bedridden man, a little slow mentally, unable to communicate freely with the outside world. If he were under the constant care of a nurse on whom he had become almost totally dependent, for example, that would be a situation where undue influence *could* be exerted. Over the course of several months or years, the nurse might suggest that the man's children do not care about him but that she loves him. She might also remind the man how dependent upon her he is and imply that her caretaking would stop if he did not make her the sole beneficiary of his will.

If this testator did so, his children would almost surely claim the nurse had exerted undue influence. If they could prove the facts recited in the above scenario, they would have a good chance of prevailing. But who is to say the testator did not simply get disgusted with his children for not showing enough interest in him, and decide to reward his caretaker for her concern and dedication? That is what she would likely argue.

In evaluating the competing arguments, the court would ask questions and look for some of the conditions that experience has identified in cases of undue influence by a person named as a will beneficiary. Some of these questions would be:

■ Was the testator physically weak and/or mentally impaired?

- Was there a close or confidential or care-taking relationship between the testator and the person accused of the undue influence?
- Was this close relationship developed only recently, just shortly before the writing of the will being challenged?
- Was the person being accused of undue influence involved in the actual writing of the will? Did this person take possession of the will after it was written?
- Were there efforts by the beneficiary to limit or obstruct contacts and communication between the testator and others, especially his family?
- Was the will out of line with what would reasonably be expected? This might ultimately be the most important factor.

In the above situation, for example, if the testator had three dutiful, attentive children, one would *not* expect him to omit them entirely from his will, in favor of the nurse. If he did so, that would be out of line. If he left his loyal caretaker not the whole estate but just five hundred dollars, that would probably not cause the judge to raise an eyebrow.

The above factors are not exhaustive and

there would be no formula underlying the court's decision. It would be based on the totality of the circumstances of each unique case. The thing to remember is that almost everyone who has ever been left out of a will feels slighted and is sure the testator must have been incompetent or unduly influenced by someone. This is understandable, especially in situations that really do appear unfair. But having a will invalidated on the basis of undue influence presents a difficult uphill battle.

Problems with Trusts and Trustees

After the grantor dies, a trust can be challenged in court on many of the same grounds as a will. The rules about mental capacity and undue influence in the making of wills apply to trusts. As with a will, one who attacks a trust bears a tough burden of proof.

● **Trustee misconduct** The previously mentioned legal and practical observations about executor misconduct apply to a trustee as well. Because these positions can be so easily abused, both have a special duty under the law to be fair and honest. But trustees do misbehave sometimes. I have gotten enough questions on this issue ("Can he do that?") to make it worth bringing this potential red flag to your attention several times here.

A living trust generally "keeps on going" after the grantor dies. It avoids probate. That's a terrific advantage, right? Not when there is trustee misconduct. A trust is not supervised by probate court; therefore beneficiaries can't simply appear before a probate judge and explain, without an attorney present, what the trustee is doing wrong. Instead, a formal lawsuit against the trustee must be filed in another branch of the court, with a much greater delay and significant expense. Since the remedy for a bad trustee is so difficult to obtain, it is especially important to avoid this problem and choose your trustee (and successor trustee) wisely.

● **A trust beneficiary's rights** A trustee's mismanagement (or worse) is often not immediately clear. A common question from beneficiaries is, "I'm afraid my brother [the trustee] is cheating me. How can I get a copy of the trust?" Of course, a testamentary trust (created in a will) can be read at the court-house—but only after the will is taken to pro-bate court. While the testator is alive, his will and everything in it is private. Similarly, while the maker of a typical living trust is alive, future beneficiaries (such as his children) have only an expectation of what they might receive. They have no rights yet to any information about their inheritance.

However, when a living trust grantor dies, state laws vary as to what information beneficiaries are entitled to. If you want a copy of the trust, don't forget to try the obvious first: a letter to the trustee asking for it. Many states require the trustee to furnish a copy of the trust document to any beneficiary upon request. The trustee may also be required to keep beneficiaries "reasonably" informed about the administration of the trust, with annual reports on trust income, expenses, and assets.

{ **Warning!** When your trustee clams up, something fishy may be going on

If you are a beneficiary and have questions the trustee won't answer, it could be simple miscommunication—or it could be cause for concern. Don't delay in seeing an attorney about where you stand; if misconduct is afoot, time is not your friend.

Be realistic about your position. A beneficiary has a legal right only to what is specifically given to her in the trust. If the trust document says she is to receive $10,000 on her twenty-first birthday, for example, and the trustee refuses to write a check, the beneficiary can sue the trustee and force him to hand over that amount. In many situations, however, trust distributions are left to the "absolute discretion" and judgment of the trustee. In that scenario, a beneficiary would have little chance of prevailing in a court challenge of the trustee's unfavorable decision.

8

Preparing for the Tax Man

Too often, estate planning is merely considered to be estate *tax* planning, with primarily federal tax in mind. Experience has shown, however, that tax liability is seldom a client's predominant concern. For one thing, contrary to popular belief, very few gifts or estates are large enough to have any federal

Hint: If your estate—including IRAs, 401(k) plans, and life insurance proceeds from a policy you own—is approaching the federally tax-protected amount ($1.5 million in 2004 and 2005), plan ahead to avoid unnecessary taxes.

tax payable at all. On the other hand, plenty of people who don't consider themselves rich find that for tax purposes their estates are worth more than they thought—and certainly enough to be concerned. Nobody wants to leave an estate that owes any more tax than necessary.

To understand tax-saving principles and strategies, this chapter offers a basic survey of federal gift and estate tax law. What is included in your taxable estate for federal purposes? What exemptions and deductions exist? Tax-wise, how do lifetime gifts compare with transfers at death?

{ A Closer Look: When certainties collide: death meets taxes

State inheritance or estate taxes ("death" taxes) have historically been of much less significance in planning than federal tax. One reason is that state rates are much lower than the federal rates. Additionally, many states have for years used a "painless" system to collect state tax. They've charged the decedent only

the exact amount that federal law has been allowing as a tax credit—a dollar-for-dollar subtraction from the *federal* estate-tax tab. Paying the state's death tax hasn't been an extra burden because the decedent's tax preparer could reduce his federal estate tax by the same amount. In other words, "pay the governor instead of Uncle Sam."

But this free ride is being phased out: By 2005, the "state death-tax credit" will be gone. This change in federal estate-tax law could sap revenue from the states. State death-tax laws are therefore being modified to make up for the lost income—but it won't be painless any more. Look for additional state tax burdens in the near future. In many places, the state death tax will be applied to much smaller estates than the federal estate tax. Make this issue a prominent blip on your planning radar screen.

Your Taxable

Estate What is included in your taxable estate for federal purposes? As stated earlier, everything. Every asset is valued at its fair market value on the date of death. Remember, the size of the *probate* estate has nothing to do with the size of the federal taxable estate. For 2004–2005, if the value of a person's or married couple's combined *federal taxable* estate reaches $1.5 million, the need for estate tax planning is triggered. If your estate is worth less, no federal estate tax will be due—unless, perhaps, you have made large taxable gifts while alive. (We'll discuss this in detail later.)

Your taxable estate consists of all property interests owned by you, or by a trust you control outright, or by a trust to which you have any significant "strings attached" This includes the following frequently overlooked assets:

- IRAs of all types, and all tax-qualified retirement plan proceeds such as employer pension plans, 401(k) and profit-sharing plans, and so on.
- Life insurance proceeds, if the policy is *owned* by the decedent, no matter to

whom the proceeds are paid. (But don't be confused—it is still true that life policy proceeds are almost always received by the beneficiary with no *income* tax due.)

How the Federal Gift and Estate

Tax Works Prior to the tax law changes that took effect in 2002, *all* transfers of money or property (outright, or by will or trust) during life or at death were subject to a single, Federal Unified Gift and Estate Tax system. Every person had a certain total amount he could give away during his lifetime or leave at death fully protected from federal gift or estate tax. For many years, that tax-protected amount had been $600,000.

Then the law changed twice and added some new wrinkles. Starting with those who died in 1998, the estate and gift tax-protected amount began increasing in uneven steps. For those who died in 2002 and 2003, it was $1 million. In 2004 and 2005, the federal *estate* (not gift) tax protected amount is $1.5 million. If the law doesn't change, that figure will step up again to

$2 million for those who die in 2006 to 2008. (There isn't much point in trying to guess what will happen after that.)

Consider these tax-protected amounts as "standard" shelters from the gift tax and estate tax. They're built into the law and available to everyone, for all kinds of transfers of money or property made to anyone. (Additionally, there are some well-known gift and estate tax deductions and exclusions that are available to fully protect transfers of property from tax in "special circumstances"—for example, money to your spouse, during life or at death. We'll address these soon. For now, note that these special-circumstance transfers don't "use up" any of your standard shelter.)

The *gift* tax-protected amount, unlike the *estate* tax-protected amount, remains at $1 million per person following its one increase in 2002. In other words, during your entire lifetime, you are entitled to give away $1,000,000 gift tax-free. So now we no longer have a single tax-protected amount that applies to the *total* of lifetime gifts and transfers at death.

Once a person makes lifetime gifts totaling $1 million, he must pay federal gift tax on all subsequent lifetime gifts. But if transfers of money or property are instead made at death, $1.5 million can be protected before estate tax must be paid (for 2004–2005). Fortunately, the person receiving the gift or inheritance does *not* pay any additional federal estate or income taxes (except on any retirement accounts on which the decedent paid no income tax previously). Of course, if the estate (or gift-giver, if living) responsible for any tax due does not pay, the IRS can take its cut from a beneficiary.

As under prior law, whatever portion of a person's *gift* tax-protected amount he uses is deducted from his *estate* tax-protected amount the year of his death. So if one had made a full $1 million in tax-protected lifetime gifts, he would have only $500,000 remaining as a shelter from estate taxes at death (in 2004 or 2005).

In other words, a total of $1.5 million can be sheltered from federal gift or estate tax, but only $1 million of that total is available to protect lifetime gifts. The full $1.5 million—minus whatever portion of the shelter has already been used for lifetime gifts ($1 million maximum)—can be used to protect transfers that occur at the estate owner's death.

{ **A Closer Look:**
Wasn't the federal estate
tax repealed?

The Economic Growth and Tax Relief Reconciliation Act of 2001 (EGTRRA) increased in steps the amount that can be left to others free of estate tax by someone who dies over the next few years. Whether or not the federal estate tax will eventually be repealed is highly uncertain; it all depends on the actions—or inaction— of future administrations and congresses.

As it stands, the 2001 law performs tax magic: the estate tax is set to vanish completely for 2010. But the law has a self-repealing feature; on January 1, 2011, the law and its tax breaks will be gone. Presto! The estate tax will reappear. Unless further legislation is passed, we'll then revert to the pre-EGTRRA rules. Before the 2001 changes, the law called for

an eventual increase in the gift- and estate-tax exemption to $1 million; most observers feel that figure would prevail after 2010 if the estate tax "repeal" is allowed to expire and no new tax relief is enacted.

EGTRRA was enacted amid overly sanguine predictions in 2001 of huge—and everlasting—budget surpluses. Even then, however, few estate planners believed the estate tax would be allowed to disappear. Fewer believe so now.

Many observers think the coming years will bring a compromise. There probably will be no permanent end to the federal estate tax, but lawmakers may well agree on a protected amount considerably greater than the $1 million under prior law. As for tax planning, all you can do for the time being is formulate a strategy based on what seems likely in the next few years—and keep your ear to the ground. During 2003, opponents of total repeal talked about such a compromise, in which the tax-protected amount would be

raised to around $3 million per person. Officially this talk is meaningless, yet it signals where we might be headed.

If you use none of your gift tax exemption while alive, then a full $1.5 million of your estate can be protected from estate taxes, if you die in 2004 or 2005. If your estate is greater than $1.5 million in 2005, *the tax on the next dollar is forty-five percent* and the rate quickly rises to *forty-seven percent* for the largest estates. Fortunately, the law still allows some significant transfers to be excluded from the gift and estate tax altogether.

• Other Gift and Estate Tax Exclusions

$11,000 Annual Exclusion per Donor for Gifts The law allows you to give cash and/or property worth up to $11,000 without tax consequences to each of an unlimited number of recipients per year. (This amount had previously been $10,000, but was adjusted for inflation.) This means a married couple can give $22,000 per year, per recipient. Spouses can either write separate checks or make a single $22,000 gift and file an informational gift tax return (no payment) to indicate that it is a split gift.

These gifts do not count against the $1 million gift tax exemption or the $1.5 million estate tax exemption. An $11,000 gift requires no paperwork and is income tax-free (as are all gifts) to the recipient. To qualify, a gift must be outright, allowing the right to spend or use the property immediately with no strings attached—not a promise of a future benefit. This requirement means that gifts in trust do not qualify (unless the trust is designed in a certain way that we will examine later).

The Unlimited Marital Deduction from Gift and Estate Tax This is potentially the biggest one. Gifts of any size to your spouse, during life or at death, are not taxed and do not "use up" any of the $1 million gift tax-protected amount or the $1.5 million estate tax-protected amount. (Note that much more restrictive rules apply when the surviving spouse is not a U.S. citizen.)

Unlimited Exclusion for Gifts Made in Payment of Another's Medical or Tuition Costs Payments must be made directly to the institution, not just earmarked for this use and given to the beneficiary. This exclusion offers grandparents who wish to make gifts in excess of $11,000 per year an easy way of helping their children and/or grandchildren without the inconvenience of a gift tax return.

Gifts to Charity Advocates for nonprofit and charitable organizations like to point out that the federal gift and estate tax is entirely voluntary. In a very real sense, this is true. You always have the option to give them your estate—or any part of it—free of any tax. The IRS has a list of qualified charities, which includes all the "household names."

{ **A Closer Look:**
Shortsightedness can be costly in the long run

Many married couples reason as follows: "Yes, our combined estate is well over $1.5 million, but each of us owns only half, so each of our estates is too small for federal estate tax to kick in if one of us dies [in 2004 or 2005]. And even if our estates were much larger, each of our simple

wills leaves everything to the surviving spouse, so we're covered by the unlimited marital deduction."

That's all true—but what happens when the second spouse finally dies? (For simplicity, assume the second death is also in 2004 or 2005.) At that point, he or she will still be able to protect $1.5 million from federal estate tax. So what's wrong? The mistake was made in planning only for the first spouse's death, whereas the tax hit comes after the *second* spouse dies. After the first spouse's estate passes to the surviving spouse, he or she will be left with a total estate worth well over the tax-protected amount; that estate will be taxed heavily upon the second spouse's death. If the value of your combined marital estate is approaching the tax-protected amount, consider the marital deduction and bypass trust (A/B trust), discussed in chapter 11.

The Generation-Skipping Transfer

(GST) Tax This is an exceedingly complex tax to explain and understand fully, and it is not worth the effort for most people to know more than whether or not it affects them. The GST tax is an extra levy, *in addition to* the gift and estate tax itself, primarily on gifts to grandchildren. A gift to a grandchild "skips" the children's generation, so to speak. Before the tax, very wealthy families also used such gifts to "skip" the estate tax that would inevitably have been due if the gift had been given to their children and grown in value by the time the children died.

Everyone has a lifetime GST tax exemption of $1.5 million (that will apply to those who die in 2004 and 2005). Generation-skipping gifts in excess of that amount are subject to taxation at forty-eight percent—the maximum gift and estate tax rate in 2004.

Cash gifts of up to $11,000 per year per grandchild are exempt from GST tax, as well as gift tax. *Some* gifts in trust qualify for the annual GST tax exemption. You'll recall that some gifts in trust qualify for the exemption from the "regular" gift tax. *But the rules pertaining to the GST tax and the gift tax are different regarding this issue.* If you plan on substantial or recurring gifts to trusts for the current or future benefit of grandchildren, ask your attorney about the GST tax issue.

A Simple Living Trust Will Not Save Any Tax

Keeping property in a trust does not mean you will pay no income tax on income from that asset. For income tax purposes, most forms of meaningful, ongoing control over trust property make it a *grantor trust* under the tax code. (The mere power to revoke makes any revocable living trust a grantor trust.) For income tax purposes, the IRS ignores grantor trusts: The grantor is liable for income tax as if the trust property was owned in his individual name and no trust existed.

Remember, too, that just because a living trust keeps property out of your probate estate, this does not mean the asset is out of the taxable estate for federal estate tax purposes. If a trust is intended to keep property *completely* out of your taxable estate, you must have "no strings attached" at the time of your death. Certainly, any trust that the grantor can revoke will be included in her taxable estate. This is also true if the grantor retains the power to change the terms of the trust in any significant way.

The bottom line is simple: **to transfer and keep property** *completely* **out of your taxable estate—with a trust or without one—you must give up both control and the right to receive personal benefit.** That is what "no strings attached" means. Alternatively, if you give up only some control and benefit from property (while retaining a portion for yourself), it is often possible to transfer at least some of its value out of your estate. But can you create any kind of arrangement to remove property from your estate to save taxes while you keep full control and benefit? No, you cannot.

In all areas, but especially here, don't try to be "cute" with the tax code. If something is not allowed because of a particular rule, and someone tries to sell you a plan or trust that seems to get around it—think twice. Experience shows that 99.999 percent of the time, these "great" plans are totally ineffective. Unfortunately, you (or your survivors) might not find out until it is too late that the IRS does not accept the scheme.

So revocable living trusts (and most others "with strings attached" or benefits retained by the grantor) should be considered primarily with the intention of achieving nontax objectives, such as avoiding probate court, planning for disability, and flexibility in property management—not tax savings. Those concerned with tax savings must consider a trust that is irrevocable. As a trade-off, irrevocability presents the obvious and significant drawbacks associated with losing control over one's property. (Fortunately, we will see in chapter 11 that a *revocable* living trust *can* be used in an estate tax-saving plan—but only if it is designed to create an *irrevocable* trust upon the grantor's death.)

Shaving Down
Uncle Sam's Share Even though the nominal federal gift and estate rates are the same, it takes more money to transfer a given amount, after taxes, upon death than by lifetime gift. The federal estate tax is

levied on the whole estate "pie." Tax is paid first on everything—including money that is about to be sent to the IRS to pay those very taxes. In contrast, the gift tax is levied more like a retail sales tax: the appropriate percentage of tax is applied to the amount of the gift. This makes for a lower *effective* rate for the gift tax. A lifetime gift can therefore be a more "tax-efficient" way to transfer wealth.

As a general *estate tax* rule, it has been thought better to make lifetime gifts of property that is expected to appreciate significantly in the future, so that the increase in value would occur while somebody else, presumably the younger generation, owns the property. This avoids or delays estate taxation for many years. On the other hand, it has traditionally been deemed better to wait until the time of death to give property that has already gone up dramatically in price, such as stock you've owned since Day 1 or a home that has appreciated significantly.

The "rule" makes sense in some cases but not others, and we will shortly look at it more closely. First, it is important to understand the tax principle that gives rise to the conventional wisdom. The reason we care about whether the would-be gift is "already appreciated" or "expected to appreciate" property lies in the arbitrary distinction under the law, at least for now, as to how the beneficiary receiving the property must compute his profit (*capital gain*) for income tax purposes, if and when the property is ever sold. The key concept involved is tax *basis*, and it is appropriate to digress here, so that this important term can be considered.

● **What is basis?** *Basis* can be imprecisely, but adequately, explained as follows: when property is sold, the seller is taxed on any gain—the difference between the sale price received and the seller's tax basis in the property. Generally, the tax basis in property is the amount originally paid for it, plus the cost of any significant additions, upgrades, or improvements you have made. (Such improvements would apply to real estate investments, but obviously not to financial assets.) So, the higher the basis you can claim at the time of a property sale, the lower will be the amount of gain subject to income tax.

To keep things simple, let's consider an asset with a basis, while you own it, that is simply the price you paid. This might be stock in a blue chip company you have owned for many years. But what would be your daughter's tax basis, if she receives this stock by a lifetime gift, or as an inheritance and pays nothing for it? The answer is not "zero" in either case, but there is a big difference between the lifetime gift and inheritance situations.

Until the 2001 law changes things after 2009 (if that ever happens), and even thereafter, to a lesser extent, special rules apply by which the taxpayer can get a valuable break from the tax code when property is acquired through an inheritance. Property given by lifetime gift takes the same tax basis in the recipient's hands as the donor had—generally, the price the donor paid. This is called a "carry-over" basis.

But property received by inheritance does *not* keep the basis it had in the donor's hands; *it receives a new "stepped-up"* basis for tax purposes. The new basis, which the donee uses to calculate taxable gain if she sells, takes a "step up" to the fair market value of the property on the date of the estate owner's death. So, if your daughter sells the stock she inherited from you immediately for its fair market value, there will be little or no taxable gain. *A lifetime of appreciation in value can totally escape capital gains taxation.*

After 2009, this big benefit might be scaled back. For the time being, however, the following examples are worth understanding.

● **Gift vs. inheritance: examples of what happens to basis**

Example 1: Dad gives Junior one hundred shares of stock in a corporation. (There are no federal tax consequences to Junior unless and until he sells.) Junior sells it next year at the market price of $60 per share for a total to him of $6,000. Dad had paid only $50 per share four years ago. What is Junior's gain? In reality, Junior has "gained" $6,000 he did not have before. But this was a gift, so he takes Dad's basis of $5,000 (the price Dad paid). Junior's taxable gain will be $1,000 ($6,000 minus $5,000). This, of course, would have been Dad's true profit had he kept the stock himself and sold it.

Example 2: In 1980, Dad bought one thousand shares of stock in XYZ Co. for $1 per share. His tax basis is simply the price paid. Assume he dies and leaves the stock to Junior in 2005 when it is selling at $75 per share. Junior's basis becomes the date of death (2005) value of $75 per share. It has been stepped up, and *he will recognize no taxable gain if he sells at that price.*

● **Gifts of "already appreciated" vs. "future appreciation" property** It's important to do some forecasting before making a lifetime gift of any kind of property that has *already* appreciated significantly in value since acquisition. Common examples of this are real estate, stocks or mutual funds, and family homes or businesses. (Remember, we're only looking at taxes here, not "human" issues. Because there are several factors to consider, this kind of decision calls for guidance from your attorney and perhaps other professionals.)

If your estate will not likely be large enough to pay estate tax, but you simply want to make a gift for nontax reasons, then a gift of "already appreciated" property should be avoided, *if other property is avail-*

able. (Cash or a check will do nicely.) The family home (or other real estate that has increased in value) comes to mind in this situation. Don't forego the step-up in basis that would be given to this "already appreciated" property if it passes at your death—unless there is a reason for doing so.

{ A Closer Look: Should you add a child's name to the deed to the family home?

This question arises frequently. Typically, the parent's motivation is either avoiding probate or protecting the property from sale by the state, in the event that she requires nursing home care provided by Medicaid, a public assistance program. This deed change is usually not a good estate- or financial-planning move. It can have serious negative consequences on the parent's Medicaid eligibility, as well as on his or her financial security. Such a gift should never be made without careful con-

sideration and consultation with an attorney.

Many people do, however, have (or antici-pate) estates large enough that estate tax will be payable. So it is obviously wise to at least consider lifetime gifts (with other strategies) to reduce the amount that will be subject to this tax. But in this situation, your gift-giving decisions are more complicated. If there is "future appreciation" property that is available and in a suitable form for gift-giving, that often remains the best choice. Let the (hopefully big) increase in the asset's value occur while your daughter, for exam-ple, owns it. She likely won't have to be concerned about her own gift or estate taxes for a while, if ever. That's good; pay-ing tax later (or not at all) is usually better than paying tax today.

If there is no such property, however, making a lifetime gift of "already appreci-ated" property might still be a good idea if you foresee having estate tax payable. In this scenario, the basis step-up that would occur at death would be lost, leaving the property appreciation subject to relatively low *income* tax (capital gains tax). Keep in mind that this tax won't even be payable unless or until the property is sold, anyway. Meanwhile you will hopefully get a big non-tax benefit—seeing your loved ones enjoy your generosity.

The alternative, if your estate is already over or near the tax-payable threshold and you hold onto this appreciated property until death, is that your estate will pay tax on it. If so, the *lowest* estate tax rate would be more than twice as high as the capital gains rate that your children, for example, would pay if they received the property as a gift and sold it. (Remember, as explained previously, any gift worth more than $11,000 in one year from one donor to one recipient will be subject to federal gift tax. But the way the gift tax is applied results in a lower federal tax cost to transfer a dollar of property by lifetime gift, as opposed to a transfer at death.)

● **Challenges in long-term planning** The above simple analysis reflects (in part) how planners have traditionally approached the gift and estate tax-planning process. Unfortunately, a difficult task has become even more complex in recent years than ever before. There are now two huge clouds of uncertainty over the estate planning field.

First, at what figure will the gift and estate tax-protected amounts "finally" settle? As discussed, there is a good chance that amount will be increased "permanently" in future years, but when and how much are anybody's guess. Meanwhile, we know the estate tax-free amount *will* change even if Congress does nothing more: the current law calls for increases later in this decade, full estate tax repeal for one year, followed by a "repeal" of the repeal in 2011, which would leave us with pre-2001 law.

The second big uncertainty concerns the fact that the estate tax-protected amount is $1.5 million per person in 2004 and 2005, and set to increase thereafter, but the gift tax-protected amount is stuck at $1 million. So now some people have to decide if they should make a taxable gift today to save on estate taxes later—without knowing if the estate tax will even apply to them when they die.

How can you do long-range tax planning amid that degree of uncertainty? Very cautiously. To review all the options from the financial or tax perspective, you just have to sit down with your lawyer or accountant and crunch numbers. Make plans based on the best assumptions you and your advisers can make now, and review them every year. Keep your options open if possible. There are planning techniques and tools your attorney can use to help maintain flexibility.

{2

Applying the Basics: Estate-Planning Tools for Common Life Situations

If you understand the basic roles and structure of a trust covered in chapter 2, most of the important work is done. Those concepts and issues apply to all trusts. From here on out, all we're going to do is take a trust "chassis" and customize it with optional equipment in the form of various terms and provisions. The two basic "makes" we start with are the revocable trust and the irrevocable trust.

Because there are descriptive names for most of the trust arrangements we'll examine, people often get the idea that each is a totally different vehicle—like Ford, Chrysler, and GM. But unlike cars, you can pretty freely mix and match options among the various makes and models of trusts to create something just right for your needs. Remember, a trust is just a contract between you and the trustee. To a large extent, you can do what you want when designing it. Keep the customizability of trusts in mind when you see your attorney.

Attorneys have designed a large handful of "workhorse" trusts to deal with certain life goals and scenarios that occur repeatedly, such as the death of both a baby's parents, a special-needs child, tax savings, and so on. But if you have the right trustee, a trust can be used quite creatively to deal with issues and situations that don't come up every day, such as providing for a beloved pet. These—and all trust documents—are nothing more than a series of paragraphs with detailed instructions telling the trustee what to do in this or that situation, or giving the trustee guidance and discretion to do what appears best at the time.

Let's look more closely at using trusts to achieve particular purposes. We'll start with providing for underage children, since that's a frequent issue of great concern to clients.

9

Providing for Young Children: Some Useful Trust Provisions

Trust provisions for minors and young adults deserve some thought by parents and grandparents. With any luck at all, of course, at least one parent will

Hint: A trust can ensure that your children receive funds in a responsible manner, should anything happen to you and your spouse. When establishing the trust, make sure to address practical issues that may arise, in order to avoid confusion after you are gone.

survive the kids' childhood and this issue will cease to be relevant. But we plan for no luck at all.

A Common Dilemma

No professional training is required to recognize the quandary: all parents and grandparents want to ensure that no matter what happens, food, clothing, shelter, and education will be provided for the children and that special opportunities or problems can be addressed. But parents know it is unwise to give most young people unfettered access to significant sums of money—life insurance, for example. By putting child-raising funds in a trust, there can be rules and strings attached. To increase the chances for success, the parents can include some guidance to the successor trustee in the trust document and perhaps find an appropriate trust protector as well. (Remember, the parents need a third-party successor trustee because we're assuming now that both of them have died.)

If more than one child is involved, there are at least two broad options for handling trust assets: there can be a division into totally separate trust shares for each child, OR a continuation as one fund for the benefit of all the children. In either case, at specified ages (such as twenty-five, thirty, thirty-five), a total or partial distribution of trust assets can be called for. By then, hopefully, the beneficiary-child will be mature enough to spend or invest it wisely.

I have always favored the latter option, a "single pot" trust approach. It allows more flexibility in dealing with emergencies, special needs, or opportunities when one child might require more than the others. This is the philosophy most parents have while both are alive. The drawback of this approach, however, is that it puts an extra burden on the trustee and/or trust protector. They could be called upon to face financial decisions that even parents find among the most difficult in raising a family. (Of course, if we are talking about a trust created by a grandparent, the children's parents are usually around to provide input into Grandma's decisions as trustee.)

With a "one share per child" approach, the trustee's hands are tied. He cannot give more to one child than another. Whether that works out to be a good thing or not is impossible to predict. That's why there are few questions with "right or wrong" answers. For that reason, these matters should be decided by the client, not the attorney.

{ A Closer Look: Imagining the unimaginable— the simultaneous death of parents

Many parents with young children ask, "What happens to our property if we both die at once?" The answer depends on how much planning has been done. First, have you found a capable and willing guardian for the children? Second, will funds be available to support them? Without a good answer to both questions, legal advice will not help much.

In many cases, of course, wife and husband have the same—and only the same—kids at home. Simple wills prepared for these parents are often mirror images of each other and have a clause to deal with the "common disaster" situation. Each spouse's will says, in effect, "All my property to my spouse, *if* he/she survives me by seven days. Otherwise, all to the children."

To analyze the result in a common disaster, focus on one parent at a time. Look at the wife; in a common disaster, the husband will not survive her. So none of the wife's property would pass to him. It would pass to the alternate beneficiaries instead— usually the children. Now look at the husband's will the same way. In a common disaster, the wife will not survive him. If his will, too, requires the spouse to survive him, then none of the husband's property would pass to her. Again, it would go to the alternates—the children.

In this type of catastrophic-accident situation, the couple's children would end up with each parent's estate—just what we want. Or is it? If a sizable amount is involved, from insurance or otherwise, the money should probably go into a trust for the kids' benefit. Otherwise, the day they turn eighteen, they can grab their shares and run.

Some "What Ifs" to Consider in Setting Up a Trust for Minor Children

Some situations arise often enough in life that it's worth addressing them now, while you're setting up a trust for your children. Once you start thinking about this, you'll probably add a few other things to your own list. Your trustee or protector will appreciate the guidance.

• **What if a teenager or young adult child needs or asks the trustee for an advance?** No matter what schedule of trust payouts you establish, or what size they are, at some point there may be a request for a lump sum advance. The trustee's response, ideally, would be the same as yours: "It depends." For a "worthy purpose," you might say yes. This portion of the trust might read:

In addition to the distributions authorized above, CHILD may request an advancement on his or her ultimate anticipated share of this trust. If, in its sole and absolute discretion, the trustee determines that the requested advancement will be used for a worthy purpose, then the trustee may make such advancement in whole or in part.

Here are three "worthy purposes" many people would agree with under the right circumstances. They might be included in the trust on a nonexclusive list, subject to the discretion of the trustee or trust protector, who makes the final call:

■ The purchase of a home appropriate to the needs and circumstances of the child
■ The acquisition of a business interest in keeping with the age, training, and experience of the child, provided that there is a reasonable probability of success in the sole and absolute judgment of the trustee (or protector)
■ The continuance of the education of any child on a full-time or part-time program in an institution of higher learning, or at a trade or vocational school.

Most serious requests (ones that don't make the trustee laugh out loud) fall into one of the above categories. Of course, you can add to the list. If you feel comfortable doing so, you can also give the trustee or trust protector the discretion to honor requests that seem appropriate and reasonable at the time they are made.

{ A Closer Look: Some purposes are "worthier" than others

Compare these two scenarios from families with sons around age nineteen who had begun college, only to discover they were already "smart enough." Eric's wealthy parents didn't have time to be involved in his upbringing. Brad had been born to wonderful parents but had lost both by the time he turned eighteen. Both boys were beneficiaries of trusts managed at the time by institutional trustees.

Brad had been mowing lawns during his high school summers. He was organized, efficient, and had enough business to hire a friend to help occasionally. Brad even hung on to enough of his earnings to provide his own spending money and pay his car insurance for his first two years of college. He was a solid "B" student, but after his sophomore year he told his trustee he was "burned out on school." Wanting to take a year off, Brad persuaded his trustee that expanding his landscaping business was a "worthy purpose," even though probably only for the short term. The trustee felt it was appropriate to advance funds to Brad to buy a second used van and a larger mower.

Eric had apparently majored in partying. He had barely scraped through freshman year when he informed his trustee that school was "irrelevant." Eric explained that he'd be better off going into "business" with two men he'd met in their late twenties. His would-be associates, while penniless, had impressed Eric with their big dreams and financial acumen. All they needed was some money to get things going. The trustee concluded, however, that an advance to allow Eric to invest in an exotic nightclub

did not constitute a "worthy pur-pose"; he declined the request.

● **What if a child becomes ill or unstable?**
If this unfortunate situation arises, it might not be a good idea to make trust distributions directly to the child. The trustee might be given instructions such as:

No funds should be given to a child if, in the sole discretion of the trustee, the child is so afflicted with emotional instability, or mental or physical illness (including drug or alcohol abuse), that he could not reasonably be expected to support herself or to prudently spend, manage, or invest funds if distributed.

If funds are withheld, the trustee should also be given wide discretion to pay whatever is necessary to provide for the child's medical care, education, and/or support.

● **What if the child's guardian needs a bigger house or car?** We have said that all trustees have the highest of legal duties to use trust assets *only* for the benefit of trust beneficiaries. Sounds straightforward enough. But what about the practical problems of the guardian you have chosen to raise your child if you cannot? At the time people select a guardian, there might not be a good candidate who just happens to have an extra bedroom available. Maybe, for example, your sister is the perfect choice, but her house is already a tight squeeze with her own family.

Should the trustee be allowed to spend money to add a bedroom or bathroom to *the guardian's* house? Or buy her a bigger car to chauffeur around her newly expanded brood? If it would make everyone's life better, your answer is probably "yes." But without prior authorization, most trustees would hesitate to make such large outlays that clearly would be of significant benefit to somebody *other than* your child, the trust beneficiary.

Therefore, it is wise to consider allowing the trustee to make payments that, although benefiting the guardian (or some other payee) personally, also assist in fulfilling the responsibilities of guardianship or provide a service or benefit to your child. These kinds of things might include, without limitation, expanding the guardian's residence, buying a larger car or a family computer, or paying for a family vacation or travel expenses under appropriate circumstances. Since it is usually impossible to forecast these needs at the time the trust is prepared, the trustee should be given guidance but authorized to use his discretion and judgment in these matters.

● **What if a child wants to use a car or live in a house owned by the trust?** There certainly might be times when it is necessary or appropriate that a child be permitted to use a residence, household goods, vehicle, or other trust property, in the trustee's discretion. If so, it would probably not be practical to require the trustee to provide the other children (if any) with equivalent property or money. That point should be explicitly stated.

{ A Closer Look: Uniform Transfers to Minors Act (UTMA) custodial account

This is a useful alternative to a trust for a child when the funds to be earmarked for his benefit might not be large enough to justify creating a trust. Almost every state has a version of this law, which provides a simple way of giving to a child while retaining some control. A gift under UTMA can be made either currently or by providing for one in a will or a trust.

The account is absolutely the child's property (only one child per account), but it is controlled by a custodian of your choice. That could be you, but you should also consider the person named as the child's guardian in your will. The custodian has broad authority to invest and spend for the child's welfare, but the account must be turned over to the child at the age of eighteen or twenty-one, depending on the state, with several states allowing an option to extend the account to age twenty-five.

The mandated turnover while the child is still young is the principal drawback of this tool. If the account balance is not expected to exceed $100,000 to $200,000, however, this can be a good college savings vehicle, because the funds would be all or mostly expended after four years of school. A cautionary note: any expenditure by a UTMA account that fulfills a legal obligation of a parent is taxable income to the parent. So if you write checks from the account at the grocery store, that's taxable income to you. Until the child is eighteen, almost any expenditure by a parent could be viewed the same way. But if the guardian is spending money to raise a child because the parents have died prematurely, that is *not* income to the guardian.

Banks and other financial institutions are quite familiar with UTMA accounts. They're easy to set up and banks don't charge a fee for doing so. UTMA is a good thing to know about, as long as its limitations are understood.

10

Planning for Children or Grandchildren with Disabilities

Providing for children with special needs is a complicated yet vitally important task. If this situation applies to

Hint: Think ahead if you plan on leaving money to a child with special needs. Without proper planning, your child's inheritance could affect his or her eligibility for government assistance. If this situation applies to you, be sure to consult an attorney to make sure your child is adequately provided for after you are gone.

your family, the following estate-planning tools can help you and your children both during your life and after your death.

What Is the Supplemental Needs Trust (SNT)?

The word "supplement" is key to understanding this estate- and financial-planning tool. Also called the *special-needs trust*, it has just one beneficiary—a disabled person receiving government assistance. The trust document directs the trustee to use trust funds to enhance the beneficiary's quality of life by *supplementing*—not replacing—whatever minimal, means-based benefits federal or state agencies provide. Those benefits are potentially available to the disabled person after his eighteenth (or twenty-first) birthday, when he is no longer the legal responsibility of his parents (or before then, if his parents themselves qualify for aid).

{ A Closer Look: Programs for the disabled

There are two primary modes of government assistance for the disabled.

1. THE SUPPLEMENTAL SECURITY INCOME (SSI) program is a means-based federal-income supplement program that provides a monthly check to help meet basic needs (food, clothing, shelter) for qualifying elderly and disabled citizens. Unfortunately, for many low-income people, SSI is their main source of income, and not a supplement.

2. MEDICAID is a state-administered system of medical care for low-income older or disabled people, and needy children and their caretakers. It is jointly funded by the federal government and the states. Within federal guidelines, each state sets its own eligibility requirements and determines the services offered. These include an array of health-related benefit programs known by a variety of names.

The supplemental purpose of the trust funds is crucial; most government assistance, indispensable to many disabled Americans, is means-tested. That's one reason special-needs trust documents must be precisely worded, with deference to eligibility limits on income and property. If there's any possibility of the funds being made available—directly or indirectly—for the disabled person's needs (such as food, clothing, shelter, or basic medical care), the trust is considered a financial asset of that person. He will not be poor enough to qualify for aid until the trust is "spent down" to a low level.

Two Types of Supplemental Needs Trusts

• **Trusts created with the beneficiary's own funds** When a disabled person eligible for public assistance receives a large sum of money, his life gets a little more complicated. There are two such situations in which this occurs: inheritance (without proper planning) and the settlement of a lawsuit for a catastrophic personal injury. In these cases, federal law allows the family of the disabled person, or the state court, to establish an SNT, provided that public funds expended for his care are paid back from the trust after the disabled beneficiary dies. These trusts are descriptively called *pay-back SNTs*.

You can see in the law an effort to balance the interests of the taxpayer with those of the disabled citizen "lucky" enough to come into a windfall. On paper, these folks can appear suddenly wealthy and would otherwise be completely ineligible for public assistance. Without the federal statute, their "fortunes" would have to be almost totally depleted before they could once again receive public benefits. Then they would have no funds available for even the small amenities of life an SNT might have provided them. On the other hand, if the SNT has money remaining upon the beneficiary's death, it seems only fair that the taxpayer be repaid.

● **Trusts created by a third party** The third party in these situations is usually the disabled person's parents or grandparents, but it does not have to be. These trusts are based on two simple rules: first, the strict *legal* duty of parents to support their children—even if disabled—with food, clothing, and shelter ends at the age of legal adulthood, eighteen (twenty-one in some states). Secondly, money paid to provide a disabled person with items *other than* food, clothing, and shelter does not reduce his SSI and other government benefits. However, depending on what is purchased, that item could be a countable asset when a government agency determines the disabled person's income and resource eligibility.

The basic care of disabled persons after the age of adulthood has become largely the responsibility of the state. So with these SNTs, no payback is required. When the disabled beneficiary dies, anything left in the trust can be paid to somebody else. Very commonly, too, the remainder of the trust is paid to a charitable organization of importance to the special-needs beneficiary and family. The government has no claim to this SNT because it was established with the parents' or grandparents' money, not the disabled beneficiary's own funds. That is the distinction upon which the payback rule depends.

What Can the Supplemental Needs Trust Provide?

There is a long list of "almost" necessities and small luxuries that most of us enjoy and would like to provide for disabled loved ones. Without impairing the disabled beneficiary's eligibility for benefits, an SNT should allow—but not require—the trustee, in his sole and absolute discretion, to use funds for goods and services (among others) such as:

- Eyeglasses and other out-of-pocket medical/dental expenses
- Transportation to and from daily activities
- Travel (including the expenses of a companion to visit relatives, for example)
- Entertainment (such as movies, bowling, magazines, books)
- Special dietary needs or food "treats"
- Materials or other costs of a hobby, educational, or recreational activity
- A computer, television, telephone, Internet, or cable TV access

Hint: Many disabled beneficiaries handle the SNT's administrative and financial tasks themselves. To main-

tain benefit eligibility, however, an SNT beneficiary should never be a trustee. In cases where the beneficiary is able to communicate his needs to the trustee, he should do so.

Generally, the trustee should not be authorized to make direct payments of cash to the beneficiary, except for a small allowance permitted by state regulations. The trust document should state that the special needs beneficiary has no power to compel the trustee to make a distribution to any party.

The document should also prohibit the trustee from spending trust funds on public-assistance benefits that would be available to the disabled person if there were no SNT. This is done, in part, by stating in the document that the trustee is prohibited from exercising authority in any way that would interfere with the availability of government benefits to the special-needs beneficiary.

Assume, for example, that the state rules for food suddenly tightened. As soon as that rule change took effect, the trustee would be duty-bound by the wording of the SNT to stop spending money for ice cream, snacks, or candy. To continue to do so would violate eligibility guidelines, making government benefits unavailable to the beneficiary. Yet the trustee is prohibited from doing any such thing. To adjust to larger, unforeseen shifts in the legal landscape, the SNT can authorize the trustee to amend the trust in any manner, *solely* for the purpose of maintaining the beneficiary's qualification for government aid.

Other Planning Issues

Maintaining eligibility for government assistance is an essential, overarching principle in all financial and estate planning for families with disabled or special-needs children. Remember that if parents leave assets directly to a child who is receiving government benefits, they will likely cause his immediate disqualification. But this critical consideration should not obscure all others. Many disabled individuals have normal life expectancies. This fact forces parents to try to make comprehensive arrangements for good long-term care of their disabled children after they are not here to do so. This is not simply a matter of qualifying for government assistance.

Indeed, there would be ample reason to use a trust, irrespective of benefit eligibility factors. After all, in many situations the special-needs child could not be expected to provide for his own support or manage money that might be given to him in an outright inheritance. If, instead of creating a trust, parents leave money to another family member with an "understanding" that the funds are to be used for the care of the disabled child, they open the door to a variety of risks that could ruin the plan. Even assuming the best of intentions, a sibling of the special-needs child, for example, might lose all or part of the earmarked money through his own difficulties. Moreover, if the sibling died before the disabled child, there would be no way to follow through with the intended use of the funds.

All these factors call for a trust to hold assets for the benefit of the disabled child. But the creation of an SNT should always be integrated with the family's overall financial and estate planning. Drafting an SNT does not in itself address a number of difficult decisions. One of these is the manner in which the SNT will be funded. Some parents feel strongly that all their children (and the SNT for the disabled child) should receive equal shares of their estate. Others look at the disabled child's special needs compared to those of the other children. Their aim is to allocate whatever estate they leave in accordance with need. This results in the disabled child's SNT taking a disproportionately large share of the inheritance. The funding issue is a family matter, with no clearly right or wrong answers. But it would be a mistake not to consider the family's larger planning picture at the time the SNT is established.

The other major decisions in setting up an SNT involve choosing a trustee. It is a good idea to have a trust adviser and/or protector as well, if at all practical. It is likely to be better for everyone in the family if siblings, for example, can assume some of the responsibilities that would otherwise fall to the trustee. Some special-needs beneficiaries are more vulnerable than others and cannot be expected to hold the trustee accountable or otherwise protect their own interests. It is therefore crucial that someone monitor the beneficiary's health, living conditions, and overall needs, and serve as a communications link between the disabled person and the trustee, if necessary. A family member, of course, is ideally suited to this role.

11

Mom and Dad's Basic Estate Tax Planning

Although tax liability usually should not be the first aspect of estate planning to consider, no spouse wants the marital estate to be cut in half by a heavy tax that many married couples easily and lawfully avoid or reduce. In this chapter we examine the trust arrangement available to accomplish this tax goal

Hint: Once the marital estate gets close to the federal tax-protected amount ($1.5 million in 2004 and 2005), the A/B trust approach is appropriate. The tax savings can be huge, and you can enjoy the other benefits of a trust as well.

and focus on how it serves that purpose. But remember that Mom and Dad's trust is also likely to have been written with other purposes as well. So keep in mind that all the family and human concerns one might hope to address with a trust can be handled by trusts that also are designed to achieve estate tax savings.

This chapter assumes Mom and Dad have a longstanding marriage and the same children. In contrast, the common "subsequent marriage" situation often involves two different sets of children and different planning challenges. That scenario is examined in chapter 12.

Saying "I Do" to the Marital Deduction and Bypass (A/B) Trust

The *marital deduction and bypass trust* ("A/B Trust") is the tax-planning cornerstone for many combined marital estates (all property owned by the husband, the wife, and jointly) worth over $1.5 million in 2004 and 2005. In this scenario, if no tax planning is done, every dollar of family wealth that eventually passes to the children in excess of $1.5 million will be taxed at rates that *start* at forty-five percent.

With the A/B trust arrangement, however, a married couple can pass a combined estate of $3 million or less to their children with *zero* federal estate tax, assuming both spouses died in 2004 or 2005. This technique is "the real deal" of tax savings—time-honored, yet with no significant catches or tricks. You really shouldn't miss out on it.

How the A/B Trust Works while Both Husband and Wife Are Alive
Remember, just think of a trust as a vat or "holding tank" into which money and property can be "poured." This is done by transferring the assets to the trustee. Usually, husband and wife serve as their own trustees, at least initially. A formal transfer of property from themselves, as grantors, to themselves, as trustees, is still required, however.

While both spouses are alive, there can be a single initial trust that is revocable and completely in their control. (The single trust for husband and wife is used especially in community property states.) As a practical matter, as well as for tax purposes, nothing changes in the way the spouse-grantors deal with their property. The only difference is that the name of the trust is used on accounts and deeds.

In the common law states (the ones that aren't community property states), most attorneys prefer to use separate trusts for the husband and wife. They are often "mirror images," but don't have to be. The tax-saving principles described here are the same, whether the spouses have joint or separate trusts, but there are some potential tax traps when using joint trusts under common law rules. It's also crucial to be aware that if separate husband and wife trusts are to be effective, it is necessary for each spouse to own property in his or her name alone—otherwise, there won't be anything to put into the "his and her" trusts.

All the rules and the scheme of ultimate property distribution are decided in advance with the help of a lawyer and written into the trust document. Many people specify the broad outline of their intentions at the time the trust is prepared, but leave the trustee or trust protector great discretion as to all kinds of details. Flexibility later on makes people more comfortable today in implementing the A/B plan.

After the Death
of the First Spouse

The initial trust ends at the first death by splitting into two new trusts ("A" and "B"). This happens simply because there is a paragraph in the initial trust stating that, upon the first death, the "A" and "B" trusts are to be created. (If separate husband and wife trusts have been set up, it is only the original trust of the deceased spouse that ends at this point, and the "A" and "B" trusts are still created.)

The trustee (usually, the surviving spouse) divides the original trust property and places some in each of the two new trusts, "A" and "B." For example, if the trust owned mutual fund accounts, the trustee might arrange to have them transferred to the "B" trust—that is, retitled in the name of the trustee of the "B" trust (even if it's also the surviving spouse). The trustee might also decide to put the vacation house in the "A" trust by preparing a deed to the "A" trustee. Again, the formal transfer is necessary even if the surviving spouse is wearing all the trustee hats.

The "B" trust (for the "Below-the-ground" spouse) is irrevocable and makes use of the deceased spouse's $1.5 million shelter from estate tax. That's the tax objective of the "B" trust, and it's important: This tax protection must be used at the time of the first death, or it is wasted. The "B" trust is established (usually) for the ultimate benefit of the children and grandchildren.

The trust is often worded so that the federal estate tax-protected amount is placed in the "B" trust. For 2004 and 2005, this is $1.5 million. The "B" trust is also called the *bypass trust*, because property in it bypasses taxation, or the *credit shelter trust*.

Warning! The threshold of the A/B trust technique is due to rise

We continue to refer to the current $1.5 million "standard" estate tax-protected amount simply for convenience. Be aware, however, that for deaths in 2006 through 2008, this amount is scheduled to increase

from $1.5 million to $2 million. If that happens, the trigger point for the usefulness of the A/B trust technique will likewise increase to that figure. Many A/B trusts now in existence use flexible language that automatically adjusts the terms of the trust to reflect whatever the estate tax-protected amount is in the year death occurs. That would *not* be a good thing for some people; if you already have such a trust, therefore, talk to your attorney about it.

The tax goal of the "B" trust is to get this money out of the couple's combined estate, so that it escapes estate taxation after the second spouse's death, too—not just the first's. To illustrate how this works, let us look at a common and costly alternative arrangement. If a couple uses simple wills alone, the first spouse to die usually passes his entire estate to the survivor with no tax at all because of the unlimited marital deduction. But in so doing, the first spouse to die has lost the chance to use his $1.5 million standard shelter from estate tax—the one available to everyone, not just spouses.

In other words, if the marital deduction is used to cover the *entire* estate of the first spouse to die, no tax will be due upon his death. In theory, his estate would then still be eligible for the standard $1.5 million in tax protection, but there would be no property left to protect. Unfortunately, it's a "use it or lose it" tax break. Upon the second death, only the second spouse's $1.5 million shelter from estate tax will be available. If the second-to-die spouse still has a substantial estate, every dollar over $1.5 million will be taxed at rates that start at forty-five percent!

● **Retaining benefits from the "B" trust** Sometimes the estate is so large that the surviving spouse can afford to part with $1.5 million upon the first spouse's death. If so, no trust is necessary to make use of the decedent's standard estate tax-protected amount; $1.5 million can pass to the children or anybody else at the time the first spouse dies, protected from federal estate tax. Most families, however, even if they are affluent, face a dilemma: tax planning is fine, but Mom and Dad usually do not want to give up such a large sum until *both* of them are gone. They want the survivor to have the benefit and security of that money. Keeping control of the full family estate is a much higher priority than tax savings in most family situations.

Fortunately, the law allows the survivor to retain substantial control over the "B" trust for practical purposes. Yet the money or property in the "B" trust will *not* be included in the estate of the second spouse to die, so it escapes estate taxation completely. The surviving spouse's rights to property in the "B" trust are significant. They include:

- All annual income produced by the "B" trust
- The annual right to withdraw the greater of $5,000 or five percent of the "B" trust principal, for any reason ("mad money")
- The right to invade trust principal, if necessary, but limited to an "ascertainable standard" relating to the survivor's "maintenance, health, support or education." (Precise wording of the trust is absolutely crucial here to avoid tax trouble.) This provision of the "B" trust is a safety net that allows the couple to feel comfortable about the whole arrangement.

What is the survivor *not* allowed to do with "B" trust funds? She should not make gifts using "B" trust property, unless specifically authorized in the trust document. She should not dip into the "B" trust principal either for expenses that go beyond maintaining her health or the basic standard of living the couple enjoyed while married. (The "A" trust could be used for these purposes, however.) As a practical matter, the limitations of the "B" trust are unlikely to constrain the way the surviving spouse chooses or can afford to live.

The "A" trust (for the "Above-the-ground" spouse) is also called the *marital deduction trust*. Property in this trust is absolutely and completely under the control of the surviving spouse. She is free to use or dispose of this property as she chooses during life or upon her death. If somebody else is serving as trustee, he must take orders from the survivor. Alternatively, the survivor can just fire the trustee. She can even revoke the "A" trust at any time.

Hint: For any trust to work, it must own property; there must be a formal transfer to it. If the A/B trust is to be established in a will, rather than as part of a living trust, an important step must be taken to get the benefit of each spouse's $1.5 million protection from federal estate tax: each spouse must own $1.5 million in assets—separately. This might involve some shuffling of title documents, but it is essential. Why? Remember that, in many families, Mom and Dad own all property jointly, with right of survivorship. If so, this property passes at death of the first spouse, outside the will (no matter what kind of will it is). Nothing would then be left to place in the trusts, and the whole plan would completely fail.

The reason the A/B trust arrangement is so useful is that it provides a means of doing two things: first, it takes advantage of *both* spouses' ability to protect $1.5 million from federal estate tax. Secondly, it achieves this tax goal while allowing the surviving spouse maximum use and control of the entire family estate. But it bears repeating: the $1.5 million tax protection is a "use it or lose it" break available only at the time of each person's death. The "B" trust is a way for the first-to-die spouse to "stake his claim" to this tax benefit, to avoid losing it. That is where the big tax savings come from.

{ **Warning!** The property you think you own may really be shared

In community property states, a spouse might have a half-interest in an asset even if her name is not on the document of ownership. Therefore, any trust in one of these states should be drafted with particular care to allow allocation of assets appropriately.

CHAPTER 12

Subsequent Marriages: Providing for a Spouse Without Giving Away the Family Fortune

A common planning goal for someone entering a second (or subsequent) marriage is to provide for his new spouse during her lifetime, ensuring at the same time that his estate will ultimately pass to his own children (or others of

Hint: If you have children from a prior marriage, the QTIP trust might be the right option for you. A useful tax-planning tool, the QTIP trust offers increased control over where your property ultimately ends up.

his choice) rather than to the new spouse's family. This goal could easily be met by drafting almost any kind of trust and including a provision directing the trustee to make regular payments to the grantor's surviving spouse for her support. The trustee could be further instructed upon the death of the second spouse to pay out the entire trust to the grantor's children, or continue it for their benefit.

If the grantor-spouse has an estate of (safely) less than $1.5 million (in 2004 and 2005), such an approach might be fine, with no particular attention given to tax planning. Remember, everyone's estate is protected from federal estate tax up to that amount with no planning necessary. But what if the estate is larger? How should the situation be handled?

When the estate is over the tax-protected limit of $1.5 million, our tax antennae should go up. But the first priority is still to take care of the surviving spouse. The question then becomes, how can this goal be realized in the most tax-efficient manner? If $1.5 million in standard estate-tax protection does not cover the full estate, what other tax-saving tools might there be?

Using the Estate Tax Marital Deduction

Generally, only free and clear transfers to the spouse qualify for the marital deduction. "When I die, my house goes to my spouse, absolutely." That qualifies—no strings. As for the idea "When I die, my house goes to my spouse for life or until she remarries, then to my children"—sorry, no marital deduction allowed. Your estate would still have your standard $1.5 million protection from tax, but upon your death your house would not be eligible for that special tax break on property interests left to a spouse.

Why not? The tax law is not intended to give your estate a big break based on a property interest that you did not give *completely* to the spouse. After all, the spouse only *has use of* the house. In this scenario, it is you who decides who ultimately gets full ownership of the house. That's the way the tax law is with respect to most such *terminable* interests in property.

The Qualified Terminable Interest Property (QTIP) Trust

To address our planning scenario, however, the law does provide specific guidelines for a *Qualified Terminable Interest Property* (QTIP) trust. This trust qualifies for the unlimited marital deduction and can serve as a useful estate tax-planning tool. But if you want your trust to qualify for the deduction, you lose some of the freedom and flexibility that a trust usually allows.

There are technical rules for drafting the QTIP trust that must be scrupulously followed:

- The QTIP trust *must* provide all income to the surviving spouse and to nobody else for her lifetime, *no matter what*.
- If the trust owns property that doesn't pay dividends or other regular income, the surviving spouse must have the right to demand that the trustee invest in income-producing assets instead.
- Nobody, not even the surviving spouse herself, can be authorized to give away trust funds or property to anyone *other than* the surviving spouse during her life-

time. (The QTIP trust may permit the surviving spouse to invade trust principal to maintain her standard of living, but this is not a requirement.)

■ When the spouse finally dies, whatever remains in the trust can go to the grantor's own children or anybody else of the *grantor's* choice. The value of the trust property, however, is included in the *spouse's* estate for federal estate tax purposes, just as if the property in the QTIP trust had been left to the second-to-die spouse outright, without a trust. (Of course, without a trust, it would have been her decision as to where the property went upon her death, which is what the grantor sought to avoid by using the QTIP trust.)

13

Charitable Donations: Gifts That Repay the Kindness

Many people find special meaning and personal fulfillment in contributing to a charity. In this chapter, we examine three tools that allow you to act on altruistic motives while simultaneously enjoying time-honored tax advantages:

Hint: Determining whether any of these charitable giving tools make sense in your situation requires crunching several numbers. The financial calculations are complex, so most people should seek guidance from a professional adviser.

the *charitable gift annuity* (CGA), the *charitable remainder trust* (CRT), and the *charitable lead trust* (CLT). One or more of these arrangements may appeal to those looking for a way to include charitable giving in their estate plans without sacrificing all benefit from the property to be contributed. The CGA and CRT provide the donor with lifetime income from an initial investment of money or property; under these agreements, the charity receives the investment balance after the donor dies. The CLT works in reverse: the charity receives the investment income during the donor's lifetime. Upon the donor's death, the trust principal goes to whomever he chooses.

Charities and educational institutions spend considerable effort promoting these and other "planned giving" arrangements. Simply call or visit the Web site of your favorite group for more information. They'll be delighted to oblige.

The Charitable
Gift Annuity Charitable gift annuities
(CGAs) are simple to implement and design. Most of the recognized nonprofit organiza-

tions offer them. A charitable gift annuity is a contract between an individual donor and a religious, charitable, or educational institution. The organization takes an initial investment of money or property (stocks, bonds, or real estate) from a donor and is responsible for managing the investment from that point on. The nonprofit agrees to make fixed payments from this principal (and the earnings on it) every month for life to a beneficiary (or annuitant, usually the donor himself). The annuity payments can begin immediately, or they can be deferred until later—when needed for retirement, for example. In return, the charity keeps whatever remains of the originally invested property upon his death.

Alternatively, with a two-life (joint) annuity, payments are made to one person for the duration of his life; after his death, the payments continue for the life of a second (survivor) beneficiary, such as a spouse. Note however, that the CGA is irrevocable—the donor cannot just "cash out" and put his money elsewhere.

{ A Closer Look:
Charitable gift annuities offer win-win solutions

Tom (seventy-five) and Edna (seventy-two) Bolton are enjoying a comfortable retirement and want a financial plan to ensure they can do so for many more years.

The Boltons' financial adviser is concerned that a large portion of their savings is invested in the stock of a single company. The stock price has risen steadily since they bought it, but that is no guarantee of the future. Tom and Edna know they should diversify their investments but have been putting it off, reluctant to take a capital gains tax hit on the appreciated value of any shares they sell. Yet they realize that, like it or not, in about a year they'll need to start drawing upon the stock to provide income.

Their adviser happens to recall the Boltons' lifelong love of animals and suggests a plan that appeals to them: the Boltons transfer a portion of their stock to a foundation that protects wildlife, and which is qualified under section 501(c)(3) of the tax code. In return, they receive a charitable gift annuity that will make quarterly payments at a 6.2 percent annual rate until the second of them dies.

When both of them are gone, the charity will benefit from their financial wisdom and generosity—plus, the transferred stock will not be included in the Bolton's federal taxable estates. Meanwhile, the capital gains tax on the appreciated value of their shares at the time of the donation will be spread over the life of the annuity, greatly reducing its impact. A portion of each annuity payment will be tax-free—a return of their original investment. The Boltons can also take a substantial income tax deduction this year if they itemize deductions. (Note that while this example is believed to be realistic, the actual figures for any individuals will depend on their ages and the annuity

rates in effect at the time of the property transfer.)

As with commercial annuities issued by life insurance companies, the rate of interest paid by an annuity is based on the age(s) of the beneficiary. The older the annuitant(s), the higher the annuity rate offered by the charity. The organization can do this because the older the annuitant, the shorter the life expectancy. So, on average, fewer payments will be necessary for older annuitants compared to younger ones. Likewise, rates on one-life annuities tend to be higher than on annuities covering two lives, also because fewer payments are probable.

The payments are backed by the assets of the charitable organization issuing the gift annuity. The government does not guarantee them. However, regulations in several states require the organization to maintain an adequate level of funds in reserve to meet its obligations.

Because of the gift involved, CGAs will not pay a rate quite as high as a typical commercial annuity. Charitable gift annuity rates compare quite favorably, however, with many fixed-income alternatives, such as certificates of deposit, money market funds, and many bonds. Other advantages of the CGA are:

- The minimum investment for a CGA is relatively low—typically five or ten thousand dollars.
- No medical underwriting is required.
- Payments to the second beneficiary of a two-life annuity begin upon the death of the primary beneficiary, avoiding probate.
- The funds or other property given in exchange for a CGA are removed from the donor's (primary annuitant's) estate and not subject to estate taxation. In the case of a two-life annuity when the second beneficiary is not the primary beneficiary's spouse, however, gift taxes could become an important issue.
- The charitable gift annuity provides an income tax deduction for the value of the charity's right to receive the annuity balance after the last beneficiary has died.

A safe, predictable return that cannot be outlived makes the CGA attractive to charitably inclined retirees who want to avoid the possibility of a prolonged downturn in the stock or bond markets.

The Charitable Remainder Trust

Charitable remainder trusts (CRTs) are similar to gift annuities in concept. Instead of purchasing an annuity contract directly from a charity, however, the CRT donor/grantor sets up a trust with the assistance of an attorney and transfers an initial sum into it, usually in excess of $100,000. She then collects taxable annual payments from trust earnings and/or principal. The *remainder* (the leftover trust principal) goes to a charity or educational institution at the donor's death. All CRTs are *irrevocable*; the donor cannot take her money back if circumstances change.

CRTs allow the donor—not the charity—to choose the amount she will receive each year. She can select a fixed dollar payment from the trust each year for life (a charitable remainder *annuity* trust, or CRAT) or a fixed percentage of trust assets valued each year (a charitable remainder *uni*trust or CRUT). As with the gift annuity, a complicated financial calculation (based on an IRS-designated interest rate) is used to place a value today on the estimated trust remainder the nonprofit beneficiary will receive when the trust ends. That is the amount the donor can take as a charitable deduction on her income tax return the year the CRT is created.

The CRUT is the more popular of the CRTs because it has features that make it particularly suitable for retirement planning. First, it offers some inflation protection: for example, if the trust payout is seven percent annually, then as the trust (presumably) grows in value each year, so, too, will the dollar amount of the donor's annual draw. With the CRAT, in contrast, the trust makes the same annuity payment to the donor every year for life ($60,000, for example).

Perhaps more important, the charitable remainder unitrust—unlike the annuity trust—is not required to dip into trust principal if investment income is insufficient to make an annual payment to the donor (although the trust can be drafted that way if the donor prefers). Many people choose investments that do not produce current income so the trust can grow over the long term, such as an undeveloped piece of land or growth stock in a company that does not pay dividends. These donors may not need the extra income until they retire, and would prefer to have as much money as possible available at that time.

The CRUT, unlike the CRAT, can be written to allow any accumulated shortfalls in the annual payout to be made up in later years, during retirement. In fact, the donor can make additional contributions to the CRUT (unlike the CRAT) whenever she has money to put aside. These features make the CRUT even better as a retirement-savings vehicle.

Hint: For those without fortunes to give away or the desire to set up a charitable trust of their own, all the recognized charities maintain their own trusts, called *pooled income funds.* Here the donor does not get to choose the timing or amount of his payout. The charitable organization manages the pooled income trust fund and each donor gets a check for his proportional share of the fund's income for that period. The investment portfolios of most of these funds are heavily weighted toward fixed-income securities, that is, various types of bonds.

{ A Closer Look:
A few practical points about
charitable remainder trusts

The following list indicates some of the benefits and uses of charitable remainder trusts with plenty of technical details omitted. This is a complex topic with a multitude of variations on a common theme.

1. The regular payments from a CRT can continue after the donor's death, for the life of a spouse or other loved one.

2. The donated property and all future appreciation on it will not be included in the donor's estate.

3. All or part of the CRT income the donor receives (which is taxable), as well as the tax savings from the original deduction, can be used to buy life insurance on the donor to fund a "wealth replacement trust." That way the donor's children's future inheritance will not be reduced, despite the donation to the charity. In these cases, everybody wins.

4. A CRT (or a pooled income fund)

can be especially useful in dodging an income tax bullet on capital gains. If a donor owns property, especially rental property, that has increased considerably in value since acquisition, there will be income tax due on the gain if and when the property is sold. For property that has been held over decades, that potential gain—and tax—can be enormous, even at a rate of fifteen percent. However, if the property is donated to a charitable trust and the trustee then sells the property, there will be no tax on the sale—the law encourages charitable giving. This allows the entire amount placed in trust to be put to work earning an income stream for the donor.

5. CRTs can allow for a painless diversification of investments. A donor who has done well in a particular investment might recognize that he should not have all his eggs in one basket. But selling that asset for the purpose of spreading around the proceeds could subject his gain to a fifteen-percent capital-gains-tax hit.

The CRT trustee, however, can sell and diversify appropriately but without losing a penny in tax.

The Charitable
Lead Trust (CLT) A charitable lead trust is essentially the reverse of a charitable remainder trust. Rather than the donor receiving lifetime income from the trust, the charity gets the "lead" benefit and receives the annual stream of income payments. When the donor dies (or at the end of a predetermined number of years), these payments to the nonprofit organization end, with the remaining trust principal going to someone of the donor's choosing (or to the donor himself, if he's still alive).

This tool can be attractive to an older person with a large estate who is looking to transfer his wealth while saving federal estate tax. For example, consider a charitable lead trust set up to go into effect at the donor's death and last for a term of ten years. Upon the donor's death, his estate can take a tax deduction for the present value of the annual payments the charity will receive over the next ten years. After the ten-year term, the trust principal goes to the donor's children or grandchildren (or anyone else). Although the children or grandchildren receive this bequest—on paper—when the donor dies, its value is greatly diminished from the original sum placed in the CLT—meaning the donor's estate is hit with less estate and generation-skipping transfer taxes. This is because the donor's loved ones must wait years before actually seeing the money (a dollar paid in the future is not worth as much as a dollar paid today).

{3

Preserving Your Estate: Keeping Creditors, Spendthrifts, and the Tax Man at Bay

What is asset protection planning, anyway? Often, what first comes to mind is safeguarding assets from the future claims of overzealous and unpredictable plaintiffs, attorneys, judges, and juries. But asset protection (or wealth preservation) is actually just one element of a good overall financial and estate plan. That plan should also protect your estate—during life and after death—from unnecessary taxes and preserve the integrity of your wishes as to how your wealth should be used for and passed to your survivors. Viewed in this broader context, asset protection consider-ations clearly should be an integral part of financial and estate planning, rather than tacked on as an afterthought.

In the next few chapters, we'll focus on some basic principles relating to protection from *future-judgment creditors*—parties now unknown who hypothetically might sue you someday. Many of the asset protection strategies considered here have long been used as financial- or estate-planning tools in their own right, to serve a variety of estate- and tax-planning purposes. For example, "dual-use" strategies—arrangements like the irrevocable life insurance trust (ILIT) and the family limited partnership (FLP)—have been useful for years in traditional estate planning and tax reduction. But their additional role in protecting assets from the reach of future creditors has been less widely recognized by the public. As the minimum estate value for payment of the federal tax continues to rise, there will be fewer people needing traditional tax planning. In coming years, therefore, these old estate-planning favorites are likely to take on new luster when touted as means of asset protection planning.

14

An Introduction to Asset Protection Planning

The material presented here should suffice as a beginning for most people's asset protection planning. The key questions to ask yourself are these: What can I do with my assets to promote a more favorable settlement if I'm the target of creditors or potential plaintiffs? How can this be done to allow for

Hint: Boosting the coverage limits of an insurance policy you already have may cost a lot less than you'd guess. No asset protection tool is simpler or more cost-effective than insurance.

maximum control of my estate, both during life and upon death?

Basic Approaches to Asset Protection

● **First things first—get adequate liability coverage** Asset protection planning for devastating legal claims (i.e., creditor protection) involves a broad spectrum of activities, from small steps to complex legal devices that reflect the widely varying exposures to risk faced by different individuals. Everyone's asset protection plan should be founded, above all, on minimizing unnecessary risk in one's personal life and business or professional practice and on maintaining adequate liability insurance. For most of us, at a minimum that means automobile and homeowner policies with substantial liability coverage. This should be particularly self-evident to those with a lot to lose, but experience shows people who ought to know better routinely ignore it at great subsequent cost.

Consider a surgeon who is rightly concerned about meritless future claims and the skyrocketing cost of malpractice coverage.

She is thinking about a promoter's pitch for a complicated, expensive offshore asset protection plan. Meanwhile, her car insurance provides coverage of only $100,000—the policy hasn't been updated since she was a struggling college student. In case of a serious accident, this doctor is exposed to enormous personal liability from a risk she is not even thinking about.

How about the law firm that courts disaster by refusing to spend money on practice-management software to avoid an overlooked filing deadline? Also, consider the landlord who just can't get around to fixing that broken handrail until somebody falls and breaks her neck. If you are in a situation like any of these, be sensible. What's the better option: (a) minimize the risk now at minimal cost or (b) pay $25,000 to put your money beyond even your own direct reach in an asset protection trust on a tiny island just south of Mars?

Before investing in any other planning, do the following to protect yourself and your assets:

■ Conduct an audit of your business or professional risk exposures and the corresponding insurance policies.

■ Consider whether, besides malpractice or "errors and omissions" insurance coverage, you have an adequate commercial general liability policy for your staff and your office premises. Does it cover self-employed (1099) subcontractors, if any, who work there, in addition to regular W-2 employees?

■ Buy as much liability insurance coverage as you reasonably can with every policy, both personal and professional. Increase your deductible amount, painfully if necessary so you can afford a higher policy limit for about the same money paid. Don't spend a scarce premium dollar to buy protection against life's little setbacks; protect against something big enough to wipe you out. Consider a personal liability "umbrella" policy. These can give excellent bang for the buck when purchased from the company that insures both your home and car.

The simple fact is that very few of us need more protection than can be purchased with liability insurance. (Physicians in some places and specialties are a notable exception.) Plaintiffs' attorneys want to get paid.

Very rarely will they recommend refusing a reasonable amount of insurance coverage offered as settlement in full. The crucial factor is having enough insurance so that in virtually any case, the plaintiff's lawyer would consider it too risky to go to trial and possibly get less, or even nothing. That's what you want a potential plaintiff to confront— an unacceptable risk in proceeding with his claim. Insurance is by far the fastest and most cost-effective way to bring about that point.

{ A Closer Look: Factoring in the cost of long-term care

Many Americans run the risk of a financial burden vastly greater than the threat of a lawsuit: the devastating cost of long-term care (LTC). For many years, LTC essentially meant "nursing home care." But most people have a strong desire to recover from illness and return to their own homes to live independently as they age. Today, LTC refers to a broad array of services that help a disabled

person experience the highest quality of life—and as much independence and dignity—as his or her condition will allow.

As the proportion of the elderly among the American population increases, more of us—especially women—will live long enough to experience the infirmities of advanced age. Most people understand that the cost of even a few years of LTC, at home or in a facility, presents a major financial liability. There are only three ways to pay for LTC: out of pocket, Medicaid (not to be confused with Medicare), and long-term care insurance. Unfortunately, many people seem to assume that either their existing medical insurance or a readily available government benefit will meet their long-term care needs. Both assumptions are completely false. (Medicare does provide services of the kind typically associated with long-term care, both in a skilled nursing facility, as well as home health care. But Medicare coverage is available only in very limited circumstances, and in no event for more than a few months. Therefore, it is a big mistake to count on Medicare for care over the long-term.)

The self-pay option will probably not be practical for most of us. If you intend to pay out of pocket for LTC (should it become necessary), be sure to include a cost inflation factor in your financial calculations, in order to reach an accurate estimate of the required funds. You may be shocked to see how much today's prices will increase over time.

Medicaid is public assistance; it is a state-administered program (that may operate under a different name locally) with federal guidelines. Medicaid clients have strict income and asset limitations. If your income and/or assets are above modest levels, the state will require you to spend the excess first. You can spend down in a variety of ways. You can use some of your excess assets or income to pay for supplemental medical insurance or other medical expenses, to support a spouse at home, and to provide a small personal needs allowance. If your income is still over-limit, you would have to pay the overage to Medicaid in order to qualify.

Your house is subject to recovery of Medicaid expenditures from your estate after you die, but not while you or your spouse lives there. Some people are tempted to qualify for Medicaid (or avoid estate recovery) by giving assets to their children—by putting their children's names on the deed to the house, for example. But such "Medicaid planning" has significant drawbacks, especially if your spouse is living at home, and should not be undertaken without consulting an attorney skilled in this area. In a nutshell, if you give away excess resources before applying for Medicaid, you could become ineligible for a very long time.

Long-term care insurance is a still-evolving product that can be purchased either as a stand-alone policy or as a rider to life insurance. LTC insurance is difficult to understand, unaffordable for many, and like all insurance, contains limitations on coverage that should be understood before it is purchased. Yet it is the only insurance product that covers custodial long-term care. An LTC policy (or rider) is a financial-planning tool. As such, it is ideally suited for some people and totally inappropriate for others. At a minimum, it is extremely important to make sure that any policy you buy covers all types of long-term care you may want in the future, whether nursing home, home health, or assisted living care.

Planning for LTC involves consideration of all the options: dedicated personal savings, Medicaid, and LTC insurance. It is therefore a subject beyond the scope of this book. But we would all be wise to put this on our financial- and estate-planning radar screens.

A Survey of the Law and Key Principles

There are at least two basic approaches to consider in creditor protection. One is to build wealth in an asset that enjoys special protection under federal law. A tax-qualified retirement plan is a good example. These include most pension, profit-sharing, 401(k), and big-company plans. (IRAs are not given special treatment under federal law, but widely varying degrees of creditor protection are found among state laws.)

Along these lines, to a large extent you are permitted to *convert* your money or property into a form that is fully or partially protected under federal or state law, such as a qualified retirement plan or life insurance. A different but not conflicting approach is to hold assets and investments in a manner that makes them unattractive to pursue for one of many legal reasons (for example, a house with a big mortgage). The latter approach is a much broader and complex topic than the former. We will look at both more fully below, but it will help to have an awareness of fraudulent transfer principles first.

{ A Closer Look: A word about offshore asset protection plans

Some equate "asset protection" with shady offshore tax-evasion schemes. These do, unfortunately, exist, but proper advance planning to keep what one has earned free from tax or other liability is neither illegal nor sleazy. As for offshore asset protection plans, the use of foreign legal entities is not wrong or unethical, per se. There can be a proper role for these arrangements in planning for the very wealthy and for some people in high risk-of-liability situations. Well-respected estate-planning attorneys use offshore techniques, but they are not for the typical client. (By the way, they are never used by reputable attorneys to avoid the reporting of income.) Foreign asset protection devices are beyond the scope of this book.

● **What's not allowed by law—fraudulent transfers** Assume somebody is served with a lawsuit today alleging seven-figure liability for negligence. Never mind if the claim has any merit or not. In order to remove the plaintiff's incentive to pursue the case, what is to stop the defendant from rendering himself penniless? Tomorrow morning, can he formally retitle and transfer all property and accounts to his adult daughter? Yes. Has any crime been committed? In most situations, no. However, each state has a law called something like the Fraudulent Transfers Act (FTA). They are all similar. The law allows the court to set aside such transfers and put the property back within reach of the plaintiff, so funds will be available to satisfy a judgment if he ultimately prevails.

{ **Warning!** Where you see a plaintiff, the court sees a creditor

Before the defendant is judged to owe the plaintiff anything at all on the suit—even before the suit is filed—the law considers the plaintiff a creditor. A transfer by a defendant is deemed fraudulent if the defendant is found to have made the transfer with the intent to "hinder, delay, or defraud" the creditor.

The statute requires the judge to evaluate the defendant's conduct in real life, not just in the courtroom. With 20/20 hindsight, the judge will determine when, how, and with what motivation the defendant's wealth was placed in a form that is now claimed to be unreachable. In fraudulent transfer cases, the court has especially broad discretion to do "the right thing." Because of this, despite the fact that the actual statute is in black and white, its practical application is not always crystal clear. But the "smell test" most of us rely on in everyday life is also applied by judges in every state and in the U.S. Bankruptcy Court, where many of these cases arise. Do not get into any transaction that doesn't pass it.

There is a lot of plain common sense in this process and most judges have more than a fair share of that. The law provides a list of factors for the court to use in evaluating the defendant's intent, but they really do all boil down to the "smell test." Transactions involving the defendant's family and other insiders will surely face extremely close scrutiny by the court. Such transactions, as well as those that suddenly leave the defendant insolvent, are marked by what the law calls *badges of fraud*.

Our hypothetical plaintiff/creditor clearly could make a good claim under the fraudulent transfer law in the father-daughter "last-minute giveaway" situation. The claim would actually be against the person who took the asset(s)—here, the daughter. Of course, unless and until any plaintiff wins a case and obtains a judgment, he cannot begin the procedure of taking ownership of the defendant's property. The best he can do is tie it up. Once the plaintiff wins a judgment, he will file a motion requesting a form of additional *relief*—a judicial order to allow him to take, not just tie up, the defendant's property or money. For example, if the defendant has an apartment building titled in his own name, the plaintiff might ask the judge to order that it be sold at public auction. Such a request would likely be granted. After all, at this point, the plaintiff has won. The defendant has lost, and should not expect any kind of break from the court.

Keep in mind that a creditor-protection strategy is supposed to bring about a favorable settlement, either before trial or after, in the collection stage. (We're assuming here that the plaintiff either has or would prevail at trial.) If the plaintiff has gotten a judgment for a certain amount and the defendant is not able to persuade him to take less, it's back to the courtroom for the real test of the defendant's strategy. The best the defendant can reasonably hope for is that the court will abide by legal precedent and not bend over backwards to find a way around his arguments. But the defendant has to have a leg to stand on in claiming protected status for one or more of his assets. The law is not written to accommodate swindlers or those who fail to meet legitimate financial responsibilities. If the defendant has not made the right arrangements well in advance, even the slickest lawyering probably won't help much at this point.

The law always considers fraudulent any transfer made to *intentionally* "hinder, delay, or defraud" any creditor. In less obvious situations, the statute provides that a transfer of money or other property made by the defendant can be considered fraudulent as to someone who later files suit against him— *even if the basis of the claim arose* **after** *the transfer was made*. That fact surprises many people. So whatever you do, do it before any claims are even on the horizon.

● **Actual and constructive fraud** When a transfer of assets was plainly (to the judge) made to intentionally "hinder, delay, or defraud," the decision to void the transaction is clear-cut. This is *actual* fraud. (*Voiding* a transaction simply means undoing it with a judicial order. The property and the parties are put back where they were before the transaction.)

Assuming the motivation behind the transfer is not obvious, the court will turn to other statutory guidelines, looking for evidence of *constructive* fraud. The defendant's innermost intentions are irrelevant in proving this kind of fraud. For the court to make a determination that constructive fraud was involved in a transfer, two conditions must exist:

1. The defendant must not have received a reasonably equivalent value in exchange for what he transferred—in other words, it was a giveaway. (If he did get good value in return, of course, then he is no poorer than before the transfer. That's an important point.)

2. After the transfer in question, the defendant must have been left with assets that were unreasonably small in relation to the business being conducted with the plaintiff.

Let's assume, for example, that a brain surgeon makes a large gift and gets sued six months later. Obviously, since it was a gift, she received no value. The issue would then be whether or not—right after the gift—she had reasonably adequate remaining wealth and/or insurance to cover the potential liabilities that come from being a brain surgeon.

The FTA sets forth a definite statute of limitations—a period after a given transfer of property within which a plaintiff must make his attempt to set it aside. If this is not done, no action is possible thereafter under the FTA. This is an effort by the law to give plaintiffs their chance, but to provide a cut-off that will allow some degree of certainty in an individual's personal financial planning. (After all, any of us can be sued.) Generally, the cutoff for undoing a transfer is four years after the transfer was made. States have varying statutes of limitations, however, and other provisions regarding this important detail. Additionally, in an effort to reach the "right" result, some courts have inconsistently applied the limitations period, ruling (arguably, incorrectly so) that it had not yet expired under the facts of a particular case. For example, courts have ruled that the limitations period did not even begin until the date the claim was made, as opposed to the date of the transfer.

● **What can you do in advance?** One key to asset (creditor) protection planning is to put one's wealth in a form that is less appealing to creditors. This might involve shifting funds into an asset that enjoys special legal protection, or making good-faith transfers of cash or other property and taking in return something of equivalent economic value, but which creditors don't want. In such transactions, no wealth is truly given away. It bears repeating: whatever you do, do it before any claims are on the horizon. In sophisticated asset protection arrangements, for example, a potential defendant will acquire an interest in one or more limited partnerships (LPs) and/or limited liability companies (LLCs). Unfortunately for creditors, however, it so happens that an interest in a LP or LLC is not attractive because, as a practical matter, it is difficult to do anything with it (we will see why later).

In coming years, we might see courts chip away at the strategy of using LPs and LLCs for asset protection. It can be strongly argued that when somebody gives cash and takes a LP or LLC interest in return, he has *not* taken fair value, as far as the *creditor* is concerned. After all, the Fraudulent Transfer Act is designed to help creditors seeking payment of lawful debts. If a debtor ties up his assets in an investment the creditor cannot get to or does not want, the debtor might just as well have given the money away to his friends. On a common-sense level, the argument makes a lot of sense. Someday, courts might take that point of view widely.

For now, we just have to plan based on the law and circumstances as they stand for the foreseeable future. But remember, courts have great leeway to reach a "fair" result in these situations, so the law is subject to change. Much will always depend on the particular facts of a given case. But this is just one reason why (a) no asset protection plan is one hundred percent ironclad and (b) the earlier a potential defendant implements a plan, the more likely it is to pass muster later.

● Transferring assets into "protected" forms

Homestead Exemption The value of the family home is to some extent exempted from property that can be taken by creditors in almost every state. In a handful of states, most notably Texas and Florida, there is an unlimited exemption so that wealthy corporate criminals and quasi-criminals have retained and even built new multimillion dollar dwellings there, totally protected from creditors in U.S. Bankruptcy Court. (Note that the federal courts within a state honor the homestead law of that state.) These abuses are under attack in Congress and calls for bankruptcy reform have included reducing the homestead exemption to a uniform level of $125,000 across the country. (Few state exemptions are now that high; most are fairly modest.)

Retirement Plan Assets and IRAs The federal retirement law most of us know as "ERISA" (Employee Retirement Income Security Act) has a provision that offers solid creditor protection for many popular retirement accounts or qualified plans such as the 401(k), profit sharing, and traditional pension plan. (Note, however, that qualified plans *are not protected if the only covered employees are the business owner and/or spouse*.) The ERISA shield is all the asset protection (besides insurance) a lot of people need, but there is a potential chink in this armor: failure by the plan administrators to strictly adhere to the rules provided by the statute and the IRS can result in ERISA disqualification—and no protection. The chance of an unintentional or "minor" error is real, especially among small companies without a full-time human resources director or benefits administrator.

It is not uncommon that family businesses sometimes conduct their affairs with less formality than those with unrelated parties. Plan documents *must* be kept up to date and required filings submitted in a timely fashion. These plans *must* cover all employees and *must not* make unauthorized loans, for example. In cases in which the employer has not shown any respect for the rigid demands of the law, it is unlikely the judge would afford the retirement account any protection.

You should also be aware that the creditor protection of ERISA does not apply at all to many types of what people generically refer to as "retirement accounts." Most significantly, there is no federal creditor protection for IRAs (including SEP-IRAs). There still might be significant or even total creditor protection for an IRA under *state* law, but these laws vary widely. The very fact that IRAs must rely on the protection of state law—subject to thousands of local judges— rather than federal, puts them a notch below ERISA-qualified plans on the protection scale.

Life Insurance and Annuities There are a multitude of personal and business scenarios where life insurance comes into play. It is impossible to generalize even in the simple, common family situation in which the defendant is the owner of a life insurance policy on his own life with a spouse and/or children named as beneficiaries. These assets get limited protection in bankruptcy (which, of course, is always a federal proceeding). The state courts vary widely in the protection from creditors given to life insurance and annuities. In some states, the protection is complete. In others, there is a partial exemption of life insurance and annuities from creditor claims. For example, the law might protect a life insurance death benefit, if payable to the dependents of the insured defendant, but not the full cash value of the policy.

{**Warning!** Don't designate your estate as the beneficiary of life insurance

Whatever protection from creditors a life insurance policy has under a state's law, it is lost if the designated beneficiary is the insured defendant's own estate. Naming "my estate" on the beneficiary designation form or leaving it blank makes the policy proceeds a probate asset. This subjects the proceeds to general creditor claims. It also increases any taxes, fees, or expenses contingent on the size of the probate estate. In a typical family, nonbusiness setting, the beneficiary of a life insurance policy should always be a named individual, or a trust for that person's benefit.

15

Protecting Your Wealth with an Irrevocable Life Insurance Trust

For asset protection and other reasons, an *irrevocable life insurance trust* (ILIT) is usually the best way to own a life insurance policy. Yes, it is perfectly fine to name a young child's trust, for example, as the beneficiary of your life policy. But when asset protection or potential estate

Hint: The focus here is on ILITs and asset protection. But keep in mind that ILITs can also serve the same purposes as other trusts and include most of the desirable trust features we examine throughout this book.

tax liability are concerns, the biggest issue is not, "Who gets the money?" The first question is, "Whose policy is it?"

"Life insurance trust" is a widely used but somewhat unfortunate name for a trust that is not really a special breed. It's just any (usually) irrevocable trust that is permitted by its terms to buy insurance. The trust should be authorized to hold a wide range of investment vehicles, with no requirement that life insurance be purchased. The IRS has never liked the fact that life insurance enjoys some powerful and unique tax advantages. Although the name "irrevocable life insurance trust" is descriptive and convenient for discussion and teaching purposes, consider giving your "insurance" trust a name without the word "insurance" in it. Even though the ILIT is an extremely valuable, mainstream estate-planning tool, there is no legal requirement to call attention to the trust just because it owns life insurance.

How the Irrevocable Life Insurance Trust (ILIT) Works An insurance policy on your life is a piece of property and there-

fore has value. Whether you own this property or not has many implications. For example, creditors want to know if it belongs to you so they can seize it and keep its cash value, if any, provided state law allows it. The IRS wants to know so that when you die the death benefit can be included in your taxable estate if a basis is found for doing so. As far as the IRS is concerned, if you have the right to decide to whom the death benefit goes, you own the policy for tax purposes.

If an ILIT owns a policy on your life, the coverage is there for your loved ones, but the property does not belong to you. (Remember, as an irrevocable trust, the ILIT is an independent legal entity.) Therefore, it makes no difference what the state law says about creditor access to life insurance. You cannot control it; it is not your asset to protect. Assuming the ILIT was not funded with a fraudulent transfer to begin with, this is very good protection against creditors. Likewise, if an ILIT owns the policy, it is not part of your estate for tax purposes.

Note that while the ILIT takes over the role of policy *owner*, your beneficiaries can remain the same. Importantly, death proceeds can still be received by your loved ones income tax-free, as usual. If there is no need to manage funds for the beneficiaries, they can receive their shares in a lump sum. Alternatively, the ILIT can be written appropriately for dealing with your goals, just like any other trust, with provisions for young children, keeping money away from your son-in-law, and so on.

ILITs and the Estate Tax

An ILIT allows you to avoid estate taxation on a policy's death benefit: since the trust owns the policy, the benefit is kept out of your taxable estate. However, you—the estate owner/insured/grantor of the trust—must avoid all "incidents of ownership" in the policy once it is acquired by the trust. The IRS looks way beyond the obvious for any controlling "strings" or links between the insured estate owner and the policy on his life. If any such connection is found, the IRS often argues it is an "incident of ownership," requiring that the policy proceeds be included in the decedent's taxable estate.

Unfortunately, "incidents of ownership" is not a clearly defined concept. Certainly, the insured should not also be the trustee. A spouse is a permissible trustee, but there are several potential problems that you and your attorney will have to consider in choosing anyone closely related to you.

{Warning! IRS audits ignore theory in favor of practice

When the IRS audits a taxpayer or takes a position on something—such as supposed "incidents of owner- ship"—it performs its examination with 20/20 hindsight. The examiners do not care how good an arrange- ment looks on paper. Instead, they focus on what actually happened, and what the final result was. This advice applies to all tax questions and strategies, not just trusts. That's one reason why it is dangerous to get too "cute" with tax planning.

In addition, the insured should not have any right under the trust agree- ment to:

NAME OR CHANGE THE POLICY BENEFICI- ARIES

REPLACE THE TRUSTEE (except per-

haps to replace one institutional trustee with another)

MAKE POLICY LOANS.

Of course, like any irrevocable trust, an ILIT cannot simply be terminated. So be careful, and make sure to understand in advance what you are doing—and giving up.

Ideally, you should first set up the ILIT, then let the trustee apply for and buy a new policy, perhaps using a cash gift from you. To put a little more distance between you and the policy, don't be involved in the arrangements any more than necessary. Sign the application only as "The Insured" *not* as the applicant or owner. This is better than transferring an existing policy into the trust because it avoids a potential estate tax problem: policies transferred to a life insurance trust within three years of death will be included in your estate anyway. Most other property is not treated this way. It's an example of why special expertise and planning are necessary to properly obtain all the benefits of life insurance.

Hint: The trustee of an irrevocable life insurance trust must be viewed by the IRS as truly independent. If the trustee is believed to be a mere puppet of the grantor, the policy proceeds will not be removed from the taxable estate. This is one advantage of using an institutional trustee, rather than a spouse. As a concession to practicality, however, a spouse serves as trustee in many cases. He or she should consult an attorney before taking any action on behalf of the trust.

ILITs and the Gift Tax

Sometimes it is not practical to get new life insurance when the ILIT is created, so the grantor transfers his existing policy to the ILIT. Since a life insurance contract is a piece of property, this is a gift subject to the federal gift tax. But the gift tax value of the policy is *not* equal to face value. For whole-life policies in force for many years, the gift tax value is roughly equal to the policy cash value. For term policies, the gift tax value is the hypothetical cost of buying the same policy on the date of the gift.

If the policy is not paid up, what about

payment of future premiums? Where does the trustee of the ILIT get the funds? Typically, that money comes from the insured— the trust grantor—in the form of annual gifts to the trust on behalf of each of the beneficiaries. (That can be anyone. In a family scenario, usually it's the spouse and children.) But won't each one of those gifts be taxable, year after year? Potentially, yes. Here's where a long explanation is necessary to make a fairly small point, but it's worth following just to see how tricky this stuff can be.

Recall that the law allows an annual tax-free gift of $11,000 from anyone to any number of recipients. That's fantastic, but read the fine print. The gift has to be a "present interest" in property to qualify— something the recipient of the gift can use right now, like cash, stock, land, or a car. A life insurance policy or cash gifts for premiums, or anything else placed in any kind of trust, will certainly be of value to the trust beneficiaries—but not today.

Gifts into trust are typically *not* something the trust beneficiaries can use presently; if the grantor wants them to have the money now, he can just give it to them. (Who needs a trust?) So the annual $11,000 gift tax exclusion would apparently not be available to protect these gifts from gift tax. *Without special measures, every dollar given by the ILIT grantor to the trustee for premium payments would be gift taxable.* Each gift would chip away at the grantor's $1 million lifetime exemption from this tax. When that is used up, any subsequent lifetime gifts to anyone would require a gift tax payment to Uncle Sam.

Premiums for a sizable insurance policy often run into the tens of thousands of dollars and more per year. So a long stretch of such payments, paid for with taxable gifts from the grantor, could erode a good bit of his $1 million lifetime shelter from gift tax. That would also leave less of the grantor's estate protected from estate tax upon his death.

Keep in mind that almost half of every unprotected dollar would be lost to the estate tax. So even for estates that are "just a little" over the tax-payable threshold ($1.5 million in 2004 and 2005), there could be a lot of money involved. Hasn't somebody come up with a way for the grantor to give the trustee $11,000 per trust beneficiary as a *tax-free* gift every year—a present interest, like a bag full of cash to each one of them?

Yes, somebody has—but nobody remembers his name. His client's name was Mr. Crummey, however; and it has been committed to estate-planning immortality. The attorney was not only smart, but gutsy. Most of us try hard *not* to go to war with the IRS or make a client famous, but he did both.

• **The Crummey trust** The *Crummey trust* takes its name from the 1968 federal court of appeals decision in the case of *Crummey v. Commissioner of the Internal Revenue Service*. Its key feature when used in trusts really should be called the Crummey *provision*, or power, because it is limited in scope and is only one portion of a trust document. But it was such a big break that many people refer to any trust that has the provision as a Crummey trust. This provision is intended to get around the aforementioned gift tax problem.

Here's how it works: The grantor makes a cash gift to the trustee of up to $11,000 per year, per beneficiary, for his or her benefit.

(Note that although the grantor cannot end the trust or take his money back, future gifts can certainly be halted, if plans change.) The Crummey trust beneficiaries are given a short period of time after each gift (thirty days, for example) in which they are permitted by the trust document to withdraw the money from the trust—it's a gift, free and clear. If the time passes and a beneficiary has not exercised his "Crummey right of withdrawal," the money stays in the trust, and the trustee can use it to make premium payments.

In the original Crummey case, the court decided that this limited access is enough to make a gift a present interest. On these conditions, a gift to a Crummey trust qualifies for the annual $11,000 gift tax exclusion—at least it has so far. The right to withdraw the gift must not be illusory and the Crummey-trust beneficiaries must be formally advised of it in a letter each year. It's the trust beneficiaries' money if they want to take it—that's the crucial factor. The grantor hopes they won't do that, but there can be no agreement to that effect. The IRS is skeptical of ("hates" is probably more like it) Crummey gifts, so it is wise to be extra-careful in complying with all technical rules. Of course, it is foolish to draft or administer trust provisions like this without an attorney's help.

{ **Warning!** You have good reason to scrutinize a Crummey trust

Good estate-planning attorneys have long used the Crummey trust as a common feature of the estate plans they design, but the Crummey-provision rules are not statutes. Instead, they are creatures of past and future judicial decisions, and therefore subject to modification. For this reason, pay extra attention to the details of a Crummey trust as your attorney spells them out.

{ **A Closer Look:** Weighing an alternative to the Crummey trust

There is another option that should work fine for many families with mature children or grandchildren as

beneficiaries. Make an outright gift of cash ($11,000 or less), without using a trust, but announce the hoped-for use of it—the purchase of insurance on your life, perhaps, or some other investment. If a child owns, pays for, and is beneficiary of a policy on the life of a parent (or grandparent), the policy proceeds will be received with no estate- or income-tax consequences to anyone. (Each child should pay a proportional share of the premiums. That way no child can be said to have made a taxable gift to the others by paying for a policy that will benefit them.)

Of course, any asset purchased by a child, including life insurance, will be his property. As such, it is subject to the claims of the child's creditors—and to the risk of being cashed in later and spent.

A Final Word

about ILITs Sheltering every possible dollar from confiscatory estate taxation is an important goal, of course, as is the asset protection that an ILIT offers. For many of you, however, the real value of using a trust to hold insurance is to provide for the use and management of the policy proceeds according to your wishes. The beneficiaries might not be old enough to manage a sizable lump sum of money. Even if age is not a problem, lack of financial and investment savvy might be. Remember that just like other trusts, an ILIT can be written so that the proceeds are paid out in a way that makes sense for the beneficiary's circumstances and needs.

Too often, an irrevocable life insurance trust is requested and prepared as part of a family estate plan, almost as an afterthought. Little time is spent in some cases to think about how to make the trust work for the grantor and beneficiaries beyond its tax-saving function. This is unfortunate and people would be wise to broaden their outlook. Estate planning should be more than just tax planning.

16

Protecting Beneficiaries from Themselves

Spendthrift and incentive provisions can be viewed as two sides of the same planning coin and, indeed, they work to complement each other in the same trust. They are appropriate to include in almost any type of trust because they address two concerns of everyone making plans to pass wealth to the next generation:

Hint: Trust incentives can be as creative as you like: detailed and specific, or broadly-worded. Just be sure to think about the "what ifs" and the possible pitfalls of trying to rule from the grave.

1. How do I protect transferred wealth from a beneficiary who might spend or invest money unwisely or live recklessly?
2. How do I encourage a work ethic and a productive, responsible lifestyle in my children, rather than giving them on a silver platter what I have worked for all my life?

Spendthrift
Trust Provisions

Like the Crummey trust, a *spendthrift trust* is so named because of a single provision or clause in the document. A spendthrift clause is a simple and valuable feature included in almost every trust. It has long been used in every state to do two things: First, the spendthrift clause prevents a beneficiary who goes on a drinking or spending binge, for example, from selling the right to his future trust payments to a loan company for a lump sum of cash. Secondly, it takes the trust "off the table" for creditors in the (unfortunate but likely) event the beneficiary is sued as a result of his financial or other irresponsibility. Below is a typical spendthrift clause. It becomes a lot more readable by focusing only on the words in bold type:

This trust, as well as **the benefits hereunder,** *both income and principal,* **which are payable to any beneficiary, shall not be subject to sale, transfer,** *encumbrance,* **assignment,** *alienation, attachment,* **or the claims of creditors,** *spouses or divorced spouses, or others,* **for the debts, obligations, or activities of any beneficiary** *or beneficiary's legal representative.*

{ A Closer Look: A sad example of how well the spendthrift clause works

A thirty-five-year-old man driving while drunk killed a mother of two. He was prosecuted for manslaughter, but the victim's family desperately needed compensation for the loss of her income. Although the defendant had the minimum liability insurance allowed by law, it was common knowledge that he had recently inherited a lot of money. The family sued for wrongful death. The jury decided in favor of the family, awarding it almost $1.5 million in damages.

Unfortunately for the family, the

defendant's inheritance actually took the form of quarterly trust payments of $25,000 from his late father's trust, made at the discretion of a bank trustee. The trust contained a spendthrift clause similar to our example. Legally, the trust principal was not the defendant/beneficiary's property; therefore, it was not available to pay the victim's judgment. Courts around the country have ruled along similar lines for many years. Topping it off, the trustee suspended payments to the beneficiary in anticipation of the several years he will spend behind bars. Even in heartbreaking situations like this, the courts virtually always honor spendthrift provisions.

The spendthrift clause keeps a creditor from receiving directly from a trust what the beneficiary was supposed to get. Once a payment from that trust has been made to the beneficiary, however, it is no longer subject to the clause—it is now the beneficiary's money, meaning creditors are free to go after it. If a trust calls for a definite monthly payout of one thousand dollars, for example, a beneficiary's creditor cannot expect the court to "just order the trustee to send the beneficiary's check to me from now on."

Still, in the above example, the beneficiary would be receiving regular trust income and the creditor knows it. This problem can be solved by the use of a trust from which distributions are made in the sole and absolute discretion of the trustee, at least until a certain point or the attainment of specified conditions. The trustee would have the authority to delay or even entirely withhold payments to a beneficiary who faces a current or potential lawsuit or has bill collectors chasing him. Since distributions from such a trust are completely discretionary, the beneficiary himself has no right to anything at all. This should stop creditors cold, and it will probably slow down the beneficiary as well.

Hint: As additional protection for both the beneficiary and the money, the trustee should also be authorized to make distributions "for the benefit of" the beneficiary, rather than directly to him. That way, payments can be made on behalf of the beneficiary to a landlord, utility companies, schools, medical providers, and so on. This method of distributing funds can also protect the beneficiary from himself. (For example, in the case of a substance abuser who decides to get treatment, it is better to send a check to the rehab center rather than to the abuser.)

{ **A Closer Look:** Unique laws in Alaska, Delaware, Nevada, Oklahoma, Rhode Island, and Utah

For ages, a trust created by a grantor that included himself as a beneficiary has been called "self-settled." As such, it has always been available to his creditors, to the full extent that the trustee even had the *discretion* to distribute assets to him—never mind whether distributions were actually made. We have learned that trustee discretion as to payouts is the key to protecting distributions to a beneficiary plagued by lawsuits or creditors. But this protection of trust assets from a beneficiary's creditors generally only applies when the beneficiary is not the grantor. As one judge wrote, it violates public policy for an individual to have an estate to live on, but not an estate to pay his debts with.

Since the mid-1990s, however, six states—Alaska, Delaware, Nevada, Rhode Island, Utah, and Oklahoma—have enacted controversial laws that *do* purport to give creditor protection to the grantor himself, *as a beneficiary*, if he places assets into a trust that meets certain conditions. These trusts are collectively referred to as *self-settled spendthrift trusts* or *domestic asset protection trusts* (DAPTs). There are still many uncertainties about the effectiveness of these trusts, as well as significant drawbacks. But some respected attorneys believe a DAPT can be worthwhile in some client situations.

But if the trust grantor is truly worried about the beneficiary wasting his trust income, even solid protection from creditors is a limited remedy. What if there are no creditors involved? A little spendthrift clause doesn't even attempt to address all the concerns one might have regarding a beneficiary's ability to handle money—bad habits, substance abuse, lack of motivation, evil spouse, and so on.

The grantor probably wants, in all events, to provide for every beneficiary's basic welfare. So the trust should authorize the trustee to pay whatever he deems "necessary or advisable" to provide for a beneficiary's support, health, and education. Sometimes the trustee's discretionary right to dole out funds as needed is called a "sprinkle" or "spray" power. That will serve as a safety-net feature. But a trust can do more to accomplish the grantor's goals.

Incentive Trust

Provisions
Trusts for spendthrift beneficiaries should require the trustee to do more than check whether creditors are at the door. Planning with problem issues in mind

requires writing conditions or restrictions into the trust, such as making trust payments contingent on certain events—getting a job, for example, going to school, or not getting arrested. A few attorneys have included these kinds of useful provisions in the trusts they draft for years. But only recently have they become widespread and touted as a special breed.

Anyone truly concerned about waste and irresponsibility on the part of trust beneficiaries should consider adding incentive features into what we have been calling a spendthrift trust. This is a double-sided approach. The beneficiary gets more by doing well, and less by doing otherwise. (Again, remember that spendthrift and incentive features are options or "add-ons" that can be used in a wide variety of trust documents that have other purposes as well.)

{Warning! Make the bonus clause legal—and uplifting

Incentive provisions cannot violate public policy. If challenged in court, for example, the trustee would probably not be allowed to honor a provi-

sion stipulating, "Nothing for my daughter if she marries a man of different ethnicity." On the other hand, any of these conditions would be honored:

"Nothing for my daughter if she fails a drug test."

"Nothing if she fails to maintain a C average in school."

"She gets a $10,000 bonus if she graduates with a B average, $25,000 for an A average."

The grantor can be as imaginative as he wants in designing the incentives and disincentives. The legal barriers are not great. The questions to consider are practical:

- How far is it wise to go in trying to rule from the grave?
- Will your descendants end up resenting your effort to make them jump through hoops or choose one vocation or lifestyle over another?
- How specific should your conditions be?
- Some incentives are open-ended and broadly worded—a payout to match the beneficiary's income shown on his tax return, for example, or a distribution to

make the down payment on a home, or to start a business appropriate to the beneficiary's background and training. It is easy, however, to get too detailed. If you say "college" but your son has an aptitude and interest in automotive repair, is there to be no incentive for trade school? There are no "right" answers. You just have to think these things through.

The other practical obstacle is having someone in place to make the kind of judgment calls that will clearly be necessary. This can be a big one. While alive, of course, the grantor himself can make these decisions. But later, it will be the trustee, perhaps aided by a trust protector or family adviser. So a balance must be achieved between the complexity of the plan and the ability of the trustee and/or protector to render sound, informed decisions to make it work.

CHAPTER **17**

Minding Your Business: Protecting Investment Interests

Family limited partnerships (FLPs) and limited liability companies (LLCs) are *limited liability entities*. They serve a variety of purposes in the operation and management of businesses and investments. Here our focus is on their use in asset protection. We'll discuss the for-

Hint: The LLC is rightly touted as the entity of choice for many businesses. However, the LLC does not offer any income tax advantages over the traditional Subchapter-S corporation.

mer first. Keep in mind, however, that this area of the law is complex, and we are painting with a broad brush.

Some Background in Partnership Law

What are limited partnerships? First, one must understand what a general partnership is: two or more individuals who have agreed to collectively own and manage some form of property or business. The neighborhood children's lemonade stand is a good example. But each partner, personally, is fully liable for one hundred percent of all partnership debts and other liabilities. For that reason and others, general partnerships are not recommended for business or estate planning.

How are limited partnerships different from general partnerships? They have two classes of partners: general and limited. The general partner runs the business, regardless of the percentage he owns. But the general partner has unlimited personal liability. If partnership property were insufficient to satisfy creditors of the partnership, the individually owned assets of the general partner would be at risk. For example, if the partnership owned apartment buildings and a tenant sued successfully, the general partner could be on the hook for anything above insurance coverage. Limited partners have no control and therefore limited liability— their amount at risk is limited to their ownership stake.

{ A Closer Look: What's wrong with a "regular" corporation?

Nothing. The traditional corporation we are all familiar with certainly does provide significant asset protection. The owners are generally protected from *personal* liability for debts and obligations *of the business itself.* This insulation, coupled with adequate business, homeowner's, and auto liability insurance, is all the asset protection many business owners need.

Keep in mind, however, that an owner is *always* personally liable for his own actions, no matter what form of organization the business

takes. If the owner himself is driving a company truck and runs over a pedestrian, for example, the owner can be sued individually, as well as the company. Of course, too, the corporation provides no protection at all to the owner for liabilities that arise outside the business.

This means that an owner's shares of a corporation are completely vulnerable to claims of his *personal* creditors. A creditor with a judgment in hand can take a defendant's ownership interest in a corporation, and all the rights that go with it. In a closely held corporation, this could allow the creditor to take over the business by getting the stock of a controlling shareholder. With that done, the creditor could force the corporation to sell assets or liquidate completely to satisfy the judgment. The membership interests of the limited partnerships and limited liability corporations are much more protected; a creditor gets much less, and would not be able to gain control.

The limited partnership was designed by law as a form of business organization that an unrelated group of owner/investors could use to undertake a commercial project or financial venture. But its structure also happens to facilitate estate planning and, to a large extent, asset protection.

Introduction to the Family Limited Partnership

The *Family Limited Partnership* (FLP) is a "regular" limited partnership, organized under state law, in which the partners happen to be a closely related group. In a typical FLP one or both parents are the general partners, and contribute all or nearly all of the FLP's working capital and property, while the children are limited partners. The FLP is best suited for an estate consisting largely of real estate or a family business. It is also often used for more liquid assets like stocks and bonds, but not for a professional practice or firm. (The use of money or capital resources must be a major income-producing component of the family enterprise—as opposed, for example, to a medical practice, where personal services generate the income.)

Despite the personal liability of the general partner for *partnership* debts, the FLP provides reasonably good asset protection from future claims that arise outside the partnership, such as an auto accident unrelated to business. If your mother and father's investment property is placed in an FLP, they will then own only a *partnership interest*—not the actual property contributed. By law, however, even if a creditor successfully sues the parents, he would ordinarily be entitled only to a *charging order*, which is the right to the partner's future payments from the partnership—if the partnership decides to make any. The creditor typically cannot vote to liquidate the partnership or take a chunk of the actual partnership property. That legal principle is the basis of the FLP's role in asset protection.

Another chief advantage of the FLP is the way it facilitates transferring family wealth to the next generation. A family estate might consist of several rental properties and financial accounts, for example. If all are put into the FLP pot, it is easier to give a daughter a certain number of "limited partnership units" rather than a slice of each asset. The value of these units for gift tax purposes can

be less than that of the underlying partnership assets, resulting in tax savings.

The limited partnership has been used for
a number of years, where appropriate, as a
means of holding and distributing family
wealth. The personal liability of the general
partner, however, is a chink in the limited
partnership's asset protection armor. When
this a concern and no individual feels comfortable taking on the role of the general
partner, a limited liability company (LLC) can
serve that role. (For even greater protection,
experts recommend a foreign-based corporation.) As general partner, the LLC itself
would still have full liability for obligations of
the limited partnership, but liability would
stop there. No one would be personally liable, unless he had taken some additional
action, such as personally guaranteeing a
loan.

The Limited
Liability Company Limited Liability
Companies (LLCs) are used every day to
carry on all kinds of profit-making ventures
and professional practices. Indeed, in recent years, the limited liability company has

become the business organization of choice
for new enterprises.

LLC laws were designed to offer the best
features of both the partnership and the
corporation. Most important to an operating
business owner are the income tax and liability characteristics. The LLC allows "pass-
through" taxation, like a partnership, so that
only the owners, not the business itself, pay
tax. (The owners of an LLC are also called
members.) Liability of the owners for debts
of the business is limited, however, as in a
corporation, to whatever stake the owner
has invested. The fifty LLC statutes vary
widely in significant details, but all share
those key advantages.

Most readers of this book will be less interested in the everyday, business opera-
tional "nuts and bolts" of LLCs than in two
other aspects: asset protection and the
transfer of wealth to the next generation. In
many states, the creditor-protection characteristics of an LLC are virtually the same
as those of an FLP (assuming the FLP has a
corporation or LLC as general partner). For
this reason, the *family* LLC will play a role in
many sophisticated asset protection plans
from now on, especially those involving on-

going family businesses. As for estate planning, like the FLP, the chief appeal of the *family* LLC in estate planning is in enabling convenient, annual gift-giving. In some circumstances, this also allows family wealth to be transferred from parents to children in a tax-efficient way.

The choice between FLP and family LLC in your particular situation might ultimately depend on practical considerations involving state-specific details in the law or the state's business organization tax structure. Many attorneys feel more comfortable with the FLP because they and the courts have worked with it longer. A lot of issues and questions have arisen (as with anything legal), and judicial decisions have resolved them. So everybody knows where he or she stands. Your own lawyer and other advisers should know best; this is not do-it-yourself stuff.

{ A Closer Look: Limited liability entities for professional practices

There are a variety of limited liability entities that provide protection to a

practitioner from what the law calls *vicarious liability*—personal liability arising from the malpractice or harm caused by employees or the *other* professionals in the group. Note, however, that the limited liability entity itself will be jointly liable with anyone who commits a wrongful act or malpractice while acting on behalf of the organization in rendering professional services.

For this reason, it is seldom a good idea for the professional corporation or partnership to own real estate, or valuable equipment, or to keep more cash in the bank than is needed. Instead, another business entity should be formed, ideally with non-professionals among the owners as well, to perform functions such as acquiring and leasing office space to the practice.

How Family Limited Partnerships

Work The family LLC can function much like the FLP in terms of both asset protection and estate planning. Because the FLP has been around longer, however, we'll refer primarily to it in our further discussion although the principles, issues, and problems noted are largely the same for both entities. The operation and benefits of an FLP are best illustrated through use of an example.

Parents with an estate of $3 to $4 million want to protect their property from future legal claims and eventually transfer it to their children. Saving estate and gift tax is important but, more importantly, they don't want to give up the control they believe is inevitably lost by making substantial lifetime gifts. Their lawyer suggests creating an FLP and contributing property such as stock in the family company and/or real estate.

One hundred limited partnership units, each representing a one-percent ownership interest, are issued. The parents assume two ownership and management roles. Wearing the hats of general partners (or through a LLC general partner they have established), Mom and Dad take two units and then hold ninety-eight units in their other capacity as limited partners. At this point, they fully *control* the partnership business and property in their role as general partners, and they also *own* one hundred percent of the partnership.

Assuming the funding of the FLP was not a fraudulent transfer, the parents enjoy considerable (but by no means ironclad) asset protection under state law under this arrangement. State limited partnership law limits the liability of the limited partners for claims against the partnership itself. The general partner is personally liable, but if they use a controlled LLC as the general partner, the parents themselves are not.

As for claims that arise against either parents or children from outside the FLP, a creditor—after winning a judgment—would probably only be able to get a charging order from the court. But this would give the creditor no control over the FLP or the assets it owns. A charging order generally *only* entitles the creditor to any distributions that the general partner decides should be paid out to the limited partners—parents or children. That unappealing prospect typically makes settlement a lot more agreeable to creditors, especially if it is a personal injury type of claim and the parents have adequate liability insurance in place.

{ **Warning!** The legal status of the charging order is changing

The legal landscape continues to shift and evolve around the charging order as a means of enforcing a creditor's rights. Because of perceived abuses by debtors and injustices to legitimate creditors, some state courts and legislatures have chipped away at the charging order's protective features in a variety of ways. If asset protection is an important factor to you in considering an FLP or LLC, monitor this legal trend closely; ask your attorney how the issue is developing in your particular state.

● **Giving while retaining control of your assets** The transfer of an ownership interest in the family company or the family investment portfolio might help provide the younger generation with a sense of involvement and interest in business and investment. But what about the parents' fear of losing management control by giving away an increasing share of ownership to the children (or grandchildren) over time?

No problem. Unlike a direct gift of company stock, the gifting of FLP units does not also grant increased management control of the company. The parents (or grandparents) remain firmly in control, due to their role as general partners (or as the managers of a LLC that is set up to be the general partner). This has nothing to do with their ownership percentage. To ensure continued family control, the partnership agreement can restrict the transfer of a partnership interest to outsiders. Alternatively, the agreement can require that the share of any partner who wants to sell out must offer the share first to the parents at a fair market price.

● **Protection of assets from divorce claims** FLP ownership units gifted by the parents to a child are not easily converted to cash or commingled with other assets. Since the gifted units remain separate and clearly identifiable as such, they will usually not be on the table if the child ends up in divorce court dividing property some day. (If the child *purchases* an ownership interest with marital funds, then it is an asset of the marriage subject to division in divorce.)

• **Convenience and cost efficiency** Another advantage of using the FLP to hold family wealth is the convenience and possible cost savings of centralized asset management. If the family owns real estate in another state, placing it in the FLP can also avoid the need for probate proceedings in that state. (A will or trust would still be needed in the family's home state, however, to dispose of any FLP units still owned by the parents when they died.) As mentioned, lifetime gift-giving can be made much more convenient with the FLP. This is an important function of an FLP, whether taxes are a concern or not.

{ Warning! It's up to you to monitor developments in the law

Estate planning techniques that use the FLP and LLC are not in the same league of time-honored traditions as the ancient laws that govern wills and trusts. New court decisions come out all the time, as do public and individual taxpayer rulings by the IRS. Nowhere do these factors change the playing field more significantly than in asset protection and estate planning. Always seek out the best advice you can find; review your plan, at least briefly, every year.

Some Final Asset Protection Pointers

If you own two or more business interests, don't put all your eggs in one basket. Use multiple legal entities to own and operate them, to the greatest extent practical. That way, a claim (or judgment) against one is not a claim against them all. Certainly, property that is especially risky or open to liability should never be kept in the same business entity as other property. If you operate a skyscraper demolition business, for example, keep it legally separate from your sidewalk flower kiosk.

■ An operating business or professional practice should usually lease, not own, equipment and other property, especially real estate. These assets can be owned by another entity in which you have an interest. For example, a group of doctors (preferably, with some outsiders) might form an LLC to own and manage their office building. A claim against the medical practice would typically not put the building at risk, because the practice would not own it.

■ Follow the filing and other administrative rules pertaining to the FLP, LLC, or any other business entity you use. Adhering to state law formalities will not, in itself, ensure that the FLP or LLC provides the insulation from liability you hope for. But if these formalities are *not* respected, the court will likely disregard the entity. This is especially important in the context of family, where informality is tempting. When the family patriarch, for example, uses the FLP checking account as a personal piggy bank, he will almost surely not get the asset protection or tax savings he expected.

Part Four:
Estate Planning with Retirement Assets

Employer-qualified plan retirement accounts such as 401(k)s, profit sharing and pension plans, and individual retirement accounts (IRAs) are different from other assets. Like all other property, retirement accounts are part of one's taxable estate. Wealthier individuals willl therefore face a significant tax bite before the money is even transferred to their beneficiaries. Unlike other property, however, previously untaxed retirement contributions—and the earnings that have accumulated over the years—are eventually subject to income tax, payable by anyone receiving a distribution. With some estates, after Uncle Sam takes almost half "off the top" and a high tax-bracket beneficiary (such as a successful daughter) then pays income tax on her distribution, the family ends up keeping a small slice of the pie.

People often postpone retirement distributions for as many years as possible (provided the full account balance is not needed right away). This allows for continued income tax-deferred growth of the account, and delays the eventual need to pay income tax on these funds. While the government has simplified the rules determining required minimum retirement distributions, some complexity is added if the account owner wants her distributions to go to a trust after she dies. In the following chapters, we'll explore the rules pertaining to this situation and how trusts and retirement plans can work together.

18

Distribution Solutions for Beneficiaries

It is not at all uncommon for retirement assets to represent most or all of a person's wealth at the time of death. As we have seen, however, a will has no authority over these assets—they are outside probate, controlled by a beneficiary designation form. (They become

Hint: It's the income, not the estate, tax that makes planning with retirement assets tricky. That's why good advice is important for everyone, not just those few with federal estate tax concerns.

subject to probate, however, if the account is payable to your estate. That is usually a mistake). If you are a beneficiary, it would be wise to consult your financial adviser or attorney before taking any action so that your own choices are clear. Conversely, if you are the one planning your estate, it's useful to review what options exist, so that you can best benefit your beneficiaries.

This is not rocket science. But make no mistake: estate planning and retirement distribution planning can each be complicated in itself. Integrating the two requires considerable knowledge—more than can be amassed from a book such as this one. Even though your final plan itself will probably not be too complicated, navigating confidently to that point requires familiarity with a wide variety of laws and regulations that change frequently, not to mention a thorough understanding of your overall situation and needs. That's why the best we can do here is alert you to some planning opportunities and pitfalls.

Taking Distributions after the Account

Owner Dies What are a retirement account beneficiary's options after the account owner has died? If no planning is done by the retirement account owner other than naming his beneficiaries, the majority of them will have two options upon his death:

1. Take whatever share of the account they have been given in a lump sum.
2. Take only the *required minimum distribution* (RMD) each year.

The RMD is based on the life expectancy of the beneficiary, according to an IRS actuarial table. The account balance is divided by the number of remaining years in the beneficiary's life to calculate how much must be distributed each year. A young beneficiary, for example, has many years of expected life. In his case, the account balance would be divided by a relatively high number, resulting in a relatively low payment required to be distributed from the account to him each year.

But why would any beneficiary want to

take his distributions in the smallest annual installments allowed, rather than a single big one? First, if the beneficiary takes a big lump sum out in a single year, he will probably bump himself up to a higher income tax bracket. Second, he may want to delay the payment of income tax and continue the benefit of tax-deferred growth. Most retirement account contributions are made with dollars that have not yet been subject to income tax. No tax is paid as the account (hopefully) grows in value over the years, but ordinary income tax is payable on any funds that are withdrawn. That's why there is an RMD—the law requires that at least some portion of the account is distributed each year to ensure that the account does not grow *too* much without Uncle Sam taking his cut.

In theory, therefore, it makes good sense to maximize the income tax-deferred growth of the funds by taking only the minimum required by law. Among attorneys and financial planners, this is certainly the most widely acknowledged estate-planning goal for retirement assets. Although there is no single best approach to retirement fund distribution planning, there is obvious value to letting the money ride for as long as possible—minimize withdrawals and maximize the benefit of tax deferral. Planners consider a retirement account owner fortunate, tax-wise, if he has a beneficiary with a long life expectancy (e.g., a child), over which the required distributions can be stretched out—the longer the better. Money not withdrawn can continue to grow, sometimes for decades, adding to the financial security of the account owner's surviving family.

Among those whose children are already well-off themselves, it makes sense to expect that inherited retirement assets will be left (largely) alone, since these beneficiaries have the means to resist the temptation of withdrawing the funds. For many others of us, however, it is silly to assume that the account beneficiaries will give tax deferral a moment's thought. To the contrary, experience shows that most would be happy to cash out the account before the ink is dry on the death certificate.

So if you consider it important that the retirement funds get the longest possible tax-deferred growth—or simply want to ensure the money is not wasted in six months—you can enforce your wish by using a trust(s) as the designated beneficiary (see chapter 19). Be aware, however, that IRA and retirement plan custodians and administrators differ in the extent to which they will cooperate with an account owner who wants, for example, to use a customized beneficiary designation form designed by his attorney. This would be necessary to designate a trust as account beneficiary, and is therefore an important practical issue to resolve during the planning process.

{**Warning!** Research twice, act once

Distribution options and decisions should always be considered carefully. Get solid professional advice before you take the first step. Take as much time as you feel necessary to educate yourself about plan provisions. The rules can be strict and confusing—not only in the law itself, but also among the various plan documents and IRAs seen around the country today. A particular retirement plan document may keep you from following a course of action

that would otherwise be legally permissible.

New Rules

Increase Flexibility The most important planning developments in recent years have resulted from a major change in the law in 2001 and subsequent IRS rulings. Now, the designated beneficiary(ies) of a retirement account does not have to be determined until September 30th of the year *after* the year the original account owner dies. This is not as outrageous as it sounds, but it does offer significant flexibility that can come in handy in certain situations.

Of course, it is not possible for anyone to *add* a beneficiary whom the original retirement account owner did not name himself. But now, in the interest of overall family financial planning, somebody who is named as a retirement account beneficiary has time to make herself "disappear" as such. First, let's explain how this is done, then why.

● **Disclaiming one's share of retirement assets** The "how" is easy. If a person is a retirement account beneficiary on the day the account owner dies, there are two ways she can cease being one by September 30th of the next year: she can take her share in full or she can *disclaim* her share. A disclaimer is a legal document that says, "I don't want it; somebody else take it." The disclaimed property (the retirement account, in this example) is then treated as though it were never received; the share is divided among the other beneficiaries. It is critical, however, that no benefit from the property is, in fact, received before the disclaimer. Once the beneficiary takes a payment, the option of disclaiming will be lost.

Why would somebody want to disclaim a retirement account? It might be a widow, for example, already in a high tax bracket. If she were named as the primary beneficiary, but did not need the money, why take it? Assuming she would eventually leave her estate to her children anyway, why not start now by disclaiming the retirement account? If the kids are in a lower tax bracket, the family overall will save income tax. Moreover, if the widow kept the retirement account, it would only increase the potential tax liability of her estate when she dies.

A person can also give up his official status as a beneficiary by taking his share in full—simply "cashing out." Obviously, he's still a beneficiary in the ordinary sense of the word. But not for further retirement account purposes. Once he receives his share, he's out of the planning picture. Of course, cashing out suits plenty of people just fine. They just want to take the money and run. But doing so can also make good planning sense in some situations, from the overall family perspective.

● **How to take advantage of the new rules** To better understand the preceding point, assume that a widow and her two successful daughters have all been named as primary retirement account beneficiaries. Assume further that this mother does not want to disclaim her share of the retirement account, because she has been counting on receiving the money.

If we assume, finally, that the daughters are able and wise enough to prefer only the required minimum distribution each year, this could present a family planning dilemma. Why? The answer depends on one additional fact we have not covered: once the beneficiary designations are set in stone on September 30th the year after the retirement account owner's death, the life expectancy of the oldest beneficiary (shortest life expectancy) is used by the IRS to calculate the minimum required distributions to all. The IRS will minimize the advantage of tax deferral, absent any planning.

Obviously, if there are only two beneficiaries of the retirement account and they are sisters close in age, the difference in life expectancies will be small. Even though the older sister's age will be used to calculate minimum distributions, the younger one would be losing little in the way of tax advantage. Not so if Mom is a beneficiary, however. Being forced to use their mother's much shorter life expectancy would greatly limit the potential power of tax deferral for the daughters. So Mom might decide to take her share in a lump sum. Having done so, she would no longer be considered a beneficiary on "determination day" (September 30th of the year after the account owner's death). Minimum annual distributions could then be based upon the long lives of her children.

Actually, there is another, probably better option for all in the above situation: the beneficiaries of a retirement account can now establish separate sub-accounts for themselves before the end of the year following the retirement account owner's death—*if* the account or plan allows it. That way, each beneficiary's account can be paid out based only upon her own life expectancy. This kind of postmortem planning was not possible under prior law.

19

Using Trusts as Designated Beneficiaries

The conventional wisdom is that, in the best-case scenario, retirement assets are best left outright (without a trust) to the account owner's spouse. This is chiefly because only a spouse is permitted to roll over the account into her own IRA and designate new, younger

Hint: Using a carefully drafted trust as beneficiary, the same tax advantages are available as when naming an individual. But remember that a trust can have the nontax features and benefits we've looked at, too.

beneficiaries. (In a typical case, this would be the spouses' children whose life expectancies could be used to stretch out withdrawals and allow income tax-deferred family wealth to build.) Additionally, the unlimited marital deduction would delay the estate tax attributable to the account, if any, till the second spouse dies.

Many people, however, are not in the "ideal" situation. For those without a spouse, tax deferral might not be a sufficient reason to rush right out and find one. Even among married people, it is sometimes not appropriate to designate the surviving spouse as the retirement beneficiary. The survivor might be disabled or otherwise impaired with regard to handling financial matters, for example.

Very commonly, the account owner's spouse is not the parent of his children, so the owner faces a dilemma: how to use his retirement assets to provide lifetime security for a surviving spouse, while ensuring that whatever is left passes to his children, not the spouse's family? Alternatively, the retirement account owner might have young or irresponsible children and be uncomfortable leaving them access to a large pool of cash.

In a nutshell, people who use trusts with tax-deferred retirement money have the same assortment of estate-planning goals as everybody else, and the same tools and options as well. The potential tax advantage is just a big, added benefit.

But a retirement account owner cannot hold his account in the name of a trust while he is alive. So our focus switches here to the manner in which retirement money can be distributed to a trust, which can then use the funds according to the terms the account owner has established. Not only is this subject somewhat complicated, but it changes frequently. Remember that our broad-brush coverage is intended only to provide some background prior to your meeting with an experienced attorney or planner to evaluate your circumstances and options.

Requirements of
the Trust Document Until a few years
ago, those who wanted to use a trust to receive retirement account distributions as part of their retirement and estate planning had to make a compromise. Naming the trust as the designated beneficiary was per-

mitted, but as a nonperson, a trust was given no life expectancy over which withdrawals could be stretched. People who designated "my trust" (or "my estate") as the retirement account beneficiary volunteered for an accelerated payout method. Decades of potential tax deferral were lost.

In recognition of the increasing use of trusts in so many situations, the rules were changed so that the life expectancy of the oldest trust beneficiary (shortest life expectancy) can be used to calculate required minimum distributions. To get the most from this rule—the longest income tax deferral—it is obviously best not to include a trust beneficiary who is much older than the others. (Consider using a separate trust for the older beneficiary.) The requirements the trust must meet to obtain this stretch-out are not burdensome, but strict technical compliance is essential. They are summarized below:

1. The trust must be valid under state law.
2. The trust must be irrevocable upon the retirement account owner's death, if not before.
3. The beneficiaries must be identifiable in the trust instrument.
4. If the retirement account owner himself

has not done so already, the trustee must provide to the retirement account custodian or administrator a list of all the trust beneficiaries with an outline of what they are to receive under the trust. This must be done by October 31st of the year after the account owner's death. Alternatively, a copy of the entire trust document can be submitted.

There is a drawback to using a trust in some situations. If the trust document calls for separate sub-trusts to be created upon the retirement account owner's death for each beneficiary, that's permitted. But only the oldest beneficiary's life expectancy is used to calculate the minimum required distribution that each must receive from the retirement account. This is unfortunate. As we saw above, if there are several *individual* beneficiaries (without trusts), and if the retirement account or plan allows it, the law now permits them to create separate sub-accounts and take distributions based on a separate calculation for each. That gives everybody the maximum tax deferral they're entitled to.

But the IRS has been unwilling to allow

this separate calculation treatment when a trust is used as a middleman. Therefore, to get the benefit of a trust and a separate pay-out calculation for each beneficiary, it appears you will have to set up a trust for each one of them before you die. Then, the retirement account beneficiary designation form must be filled out to show that the account is to be split up among these separate trusts.

{A Closer Look:
Take care when your
beneficiary is a trust

Here's a trust-drafting pitfall: Suppose you've set up a trust to be the beneficiary of your IRA. You assume the lives of your loved ones will be used to calculate minimum distributions. The trust also happens to authorize the trustee to help pay your estate's debts, expenses, and fees— outlays your executor might incur in probate court, for example. This is not an uncommon scenario. So what?

The IRS might take the position that if the trustee is allowed to pay estate expenses, then the estate is really a beneficiary of your IRA, too. You'll recall that naming "my estate" as beneficiary is usually not a good idea. For one thing, it puts the IRA on the probate table for creditors, if any. But your estate also has the shortest "life expectancy" of all your beneficiaries—zero. This would mandate a more accelerated distribution schedule. The plan to spread payments throughout the lives of your *intended* beneficiaries would be ruined.

Here again, however, the delayed date for beneficiary designation could come to the rescue. If all debts and other expenses of the estate were paid out of the IRA by September 30th of the year after the IRA owner's death, then the estate would have been paid in full, and would no longer be considered a beneficiary. At that point, only the real, human beneficiaries would be considered for required payment calculations.

The QTIP Trust

as Beneficiary

When the retirement account owner's current spouse is not the other parent of his children, the outright bequest of the account to the surviving spouse would most likely result in the account balance eventually passing to the spouse's descendants. This is usually not what the account owner wants. He typically does want to provide lifetime support to his survivor, however. The QTIP trust might be called for in this situation.

Funds in a QTIP trust qualify for the estate tax marital deduction, even though the surviving spouse/QTIP beneficiary gets *income* only, not control of the trust principal. This allows the retirement account owner to delay the payment of estate tax on that money; it will be part of the taxable estate of the *beneficiary*—the second spouse to die. It also ensures that the principal ultimately will go to his own children; his widow is entitled only to *income* produced by the trust.

When a QTIP trust is the retirement account's designated beneficiary, the trust document must be written with particular care as it relates to the surviving spouse's right to income earned by the assets of the trust. Note, for example, that the right to annual *distributions* from an IRA is not the same as the right to all the *income* produced by whatever is in the IRA account—stocks, bonds, mutual funds, and so on. The survivor must have a right to all such income, on an annual basis, for life—never mind what the required minimum withdrawal from the IRA might be.

{ **Warning!** To avoid a hit from the tax man, watch your p's and QTIPs

If the QTIP trust is not precisely worded, the surviving spouse's interest will not qualify for the marital deduction for estate tax purposes. In an estate large enough to face a tax payable, a small drafting error could be very costly. Likewise, the retirement account's standard beneficiary designation form must be modified to reflect these requirements. (The attorney who prepares the trust document will probably have to draft a customized form.)

Note that a surviving spouse/QTIP bene-ficiary must have a *right* to all the income, but does not have to take it. If the QTIP trust document gives the spouse power to com-pel the trustee to withdraw and pay to the spouse all the income earned on the retire-ment account assets at least annually, that will suffice. This allows actual distributions to be minimized, resulting in longer tax-de-ferred growth, if the spouse chooses to take less than she is entitled to.

Some Final Points on Estate Planning with Retirement Assets

Outlined below are some of the more important points to re-member when considering retirement as-sets in your estate-planning efforts, whether you name a trust as a beneficiary or not.

• **Regarding spouses** A surviving spouse must be the beneficiary of an employer-sponsored qualified plan, unless this right is waived in writing. (This is *not* true of IRAs.) Be aware of this fact in making any plans.

Remember to remove your former spouse from all IRA and employer plan beneficiary forms after a divorce. A divorce automatically revokes your will, as to the ex-spouse, but it does *not* revoke anything for which you listed the ex-spouse as a beneficiary such as retirement accounts or life insurance.

• **Paying estate taxes** Remember that all your IRAs and employer-sponsored retirement plan accounts of every variety will always be part of the taxable estate for federal purposes. For large estates (over $1.5 million in 2004 and 2005) facing federal estate tax, the overall plan should establish the source of funds to pay the estate tax that will be due on the retirement account. Not taking this issue into account can result in two kinds of problems.

First, if there are no arrangements for the retirement account to "contribute" its proportional share of the estate taxes, an unintended outcome of your plan of distribution is possible. For example, many wills direct the executor to "pay all my taxes." In that event, the executor would have to use only probate assets (such as CDs in your individual name) to pay the estate tax on the retirement funds, which are not part of the probate estate.

The retirement account beneficiaries would therefore get a free ride on taxes, while whoever inherited the probate property would shoulder the estate's full tax burden. In many situations, this would not matter, because the decedent's children would all be equal beneficiaries of every asset in his estate—probate as well as nonprobate. But this is not always the case, so the source of any estate tax to be paid should be considered.

Secondly, on the other hand, if withdrawals from the retirement account are to be stretched out for maximum income tax deferral, it is best not to use this money to pay estate tax. In other words, it is better to use funds that are not eligible for tax-advantaged growth. Otherwise, almost half the tax-deferred account itself would immediately have to go to Uncle Sam—then there is income tax on what's left over (except for Roth IRAs). Life insurance on your life, owned by the retirement account beneficiary or an irrevocable trust can fill this need. (Remember, if you own the policy yourself, it becomes part of the taxable estate and largely defeats the purpose of having it.)

● Naming a charity as your beneficiary

Retirement assets are ideal for carrying out your charitable intentions. Charitable organizations like to point out, quite correctly, that the payment of taxes at death is voluntary. When you name a charity as the beneficiary of an IRA or other retirement plan, the account passes to the charity totally free of estate taxes *and* income taxes.

Some people use part of the anticipated tax savings to pay for a life insurance policy. It's a means of "wealth replacement," so their survivors are not left without an inheritance.

If a charity is to be the beneficiary of only part of your retirement assets, it is better to dedicate a separate IRA to it. When a charity (a nonperson) shares a beneficiary designation form with real human beings—your son and daughter, for example—they would be foreclosed from taking distributions stretched over their life expectancies. (If this situation arises, however, it may be fixable by September 30th of the year after the account owner's death.)

● Primary and secondary beneficiaries

When filling out beneficiary forms for retirement accounts, be sure you recognize the difference between multiple *primary beneficiaries* of the account, who will all share, and *secondary beneficiaries* (also known as alternate or contingent beneficiaries), who will take a share only if the primary beneficiary dies first (or disclaims the share).

For example, a common designation is, "Primary beneficiary: Spouse. Secondary beneficiaries: Child A, Child B, and Child C, one third each." This means, "All to Spouse, if alive. If not, then—and only then—to the children in equal shares."

Do *not* leave the entire account to one child out of several, assuming he will share. Sure, he probably would, but this is asking for trouble and is completely unnecessary. Just divide the account on the beneficiary form.

If more than one child is a beneficiary, indicate what is to happen should a child predecease you. You will probably want his share to pass to his children rather than his siblings, but that result may not occur automatically.

● **Beneficiary forms** IRA and employer-plan beneficiary forms can be a real problem. Whether the beneficiaries are trusts or individuals, all your instructions must be included there, but there is often no room.

If necessary, insist on preparing your own form and get an acknowledged copy from the administrator or custodian. If you don't get cooperation, move the account elsewhere. This is an important estate-planning matter, and you are not the first or only person who needs this service. If a bank or other financial institution does not want to accommodate you, it does not deserve your business.

● **Roth IRAs** Roth IRAs are funded with after-tax dollars. Unlike traditional IRAs, no distributions are *required* from a Roth IRA during the owner's lifetime.

After the Roth IRA owner dies, required distributions must be made, with options similar to those for a traditional IRA. The account can be fully paid out in (about) five years, or annual installment payments can begin to the designated beneficiary, if there is one (the beneficiary's life expectancy dictates the required minimum). If the designated beneficiary is the Roth IRA owner's spouse, the surviving spouse can roll the account over to his own Roth IRA (not a traditional IRA).

{Appendix

A List of Executor Duties and Tasks of Probate

State laws and local practices differ so much that it is impossible to outline a precise sequence of steps an executor must follow. The probate court in your state undoubtedly makes more detailed instructions available in print and,

Hint: Sit down with a lawyer for an hour with a list of questions before taking any actions as executor. Remember: if a do-it-yourself legal error is made, it won't come to light until later, when it can really mess things up. It's not worth the worry, so consider letting your lawyer handle the more complex situations.

possibly, online. Of course, the court clerks can help you to some extent, but they are justifiably leery about providing anything that might be construed as legal advice.

Here are the likely steps, together with a few practical pointers, taken by most executors. The items near the top of the following list have to be addressed before you can do much else. The rest can be taken care of shortly thereafter, in no definite order.

● **The nuts and bolts**
1. Get at least ten certified copies of the death certificate, with raised seal. The funeral director should help you get them shortly after the funeral at nominal cost. You'll need the copies for many purposes and won't be able to do much without them.
2. Begin a time sheet to start recording the hours you spend on official executor duties. This is good to have for all to see, whether or not you ultimately take any compensation.
3. Secure the decedent's residence and other property, if necessary, and be sure all hazard and liability insurance is kept in full force and effect.

4. Notify the automobile insurance company immediately if a new driver will be using the decedent's car, pending formal transfer.
5. Arrange for the handling/forwarding of decedent's mail.
6. Cancel or remove decedent's name from credit card accounts and destroy cards.

● **The probate process**

1. Obtain, complete, and file the Petition for Probate, or take the equivalent first step in your state. Have the death certificate and cash in hand for filing fees (or be sure the probate office takes checks).

   You might be asked generally about the nature and value of the decedent's probate assets and the identity of his next of kin. Other than that, the rest of the information you'll need will probably be on the death certificate.

   Follow instructions to get Letters Testamentary. This might involve a brief trip to probate court so the judge can appoint you as executor in open court. Request ten copies of the Letters, maybe more. You will definitely need one for each financial institution you'll be contacting.

2. Send copies of the will by certified mail (with return receipt) to all beneficiaries, as well as to the decedent's spouse and all children, whether named in the will or not. There may be a form to submit stating that you have done this.
3. Arrange for a notice to creditors by newspaper publication.
4. Determine whether a streamlined probate procedure is available, based on the limited size of the estate and/or the beneficiaries. Does the entire estate go to the spouse? Or does it all go to the spouse and/or children? If so, there might be a fast track.
   If a simplified procedure is available, it will probably be necessary to have all beneficiaries sign a form indicating they agree to it and give up the right to a formal hearing.

5. File paperwork for allowances or set-asides, if appropriate, for a surviving spouse or children of the decedent.
   In some states, to avoid hardship, it is also possible for a surviving spouse to obtain emergency money from a bank

account that has been temporarily frozen because of the decedent's death.

● **Organizing the estate's finances**
1. Apply for an Employer Identification Number (EIN) for the estate. This is a federal tax ID that is necessary even though the estate probably will not be an "employer." Instructions can be found on the IRS Web site (www.irs.gov) or by calling the IRS at 1-800-829-4933.
2. Open an estate checking account, using the EIN as if it were a regular Social Security number. If any significant amount will be in the account for more than a few weeks, consider an interest-bearing account option or a money-market fund to hold what is not immediately needed for bills.
3. Contact each financial institution at which the decedent held an account, to determine the number and date-of-death balance for all accounts there. Except for local banks that you can visit in person, you'll have to spend time on the phone to figure out the person to whom to mail your Letters Testamentary and a certified copy of the death certificate (with raised

seal). You will need at least those items. Simply ask each place what else it requires for you to gain access to the decedent's accounts. The odds are good the first person you talk to will not know. Don't be surprised if you get the feeling they have never had a customer die before.

Some states require a release from the state taxing authority before the accounts can be made available. Usually this is easy to get, especially if the beneficiaries are all either children or the spouse of the decedent.

Were any of the accounts IRAs? If so, there should be beneficiaries named. Unless the decedent named his own estate, the executor will have no authority over an IRA account. As a practical matter, however, the executor should advise the IRA beneficiaries (who are likely to also be beneficiaries under the will) to contact the bank for the necessary forms to submit in order to claim their money. They can expect to need at least the death certificate.

Try to reconcile any differences between what you expected to find in the accounts and what was actually there. For example, you might have last year's account statements that suggest four certificates of deposit at Bank Two, but only one is reported there now. The others were probably cashed in or rolled over.

Obtain permission to open safe deposit boxes. Procedures vary widely. The most practical advice is to just ask at the bank what it's going to take to get you in. Whether required or not, the executor should be sure to have a witness to his inspection of the safe deposit box, if there is any likelihood whatsoever that the executor's word will be challenged by an interested party.

4. Notify the Social Security Administration of the decedent's death. Be prepared to return or refund the check received for the month of his death.
5. To see where the estate stands financially, make a projection of the estate's cash flow over the next few months using the best estimates available.
   Simple checking account software (such as Quicken, Microsoft Money, etc.)

is handy for this. It will automatically put everything in the correct order as you enter the dates of present and anticipated deposits and expenditures. That way you can see where the estate will be, cash-wise, as of any date.

List all fees, expenses, and bill payments you know will be coming. Include a reserve for *un*anticipated expenses (trust me).

Cash on hand (such as the decedent's checking account) and expected income (for instance, insurance payable to estate, final paychecks, etc.) should be accounted for in the cash-flow projection and entered with a future date.

Do the same for the other liquid assets of the estate such as CDs and other financial accounts that will be cashed in during the next few months and dumped into the estate pot. (Just remember, however, that this money is not really in the checking account till you put it there!)

Hint: Note that there is no penalty when an executor cashes in a CD before its maturity date.

• Real estate and household items

1. Obtain a formal appraisal of all real estate; request value as of date-of-death. (The cost for the appraisal should be $300 to $500 for a single-family house.)
2. Take inventory of all tangible household personal property. Generally, the value of this property at an estate auction is not too high. If there is no sale, the executor's honest, best reasonable estimate of value would probably be acceptable.

   How detailed and itemized an inventory will be taken will vary, depending largely on the attitude of the other interested parties. Usually this kind of property—furniture, personal effects, clothing and the like—can be lumped together in just a few broad categories.

   If there is mistrust among the beneficiaries or insinuations of misconduct, the executor should make a videotaped inspection of the decedent's residence, preferably with a witness.

   Collectibles (art, coins, etc.) and big-ticket items like vehicles should be listed separately. If possible, use some objective benchmark or reference (such as the "book" value of a car). Consider a formal

appraisal of collectibles if the will beneficiaries are likely to be suspicious or critical. It is important that everyone feel
confident in the values assigned to various items.

Hint: If you're having difficulty dividing up household items not specifically listed in the will, consider an al-
ternating selection process using a
coin flip or drawing of straws. On
each turn, the children could decide
to go for something of sentimental
importance or cash value. This will
achieve about as fair a result as is
humanly possible. More importantly,
the process itself is transparent and
equitable. Even if a child (or his
spouse) is bound and determined to
feel short-changed, it would be difficult to blame the executor.

● **Final debts and distributions**
1. Pay the legitimate final bills of the decedent from the estate checking account.
2. Pay taxes as applicable. Tax returns you
   might have to file include:

Decedent's final year individual state and federal income tax
Estate income tax, if the estate itself earns more than $600 per year in interest and other income during the period of probate administration
State inheritance or estate tax, if applicable
Federal estate tax, if the estate value is greater than $1.5 million (for 2004 and 2005.) This should be done by a professional, even if you do the others yourself.

3. When all debts and obligations of the estate are satisfied, divide what is left according to the will.
4. Keep a record of everything you've done and be prepared to make a final accounting or report if required by law, or if requested by a beneficiary.

• A sample letter for obtaining information from financial institutions
This is a useful sample letter when contacting financial institutions for information on a decedent's account. This sample is designed to obtain financial account information and collect Certificate of Deposit proceeds.

February 10, 2003

XYZ Bank
P. O. Box 1234
Somewhere, NJ 07654

RE: Estate of Michael J. Palermo,
deceased
CD Account No. 1234567
Date of Death: 1/16/03
Social Security No: —- — ——

To whom it may concern,

My father has recently died and I am the executor of his estate. Enclosed please find a certified copy of the death certificate and my Letters Testamentary.

Please provide me with the value of the above-referenced account as of the date of death, 1/16/03. Also, please close the account and send a check in the full amount of the current balance to me at:

Michael T. Palermo
300 West Short St.LLexington, KY 40507

Finally, I ask that you examine your records to determine if there are any other accounts at XYZ Bank in my father's name and, if so, to please advise me.

Thank you for your attention to this matter.
Michael T. Palermo

Acknowledgments

I would like to thank my editor, Meredith Peters, for cheerfully guiding me every step of the way through writing my first book. Meredith was invaluable in many ways, especially in spotting places where the text was unclear and suggesting how to make it better. On several occasions as well, she rescued the manuscript from the quagmire of needless detail by suggesting two sentences on a minor point instead of the three paragraphs I'd written. Meredith's meticulous attention to details that do matter, however, has greatly improved the book.

Everyone at AARP who worked hard to ensure the accuracy and quality of the manuscript also deserves acknowledgment. Allan Fallow, managing editor of AARP Books, labored over the manuscript and made dozens of helpful suggestions to improve its clarity and readability. I am also grateful to four members of AARP's professional staff—Sally Hurme, Esq., consumer advocate; Stuart Cohen, Esq., director of legal advocacy; Sterling Kerr, Ph.D., director of gift planning; and Michael Schuster, Esq., associate general counsel—for drawing on their areas of expertise to offer constructive criticism and specific advice on topics to be covered.

Janet Kuhn, Esq., of McLean, Virginia, reviewed the entire manuscript on behalf of AARP. The book benefited greatly from her expert analysis and practical experience, and for that I thank her.

Special thanks go to Hugh Delehanty, editor-in-chief of AARP Publications. Recognizing the need for public education on estate planning and related matters, Hugh was an early supporter of the book. I am honored that he considered this project worthy of AARP's participation.

My thanks as well to Michael Fragnito, vice president and publisher of general trade books, Barnes & Noble Publishing; Andrew Martin, vice president and publisher, Sterling Publishing; Steve Magnuson, vice president and editor-in-chief, Sterling Publishing; and Alan Kahn, president of Barnes & Noble Publishing. In committing themselves to this book, these gentlemen, too, acknowledged the increasing relevance of estate planning in an aging society.

Last but by no means least are those my editor calls "the truly important people."

They toil largely without recognition, yet their efforts are indispensable and I thank them sincerely: Liz Donovan, production manager; Elaine Freed Lindenblatt, copyeditor; AARP creative director Carl Lehmann-Haupt; AARP design director Eric Seidman; freelance designer Marty Ittner; and Marie Timell, who provided invaluable editorial input.

If any shortcomings remain in this book despite the assistance of so many good people, they are, of course, my responsibility. I welcome your e-mailed comments and suggestions at bookfeedback@mtpalermo. com. —Mike Palermo

{Glossary

A/B trust: See "marital deduction and by-pass trust"

ademption: Situation in which a bequest of specific property under a will cannot be honored because the item has been lost or sold before the testator's death, and is thus unavailable

advance medical directive (AMD): Document addressing a variety of medical, legal, and ethical situations that a person may confront during serious illness, incapacity, or near the very end of life

agent: See "attorney-in-fact"

ancillary probate: Probate of property owned in a state other than one's primary residence

annuitant: Person who receives fixed payments from an annuity, such as a charitable gift annuity

attorney-in-fact: One authorized by a power of attorney to act on another person's behalf; also known as an "agent"

augmented estate: Everything a person owns, including the probate and nonprobate estate; sometimes used in determining a surviving spouse's elective share

beneficiary: Person designated to receive payment after one's death according to one's will or trust, or from an insurance policy or financial account, such as an IRA

bequest: Gift of personal property in a will

bypass trust: Also known as a "credit shelter trust," the "B" subtrust of an A/B living trust; it typically contains the federal estate tax-protected amount, thus "bypassing" taxation

capital gains tax: Federal levy on profits from the sale of one's property, on the difference between the sale price received and the owner's tax basis in the property

charitable gift annuity (CGA): Contract between an individual donor and a religious, charitable, or educational institution whereby the organization takes an initial investment from a donor and agrees in return to make regular, fixed payments to the donor for life; the charity keeps whatever remains of the original investment property after the death of the donor (and the subsequent death of the secondary beneficiary, if any, named by the donor)

charitable lead trust: Trust established by a donor whereby a charity receives an annual stream of income payments from the trust; when the donor dies (or at the end of a predetermined number of years), the remaining trust principal goes to someone of the donor's choosing

charitable remainder trust (CRT): Trust set up by a donor/grantor who collects taxable annual payments from trust earnings and/or principal; upon the donor's death, the leftover trust principal goes to a charitable, religious, or educational institution

claim: In asset protection planning, a right to payment, even if uncertain or disputed

codicil: Amendment to an earlier will, requiring the same signing and witnessing formalities

common law: System of law and marital property ownership that originated in England

community property: Form of property ownership between husband and wife in Arizona, California, Idaho, Louisiana, Nevada, New Mexico, Texas, Washington, and Wisconsin

conservatorship: Custody and control of a person's money and property under authority of a court

creator: One who establishes a trust; also called the "grantor," "settlor, or "trustor"

creditor: Person or party who has a claim for payment

devise: Gift of real estate made in a will

durable power of attorney: Document in which one person (the principal) authorizes another (his or her agent) to act on his or her behalf, and which power remains effective even if the principal becomes disabled

elective share: State-specified share of a deceased spouse's estate, taken by the surviving spouse in lieu of whatever inheritance the will specified; also referred to as a "forced share"

estate: All property rights and interests owned by one or by a trust from which one benefits or which one controls in a significant way

estate planning: Process of designing a legal and practical mechanism to implement one's wishes and dispose of one's property after death

estate tax: Federal tax on money or property transferred after death from one's estate to another party (some states also have an estate tax)

ethical will: Nonlegal document (or videotape) from a person to loved ones, communicating the writer's values, beliefs, lessons learned in life, and hopes for the future

executor: Person named in the will to carry out its instructions

executor misconduct: Any action that violates the executor's legal duty to act only in the best interests of the will beneficiaries

family limited partnership (FLP): Limited partnership in which the partners happen to be a closely related group

fiduciary: Executor, trustee, agent, or administrator who is responsible for the property of another person and has a fiduciary duty to that person

fiduciary duty: Fiduciary's obligation to act exclusively in all the beneficiaries' interests in investing, distributing, and otherwise handling the property entrusted to the fiduciary

forced share: See "elective share"

fraudulent transfer: Transfer made by someone with intent to "hinder, delay, or defraud" a creditor

generation-skipping tax: Extra levy, in addition to the gift and estate tax, on gifts to grandchildren and subsequent generations

gift: Completed lifetime transfer of money or property to a person or charity

gift tax: Federal tax on lifetime transfers of money or property not specifically excluded from the tax by law

grantor: One who establishes a trust; also called the "settlor," "trustor," or "creator"

guardian: Person or persons appointed by the court to take responsibility for the care and property of another person (usually a minor or one adjudged to be incompetent)

health-care agent: A person one authorizes in an advanced medical directive to make health-care decisions if one becomes unable to do so; also referred to as a "health-care surrogate" or a "health-care proxy"

health-care power of attorney: An advanced medical directive in which one names a health-care agent to make medical decisions on one's behalf

holographic will: Will written entirely in the handwriting of the will-maker, usually with no witnesses; in many states such wills are invalid

incentive trust provision: Clause in a trust that instructs the trustee to provide a specified reward to a trust beneficiary for fulfilling the wishes of the trust creator, such as graduating from college or remaining drug-free

intestate: Legal status of the estate of a person who dies without a will; in this situation the state laws of intestacy (or "descent and distribution") determine the distribution of his or her probate property

irrevocable life insurance trust (ILIT): Any irrevocable trust that owns life insurance

irrevocable trust: Trust that cannot be revoked or modified by the grantor in any significant way

joint tenancy with right of survivorship: Form of property ownership in which two or more joint tenants (owners) in property have an undivided interest in the whole account or asset. The share of the first to die automatically shifts to the surviving joint tenant(s) upon death

letters testamentary: Certified court document conferring full authority on the executor to handle the decedent's accounts and affairs

letters of trusteeship: In cases where the terms of a will create a new trust, a certified court document conferring full authority on the trustee to administer a trust

life estate: Grant of property rights that lasts only for the duration of the life estate holder's life. When that person dies, the property permanently passes to one or more people chosen in advance by the original property owner

life-prolonging (or life-sustaining) efforts: Any medical procedure or treatment using mechanical or other artificial means to keep one's heart or lungs going when they stop working on their own **and** which serves only to prolong the dying process (this may or may not include artificial nutrition an dehydration, depending on state law); it does not include medication or procedures to alleviate pain

limited liability company (LLC): A relatively new form of business entity created by state law to combine the liability protection and other features of a traditional corporation with the desirable tax features of a partnership

limited partnership: Business entity in which the owners (limited partners) agree to share profits and losses, but don't take part in managing the business and therefore are exposed to limited liability under state law for claims against the business

living trust: Trust established by a grantor during his or her lifetime

living will: Type of advance medical directive in which one puts in writing one's wishes regarding medical treatment near the end of life, should one be unable to communicate

marital deduction and bypass trust (A/B trust): Two-trust arrangement used for federal estate tax savings by married couples

marital deduction trust: Trust that is written and funded in a way that qualifies for the estate tax unlimited marital deduction upon the death of the grantor-spouse

no contest clause: Clause inserted in a will to automatically exclude anyone who challenges the will in court (also called an in terrorem clause)

nonprobate property: Any property that passes outside of probate court, such as retirement accounts and other financial assets that have beneficiaries named, property owned by a trust, or property owned jointly with right of survivorship

payable-on-death (POD): Bank account, such as a certificate of deposit, in which one or more beneficiaries are designated to receive the account funds upon one's death, outside of probate

payback supplemental-needs trust (SNT):
An SNT in which public funds expended for
the disabled person's care are paid back
from the trust after the disabled beneficiary
dies

per stirpes: Latin term often found in the
wills of those with children; stipulates that if
one of the children dies before the will-
maker, leaving children of his or her own,
these grandchildren of the will-maker shall
split the deceased parent's share of the will-
maker's estate

personal property: Any property that is not
real estate, including tangible items as well
as intangibles such as retirement and financial assets of all types

pour-over will: Document typically accom-
panying a living trust that allows any assets
not formally transferred to the trust during
the decedent's life to be "poured over" into
the trust and become part of the trust principal upon the decedent's death

prenuptial agreement: Contract that sets
forth the responsibilities of husband and
wife for joint living expenses and establishes what each spouse is to receive upon

divorce or the death of the other; also known as an "antenuptial agreement" or a "premarital agreement"

probate court: Part of the state court system responsible for probating wills and administering estates; in some places called "surrogate's court"

probate estate: Any property subject to the authority of probate court, whether that property passes according to a will or, if a person dies without a will, as prescribed by state law

prudent investor rule: State law dictating the obligations and standards to be met by an executor or trustee in managing the investments under his or her control

qualified terminable interest property (QTIP) trust: Trust often used in subsequent marriages to benefit a surviving spouse and take advantage of the unlimited marital deduction, while ensuring that when the surviving spouse dies, whatever property remains in the trust goes to the trust creator's own loved ones

remainderman(men): In a life estate, one or more people designated by the original property owner to receive the property once the life estate owner dies

required minimum distribution (RMD): Smallest annual distribution installments allowed by law from a retirement account

residue: Ancient legal term referring to anything that remains in one's probate estate after the payment of legal obligations and the distribution of property according to any specific bequests made in the will

revocable trust: Trust the grantor can terminate or modify at any time for any reason

right of election: Right of a surviving spouse to renounce the deceased spouse's will and instead take a state-specified share of the decedent's estate

right of occupancy: Grant of property rights that ends once the right-holder ceases to occupy the property

self-proving will: Will that contains notarized clauses signed by witnesses affirming that the will-maker is of sound mind and knows he or she is signing the will; these witnesses do not have to appear in probate court to verify the document after the will-maker's death

settlor: One who establishes a trust; also called the "grantor," "trustor," or "creator"

spendthrift trust provision: Clause in many trusts that prohibits a beneficiary's creditors from reaching the beneficiary's interest in the trust in order to satisfy his debts

springing power of attorney: Variant of the durable power of attorney that "springs" into action only upon the principal's disability, rather than taking effect immediately upon signing

successor trustee: Person who takes over as trustee after the original trustee ceases to serve in this role due to death, incompetency, or any other reason

supplemental-needs trust (SNT): Trust whose sole beneficiary is a disabled person receiving government assistance; also called a "special-needs trust"

surrogate's court: Another name for "probate court"; a division in a state's court system responsible for probating wills and administering estates

tenancy by the entirety: Form of joint ownership, available only to married couples, where neither tenant can transfer his or her interest in the property independently of the other

tenancy in common: Form of co-ownership in which each tenant (co-owner) has a severable interest in the property and is free to transfer it independently of the other(s)

testamentary capacity: The requirement under state law that a will-maker be of "sound mind" when drawing up and signing the will

testamentary trust: Trust created by a will, thereby coming into existence only after the will-maker's death, when the will is taken to probate court

testator: Will-maker; one who dies with a will

transfer: Mode of disposing of or parting with an asset or an interest in an asset

transfer-on-death (TOD): Similar to payable-on-death; a brokerage or mutual fund account in which one or more beneficiaries are named to receive the account funds upon one's death, outside of probate

trust: Agreement under which one person (the grantor) formally transfers the title to property to another party (the trustee), who then manages it exclusively for the benefit of whomever is named in the trust agreement (the beneficiaries)

trust adviser: Person appointed by the trust grantor to offer nonbinding advice to the trustee; usually the adviser is a family "insider" who can assist an institutional trustee with "human" decisions involving beneficiaries

trustee: One who administers a trust according to the terms of the trust document

trustor: One who establishes a trust; also called the "grantor," "settlor," or "creator"

trust principal: Any form of property, such as a financial account or real estate, transferred to the trustee to manage on behalf of the trust

trust protector: Person empowered by the trust grantor to make "judgment calls" in decisions involving beneficiaries and to monitor the trustee's performance

undue influence: When someone in a close relationship with a will-maker exercises mental coercion over him or her in the writing of his or her will, so that the document does not truly reflect the will-maker's intent

unlimited marital deduction: Provision of the federal gift and estate tax law that allows tax-free gifts of any size to one's spouse, during life or upon one's death

valuation planning: Broad range of legal and financial strategies designed to reduce the value of property transferred by lifetime gift or upon death for federal gift or estate tax purposes

vicarious liability: Personal liability arising from the malpractice or harm caused by employees or other professionals in an organization

will: Simple statement directing how property in one's name is to be distributed after one's death

will contest: Court challenge to the validity of the will

{Index